Defining Technological Literacy

Towards an Epistemological Framework

Edited by
John R. Dakers

First published in 2006 by
PALGRAVE MACMILLAN™
175 Fifth Avenue, New York, N.Y. 10010 and
Houndmills, Basingstoke, Hampshire, England RG21 6XS
Companies and representatives throughout the world.

PALGRAVE MACMILLAN is the global academic imprint of the Palgrave Macmillan division of St. Martin's Press, LLC and of Palgrave Macmillan Ltd. Macmillan® is a registered trademark in the United States, United Kingdom and other countries. Palgrave is a registered trademark in the European Union and other countries.

ISBN 1–4039–7037–8

Library of Congress Cataloging-in-Publication Data

Defining technological literacy: towards an epistemological framework / edited by John R. Dakers.
    p. cm.
    Includes bibliographical references.
    ISBN 1–4039–7037–8
    1. Technological literacy. 2. Technical education. 3. Technology—Philosophy. I. Dakers, John R.

T65.3.D44 2006
600—dc22   2005054723

A catalogue record for this book is available from the British Library.

Design by Newgen Imaging Systems (P) Ltd., Chennai, India.

First edition: April 2006

10 9 8 7 6 5 4 3 2 1

Printed in the United States of America.

For Wendy:
My friend, colleague, and wife,
without whose support this collection would never have happened.

Contents

Part II   Considering Aspects of Design in Developing Technological Literacy

Part III   Considering Aspects of Pedagogy for Developing Technological Literacy

Part IV   Considering Globalization, Computers, the World-Wide Web, and their Impact in Developing Technological Literacy

Acknowledgments

I would like to pay particular thanks to two of my colleagues at the University of Glasgow, both of whom provided me with support with the compilation of the manuscript: Michael Peters for offering me very sound advice and direction, and Wendy Dow for her help in proof-reading and standardizing the chapters. I am extremely grateful to them both.

I would also like to thank Malcolm MacKenzie and Bob Matthew from the University of Glasgow for believing in me, Amanda Johnson from Palgrave Macmillan for her sound advice and direction, as well as the various authors for their help, advice, support, and contributions.

Foreword

Albert Borgmann

This book is the happy convergence of a need and an accomplishment. The need is for a penetrating understanding of contemporary life, more particularly of the culture of the advanced industrial countries. There is an alarming gap between the gigantic and exhausting measures we have been undertaking to transform the face of the Earth and the uncertain and half-conscious sense we have of the value of it all. Affluence has been rising dramatically in the technological societies, but has the well-being of the citizens of those societies been rising accordingly? Are our enormous efforts and their effects worthwhile?

The accomplishment is to be found in the social theory of technology. After half a century of surveying and sorting, of trial and error, there is now something like a body of coherent and illuminating theories of technology. An important fruit of this development is the fact that we can now use the term and the concept of technology to get a grip on the character and worth of the culture of the advanced industrial countries.

The task now is to bring this accomplishment to bear on the need. There is no better place to start than education. We owe young people an understanding of the moral and cultural quality of the world they are about to enter. There is much excellent schooling in modern liberal democracies around the world. We train and educate our students well. But although the skills we teach them help them to succeed, the education we try to give them in the arts, the letters, and the sciences leaves them unprepared for a society that values their skills, but is indifferent to their education and finally suffocates it. If we can teach our students technological literacy, we not only enrich their education, we also enable them to see what obstacles and opportunities they face in trying to remain educated persons once they have left school and for the rest of their lives.

This collection of articles furnishes a solid foundation for the teaching of technological literacy. It contains some of the best theoretical work on technology that has been done in modern liberal democracies around the world, ranging from philosophy via design to pedagogy. It will help in a unique and important way to make the prosperous societies good societies too.

Introduction: Defining Technological Literacy

John R. Dakers

There is, more than ever before, a growing need to understand the "character of contemporary life" (Borgmann, 1984). We are transforming our world at an alarming rate and in so doing, we are alienating ourselves from it. Our technologically mediated existence is threatening the very democratic process itself. We need to develop a new language, a new literacy, in order to both understand our brave new world, and learn how to live a meaningful existence in it. Where better to start this new literacy than in technology education?

There is, however, very little literature, or engagement in the classroom, directly relating to education about the basic technological nature of the world that young people must negotiate, or about the kinds of technological obstacles that they are likely to encounter in that world. Their views of technology influence their ability to both use and relate to it. Many young people have a tendency to perceive technology in terms of its artifacts: computers, cars, televisions, toasters, pesticides, flu shots, solar cells, genetically engineered tomatoes, and so on. Often they do not see technology in terms of the knowledge and processes that create these artifacts, nor, in particular, are they aware of the various implications for society that result from the existence of these technologies (ITEA, 2000).

The predominant focus in technology education tends more towards the development of knowledge relating to the fabrication of artifacts, this is at the expense of the development of a critical awareness in young people of the technologically mediated world they inhabit and the way in which their future lives are, and will be, shaped by it.

It is this unreflectivity, this lack of a discourse, this missing literacy, that essentially reduces the concept of technology to that of basic raw materials; to stuff that we will transform into artifacts that we perceive as necessary for our needs and wants. In this definition, we control and exploit the world to our own ends, and we continually get better at doing it.

Technology education cannot ignore this. We must guide young people's learning towards developing a critical awareness of what it is to live in a technologically mediated world. I do not suggest that we inculcate young people into developing a dystopian view of technology. Rather, I suggest that technology education (and other subject domains also) need to engage young people in a discourse surrounding technology. They need to see the benefits of technology as well as the potential dangers it can harbor. As we move into the twenty-first century, our lives are being transformed at an alarming rate not only by new and emerging technologies but, significantly, by the subversion of those technologies, intended or otherwise, that serve to dramatically alter our lives. Thus technologies such as information and communications technologies, the development of which helped to extend democracy for the good of humanity, have also enabled global networks of terrorists to engage in new and terrifying forms of warfare. The development of the automobile, the provider of mobility and freedom, but the proliferation of which has resulted in an increase in greenhouse gasses, has contributed much to global warming. The potential that nanotechnologies, coupled with the merging of flesh and machines, might offer, serves to illustrate the absolute need for us all to engage in a new literacy, a literacy that will enable us to reflect upon our new technological lifeworld.

In the chapters that follow, these, and many other issues, are discussed and debated. The authors come from a broad range of disciplines including philosophy, anthropology, psychology, sociology, and education, but all have a major interest in technology. The authors are are all well known in their respective fields and have collaborated to form a collection that will enable students of technology, engineering, and science, together with their teachers and lecturers, to engage in a new dialogue about the nature of technology as well as the impact it will have on all our lives in the twenty-first century.

References

Borgmann, A. (1984). *Technology and the Character of Contemporary Life: A Philosophical Enquiry*. Chicago: University of Chicago Press.

ITEA. (2000). *Standards for Technological Literacy*. International Technology Education Association: Virginia.

PART I

*Considering Aspects of Knowledge and Experience
for Developing Technological Literacy*

CHAPTER 1

What Is Philosophy of Technology?

Andrew Feenberg

Introduction

In this chapter I attempt to answer the question posed in the title from two standpoints, first historically and then in terms of contemporary options in the field, the various different theories that are currently under discussion.[1] But before I begin, I would like to clear up a common misunderstanding: philosophy of technology is *not* closely related to philosophy of science. Science and technology share a similar type of rationality based on empirical observation and knowledge of natural causality, but technology is concerned with usefulness rather than truth. Where science seeks to know, technology seeks to control. However, this is by no means the whole story.

Our image of premodernity is shaped by the struggles between science and religion in the early modern period. From those struggles we derive the notion that traditional societies restrict questioning of their basic customs and myths. In the premodern West, the principle of authority was the basis not just for church doctrine, but for knowledge of the world as well. Modern societies emerge from the release of the power of questioning against such traditional forms of thought. The eighteenth century Enlightenment demanded that all customs and institutions justify themselves as useful for humanity. Under the impact of this demand, science and technology become the new basis for belief. Eventually, technology becomes omnipresent in everyday life and scientific-technical modes of thought predominate over all others.[2] In a mature, modern society, technology is taken for granted much as were the customs and myths of traditional society. Scientific-technical rationality has become a new culture.

This culture is clearly "useful" in all its details in the sense the Enlightenment demanded, but it is now so all-encompassing that larger questions can be asked about its value. We judge our technological civilization as more or less worthy, more or less ethically justified, more or less fulfilling. Modernity itself authorizes, even demands such judgment. We need to understand ourselves today in the midst of technology and neither scientific nor technical knowledge can help us. Insofar as our society is technological at its base, philosophy of technology is its theoretical self-awareness. Philosophy of technology teaches us to reflect on what we take for granted most of all, that is, the rationality of modernity. The importance of this perspective cannot be over-estimated.

Greek Origins

The question of technology is raised at the very origins of Western philosophy, not as we pose it today of course, but at a metaphysical level. Philosophy begins in ancient Greece with the interpretation of the world in terms of the fundamental fact that humanity is a laboring animal constantly at work transforming nature. This fundamental fact shapes the basic distinctions that prevail throughout the tradition of Western philosophy.[3] The first of these is the distinction between what the Greeks called *physis* and *poiēsis*. *Physis* is usually translated as nature. For the Greeks, nature creates itself, emerges from out of itself. But there are other things in the world, things that depend on humans to come into being. *Poiēsis* is the practical activity of human production. We call the beings so created artifacts and include among them the products of art, craft, and social convention.

The word *technē* (plural *technai*) in ancient Greek signifies the knowledge or the discipline associated with a form of *poiēsis*. For example, sculpture is a *technē* that creates out of stone; carpentry is a *technē* that builds from wood. Each *technē* includes a purpose and a meaning for its artifacts. For the Greeks, *technai* show the "right way" to do things in a very strong, even an objective, sense. Although artifacts depend on human activity, the knowledge contained in the *technai* is no matter of opinion or subjective intention. Even the purposes of artifacts share in this objectivity insofar as they are defined by the *technai*.

The second fundamental distinction is that between existence and essence. Existence answers the question of whether something is or is not. Essence answers the question of what the thing is. *That* it is and *what* it is appear to be two independent dimensions of being. In the tradition of Western philosophy, existence has been a rather hazy concept. We know the difference between what exists and what does not, for example, as immediate presence or absence, but there is not much more to say. Most of the attention is given to essence and its successor concepts as developed by the sciences, because this is the content of knowledge.

These distinctions are self-evident. They form the basis of all philosophical thought in the West. But the relation between them is puzzling. The source of the puzzle is the Greek understanding of *technē*, the ancestor of modern technology. Strange though it seems, the Greeks conceived nature on the model of the artifacts produced by their own technical activity.

To show this, I analyze the relation between the two basic distinctions that I've introduced, *physis* and *poiēsis*, and existence and essence. The difference between existence and essence in *poiēsis* is real and obvious. The thing is present first as an idea and only later comes into existence through human making. For the Greeks the idea is not arbitrary or subjective but rather belongs to a *technē*. Each *technē* contains the essence of the thing to be made prior to the act of making. The idea, the essence of the thing, is a reality independent of the thing and its maker. Although humans make artifacts, they do so according to a plan and for a purpose that is an objective aspect of the world.

But the corresponding distinction between existence and essence is not obvious for natural things. The thing and its essence arise together and exist together. The essence does not have a separate existence. The flower emerges along with what makes it a flower: that it is and what it is "happen," in a sense, simultaneously. We can define a concept of the flower, but this is our notion, not something essential to the flower as a concept or plan is to artifacts. Indeed, the very idea of an essence of the things of nature is our construction. Unlike the knowledge that is active in *technē*, which participates in bringing into existence the objects it defines, the essences identified by *epistemē*, the science of nature, appear to be purely human doings to which nature itself would be indifferent. Or is it? Here is where the story gets interesting.

Although essences quite obviously relate differently to *physis* than to *poiēsis*, since Greek times philosophers have struggled to efface that difference in a unified theory. For Plato, who started the tradition on this path, the concept of the thing, its "idea," exists in some sense prior to the thing itself and allows it to exist and us to know it. This is exactly the pattern familiar from *technē*, but Plato does not reserve his theory for artifacts; rather, he applies it to all being. He relies on the structure of *technē* to explain not only artifacts, but nature as well.

Plato understands nature as divided into existence and essence just as artifacts are, and this becomes the basis for Greek ontology. In this ontology there is no radical discontinuity between technical making and natural self-production because they both share the same structure. *Technē* includes a purpose and a meaning for artifacts. The Greeks import these aspects of *technē* into the realm of nature and view all of nature in teleological terms. The world is thus a place full of meaning and intention. This conception of the world calls for a corresponding understanding of man. We humans are not the masters of nature but realize its potentialities in bringing a meaningful world to fruition. Our knowledge of that world and our action in it are not arbitrary but are in some sense the completion of what lies hidden in nature.

What conclusion follows from these historical considerations on ancient Greek philosophy? I will be provocative and say that the philosophy of technology begins with the Greeks and is in fact the foundation of all Western philosophy. It was the Greeks who first interpreted being as such through the concept of technical making. This is ironic. Technology has a low status in the high culture of modern societies, but it was actually there at the origin of that culture and, if we believe the Greeks, contains the key to the understanding of being as such.

Modern Alternatives

I now leave these historical considerations and turn to the status of philosophy of technology in our era. At its inception, Descartes promised that we would become "the masters and possessors of nature" through the cultivation of the sciences, and Bacon famously claimed, "Knowledge is power." Here technology no longer fulfills nature's potentialities as it did for the Greeks, but rather it realizes human plans. Clearly we are in a different world from that of the Greeks. And yet we share with them the fundamental distinctions between essence and existence, and between the things that make themselves, nature, and the things that are made, artifacts. But our understanding of these distinctions is different from theirs. This is especially true of the concept of essence. For us essences are conventional rather than real. The meaning and purpose of things is something we create, not something we discover. The gap between man and world widens accordingly. We are not at home in the world, we conquer the world. This difference is related to our basic ontology. The question we address to being is not *what* it is, but *how* it works. Science answers this question rather than revealing essences in the Greek sense of the term.

Note that technology is still the model of being in this modern conception. This was particularly clear in the Enlightenment when philosophers and scientists challenged the medieval successors to Greek science with the new mechanistic worldview. Eighteenth-century physical science identified the workings of the universe with a clockwork mechanism. Thus, strange though it may seem, the underlying structure of Greek ontology survived the defeat of its concept of essence.

In the modern context technology does not realize objective essences inscribed in the nature of the universe as does *technē*. It now appears as purely instrumental, as value-free. It does not respond to inherent purposes, but is merely a means serving subjective goals. For modern common sense, means and ends are independent of each other: "Guns don't kill people, people kill people." Guns are a means independent of the users' ends, whether it be to rob a bank or to enforce the law. Technology, we say, is neutral, meaning that it has no preference as between the various possible uses to which it can be put. This "instrumentalist" philosophy of technology is a spontaneous product of our civilization, assumed unreflectively by most people.

Technology in this scheme of things encounters nature as raw materials, not as a world that emerges out of itself, a *physis*, but rather as passive stuff awaiting transformation into whatever we desire. This world is there to be controlled and used without any inner purpose. The West has made enormous technical advances on this basis. Nothing restrains us in our exploitation of nature. Everything is exposed to an analytic intelligence that decomposes it into usable parts. Under this assumption, our means have become ever more efficient and powerful. In the nineteenth century it became commonplace to view modernity as an unending progress toward the fulfillment of human needs through technological advance.

But for what ends? The goals of our society can no longer be specified in a knowledge of some sort as they were for the Greeks. The Greeks lived in harmony with the world whereas we are alienated from it by our very freedom to define our purposes as we wish. So long as no great harm could be attributed to technology, this situation did not lead to serious doubts beyond small circles of intellectuals. But as the twentieth century proceeds from world wars to concentration camps to environmental catastrophes, it becomes more and more difficult to ignore the strange aimlessness of modernity. This has led to a crisis of civilization from which there seems no escape: we know how to get there but we do not

Table 1.1 Alternative definitions for technology

Technology is:	Autonomous	Humanly controlled
Neutral (complete separation of means and ends)	Determinism (e.g. modernization theory)	Instrumentalism (liberal faith in progress)
Value-laden (means form a way of life that includes ends)	Substantivism (means and ends linked in systems)	Critical theory (choice of alternative means–ends systems)

know why we are going or even where (Table 1.1). It is because we are at such a loss that so many twentieth-century philosophers of technology became critics of modernity.

I want now to present the various alternatives so far discussed and others as well in a chart that puts order in the discussion.[4]

Technology is defined here along two axes reflecting its relation to values and agency. The vertical axis offers two alternatives: either technology is value neutral, as we typically assume in modern times, or it is value-laden as the Greeks believed and, we will see, as some philosophers of technology believe today. The choice between these views is not obvious. From a common-sense perspective a technical device is simply a concatenation of causal mechanisms. No amount of scientific study will find anything like a purpose in it. But perhaps common sense misses the point. After all, no scientific study will find money in a $100 bill. Not everything is a physical or chemical property of matter. Perhaps technologies, like bank-notes, have a way of containing value in themselves as social entities.

On the horizontal axis technologies are signified as either autonomous or humanly controllable. To say that technology is autonomous is not of course to say that it acts alone. Human beings are involved, but the question is, do they actually have the freedom to decide how technology will be applied and develop? Is the next step in the evolution of the technical system up to human decision-makers or do they act according to a logic inscribed in the very nature of technology? In the latter case technology can rightly be said to be autonomous. On the other hand, technology would be humanly controllable if we could determine the next step in its evolution in accordance with intentions elaborated without reference to the imperatives of technology. The intersection of these two axes defines four types of theories.

Instrumentalism, the occupant of the box in which human control and value neutrality intersect, has been discussed above. This is the "standard" modern view according to which technology is a tool or instrument of the human species as a whole. As noted in the chart, this view corresponds to the liberal faith in progress that was such a prominent feature of mainstream Western thought until fairly recently.

Technology, on the determinist account, is rooted on the one side in knowledge of nature and on the other in generic features of the human species. This is why it can be described as neutral, as a rationally constructed tool serving universal human needs. Some determinists argue that technologies simply extend human faculties: the automobile extends our feet while computers extend our brains. It is not up to us to adapt technology to our whims but on the contrary, we must adapt to technology as the most significant expression of our humanity. Determinism is a widely held view in social science in which it supports the pretensions to universality of both capitalist and communist societies.

Substantivists attribute substantive values to technology in contrast with instrumentalism and determinism which view technology as neutral. The contrast here is actually more complex than it seems at first sight. The neutrality thesis to which instrumentalists and most determinists subscribe does admit that technology embodies a value but it is a merely formal value, efficiency. Using technology for this or that purpose would not be a specific value choice in itself, but just a more efficient way of realizing a preexisting value of some sort. A substantive value on the contrary involves a commitment to a specific conception of the good. According to substantivism, the values embodied by technology are the pursuit of power and domination. These values track technology like a shadow and show up in everything it touches. If technology embodies these value, it is not merely instrumental and cannot be used for the various purposes of individuals or societies with different ideas of the good. According to substantivism, insofar as we use technology we are committed to a technological way of life.

There are obvious relations between substantive theory of technology and determinism. In fact most substantive theorists are determinists as well. But the position I have characterized as determinism is optimistic and progressive. Both Marx (in the commonplace interpretations) and the modernization theorists of the postwar era believed that technology would save humanity. Substantive theory is not so optimistic and regards autonomous technology as threatening if not malevolent, rather than benign. Once unleashed technology becomes more and more imperialistic, taking over one domain of social life after another. In the most extreme imagination of substantivism, a *Brave New World* such as Huxley describes in his famous novel converts human beings into mere cogs in the machinery. This is not utopia—the "no place" of an ideal society, but dystopia—a world in which human individuality has been completely suppressed. Here people become, as Marshall McLuhan once said, the "sex organs of the machine world" (McLuhan, 1964: 46).

Martin Heidegger was the most famous substantive theorist. He argued that the essence of modernity is the triumph of technology over every other value. He noted that Greek philosophy had already based its understanding of being on technical making and argued that this starting point culminates in modern technology. Where the Greeks took *technē* as the model of being in theory, we have transformed beings technically in practice. Our metaphysics is not in our heads but consists in the real technical conquest of the Earth. This conquest transforms everything into raw materials and system components, including human beings themselves (Heidegger, 1977a). Not only are we constantly obeying the dictates of the many technical systems in which we are enrolled, we tend to see ourselves more and more as devices regulated by medical, psychological, athletic, and other functional disciplines. Our bookstores are full of "operating manuals" for every aspect of life: love, sex, divorce, friendship, raising children, eating, exercise, making money, having fun, and so on. We are our own machines.

But, Heidegger argues, although we may control the world through our technology, we do not control our own obsession with control. Something lies behind technology, a mystery we cannot unravel from our technological standpoint. Where we are headed is a mystery too. The West has reached the end of its rope. Heidegger's last interview concludes that "[o]nly a God can save us" (Heidegger, 1977b).

Heidegger's views contrast sharply with the critical theory of technology. Critical theory agrees with substantivism that technology is not the unmixed blessing welcomed by instrumentalists and determinists. It recognizes the catastrophic consequences of technological development but still sees a promise of greater freedom in a possible future. The problem is not with technology as such but with our failure so far to devise appropriate institutions for exercising human control over it. We could tame technology by submitting it to a more democratic process of design and development.

The economy offers an encouraging parallel to this view of technology. A century ago mainstream political and academic thought conceived of the economy as an autonomous power operating according to inflexible laws. Today we know the contrary, that we can influence the direction of economic development through democratic institutions. Critical theory of technology argues that the time has come to extend democracy to technology as well. It thus attempts to save the Enlightenment values that have guided progress for the last several hundred years without ignoring the resulting problems.

As can be seen from the chart, critical theory shares traits with both instrumentalism and substantivism. Like instrumentalism, critical theory argues that technology is in some sense controllable, but it also agrees with substantivism that technology is value-laden. This seems a contradictory position since, in the substantivist view, precisely what cannot be controlled are the values embodied in technology such as efficiency and domination. If this is true, the choices within our power would be like those we make in the supermarket between different brands of soap, that is, trivial and delusory. How then can we conceive the value-ladenness of technology such that human control matters?

The critical theorist Herbert Marcuse sketched an answer I have tried to develop in what I call a critical theory of technology. According to critical theory the values embodied in technology are socially specific and are not adequately represented by such abstractions as efficiency or control. Technology can frame not just one way of life but many different possible ways of life, each of which determines a different choice of designs and a different range of technological mediation. Does this mean that technology is neutral, as instrumentalism believes? Not quite: modern societies must all aim at efficiency in those domains in which they apply technology, but to claim that they can realize no other significant values besides efficiency is to overlook the tremendous social impact of differing design choices. What is worse, it obscures the difference between the current miserable state of technological societies and a better condition we can imagine and for which we can struggle. One must look down on mankind from a very great height indeed not to notice the difference between efficient weapons and efficient medicines, efficient propaganda and efficient education, efficient exploitation and efficient research! This difference is socially and ethically significant and so cannot be discounted as thinkers who share Heidegger's Olympian view sometimes claim.

Nevertheless, the substantivist critique of instrumentalism does demonstrate that technologies are not neutral tools. Means and ends are connected. Thus even if some sort of human control of technology is possible, it cannot be understood on the same terms as instrumental control of particular devices. In critical theory, technologies are not seen as mere tools but as frameworks for ways of life. Thus we cannot agree with the instrumentalist that "[g]uns don't kill people, people kill people." Supplying people with guns creates a social world quite different from the world in which people are disarmed. We can choose which world we wish to inhabit through legislation.

This is not the sort of control over technology that instrumentalism generally claims we have. Its model of control is based on a restricted notion of use of individual devices, not choices between whole technological systems with different social consequences. This is a meta-choice, a choice at a higher level determining which values are to be embodied in the technical framework of our lives. Critical theory of technology opens up the possibility of reflecting on such choices and submitting them to more democratic controls. We do not have to wait for a God to save us as Heidegger expostulated but can hope to save ourselves through democratic interventions into technology.

But critical theory is not naïve about the difficulties that stand in the way of democracy. Technology gradually subverts the capacity for democracy even as it destroys the objective world. Thus the practical difference between substantivism and critical theory is not as great as it seems at first.[5] Critical theory is relatively skeptical about the capacity of human beings to get technological civilization under reasonable control, but at least it does not exclude the possibility in principle as does substantivism. This is why it is necessary to talk not in terms of a utopian democracy of technique but more modestly of democratic interventions into technology.

What is meant by the concept of democratic interventions? Clearly, it would not make sense to hold an election between competing devices or designs. The voting public is not sufficiently concerned, involved, and informed to choose good politicians, much less good technologies. So, in what sense can democracy be extended to technology under current conditions? People affected by technological change ever more frequently protest or innovate. Where it used to be possible to silence all opposition to technical projects by appealing to Progress with a capital "P," today communities mobilize to make their wishes known, for example, in opposition to nuclear power plants or toxic waste dumps in their neighborhood. In a different vein the computer has involved us in technology so intimately that our activities have begun to shape its development. Email, the most-used function of the Internet, was introduced by skilled users and did not originally figure in the plans of the designers at all. Similar examples can be adduced from medicine, urban affairs, and many other domains in which technology shapes human activity.

Critical theory of technology detects a trend toward greater participation in decisions about design and development in examples such as these. The public sphere appears to be opening slowly to encompass technical issues that were formerly viewed as the exclusive preserve of experts. Can this trend continue to the point at which citizenship will include the exercise of human control over the technical framework of our lives? We must hope so, for the alternative is likely to be the eventual failure of the experiment in industrial society under the pressure of untrammeled competition and national rivalries. If people are able to conceive and pursue their intrinsic interest in peace and fulfillment through the political process, they will inevitably address the question of technology along with many other questions that hang in suspense today. We can only hope this will happen sooner rather than later.

Notes

1. This short chapter can give only a hint of the richness of the field. For a thorough account, see Mitcham (1994).
2. This is a summary of ideas developed in Habermas (1984). Although the usual contrast of premodern dogmatism with modern reflexivity is no doubt overdrawn, this is hardly the moment to drop it entirely. For a critique of this position, see Latour (1993).
3. The discussion in this section is loosely derived from Heidegger's (1973) history of being.
4. This chart is drawn from Feenberg (1999: 9).
5. For a comparison of Heidegger and critical theory, see Feenberg (2005).

References

Feenberg, A. (1999). *Questioning Technology*. New York: Routledge.

Feenberg, A. (2005). *Heidegger and Marcuse: The Catastrophe and Redemption of History*. New York: Routledge.

Habermas, J. (1984). *The Theory of Communicative Action*. Boston: Beacon Press.

Heidegger, M. (1973). *The End of Philosophy*. Trans. J. Stambaugh. New York: Harper and Row.

Heidegger, M. (1977a). *The Question Concerning Technology*. Trans. W. Lovitt. New York: Harper and Row.

Heidegger, M. (1977b). "Only a God Can Save Us Now." Trans. D. Schendler. *Graduate Faculty Philosophy Journal*, 6: 1.

Latour, B. (1993). *We Have Never Been Modern*. Trans. C. Porter. Cambridge, MA: Harvard University Press.

McLuhan, M. (1964). *Understanding Media: The Extensions of Man*. New York: McGraw Hill.

Mitcham, C. (1994). *Thinking Through Technology: The Path Between Engineering and Philosophy*. Chicago: University of Chicago Press.

CHAPTER 2

Technological Knowledge and Artifacts: An Analytical View

Marc J. de Vries

Introduction: Analytical and Critical Philosophy

The philosophy of technology is a fairly young discipline, compared to, for example, the philosophy of science. Most of what was published in the early days of this discipline was fairly critical. Authors such as Martin Heidegger and Jacques Ellul wrote in rather negative terms about the impact of technology on humans and on culture. These authors are commonly reckoned to be the Continental philosophers, the term "Continental" referring to the European Continent (with countries such as Germany and France). It is also common use to contrast this Continental stream in philosophy with the analytical stream. This, of course, is a strange way of defining contrasting philosophical streams, as "Continental" is related to the geographical origin of authors, while analytical has to do with the nature of what the philosophers in that stream do. The reference to geographical differences is becoming more and more problematic, as nowadays many analytical philosophers are from the Continent. Therefore a better way of distinguishing the two streams is not by referring to the background of the philosophers but to the kind of philosophical work they do. Then it seems appropriate to distinguish between two functions or tasks of philosophy: an analytical function, and a critical function (De Vries, 2005a). The analytical function deals with conceptualization (Scruton, 1996). In the philosophy of technology this means searching for answers to questions such as what technology is, what a technical artifact is, what technological knowledge is, and the like. This work can result in a "language" that facilitates proper discussions that are not hampered by different authors using words and concepts in different ways. Such frustrating discussions have been there, and a striking example is the debate about technology being "mere applied science" or not. This discussion was fruitless, not in the least because different authors meant different things by the terms "science" and "technology". Proponents of the formula "technology as applied science" had technologies such as the transistor and the laser in mind, while opponents of the same formula were thinking of technologies such as the steam engine. Each was right from his/her own perspective, but the debate was not proper this way. Here a sound analysis of the meaning of the terms "science" and "technology" would have been useful.

A lot of writings of "Continental" philosophers can be criticised for making very general claims about technology. Here again a sound analysis of the meaning of the term "technology" would be useful. One could, for instance, question if all technologies bear equally the "autonomous systems" character that Ellul ascribed to them. Apparently Ellul has not made enough effort to examine the nature of different technologies closely enough to see that one technology can be very different from the other. If the analytical function had preceded the critical function in Ellul's work, maybe his conclusions would have been different from the ones that we find in his writings now. For this analytical function it is desirable to examine closely how technology functions in practice. For that reason the emergence of the analytical philosophy of technology, that is, the philosophy of technology in which conceptualisation is the primary aim, has caused what is sometimes called an "empirical turn" in the philosophy of technology. The meaning of that phrase is that philosophers would seek inspiration for reflection in empirical studies about examples of technology. These studies can be the result of the work of historians, sociologists, (cognitive) psychologists, and so on. The interpretation of these studies usually requires a certain understanding of the technology. Most of the Continental philosophers of technology had a nonengineering and non-(natural) science background, and maybe that is a reason why they did not make use of this kind of empirical studies. This must have been annoying to engineers as the strong negative claims about the impact of technology on humans and culture were made by people who were complete outsiders and did not make real efforts to understand technology "from inside" by using empirical studies about practical examples of technology. Many of the analytically oriented philosophers of technology do have an engineering or (natural) science background, second to their philosophical background.

The empirical turn does not mean that philosophy is turned into an empirical discipline (Kroes and Meijers, 2000). Philosophy remains a discipline that can build up its own terminology and define concepts in its own way. This is similar to the situation in the philosophy of science: taking into account that science in practice develops in certain ways does not mean one can no longer think about desirable norms for what one would and would not like to accept as being science. In that respect philosophy remains a formal discipline in which empirical data do not have the final say in what is, and is not, accepted as good theory. The empirical turn, however, can prevent the claims that are made about philosophy becoming too far removed from the real world as we experience it. It is clear that here I do not share the point of view of philosophers who "naturalize" concepts such as knowledge and science, and are only interested in examining how people deal with these terms in practice.

Themes in the Analytical Philosophy of Technology

In his book *Thinking Through Technology*, Carl Mitcham identified four different ways of conceptualising technology, namely as objects, knowledge, activities, and volition (Mitcham, 1994). By "technology as objects," Mitcham means that we can regard technology as a set of objects that are the result of designing and making. Mostly we speak of "technical artifacts" when the objects are the result of technological activities. "Technology as knowledge" refers to the idea that technology is a discipline with a distinct kind of knowledge. The domain of "technology as processes" deals with designing, making, and using as the main types of processes in technology. "Technology as volition" refers to the notion that technology is part of our human will and is therefore an intrinsic part of our culture, and that technology for that reason has everything to do with values that humans hold. The Continentally oriented philosophy of technology has mainly focused on technology as volition. As a result, the ideas that have emerged in the remaining three conceptualization modes are fairly limited. Mitcham's survey indicates that in the objects domain most publications seek for taxonomies of objects, but the nature of technical artifacts has not really been explored yet. In the knowledge domain the main result is that we now recognize that there is something like "technological knowledge," which is different from scientific knowledge (Baird, 2004; Laudan, 1984; Vincenti, 1990), although in practice the two can be almost indistinguishable, in particular in the situation of industrial research (De Vries, 2005b). But what defines the specific nature of technological knowledge is still not well explored. In the activities domain Mitcham refers to research in the field of design methodology. Here indeed a lot of insights have been gained, but most of them are not really of a philosophical nature. They are mostly the work of practitioners reflecting on their own practice, or psychologists, who explore what goes on in the designers' minds, and not really methodological studies in the philosophical sense, that is, studying the metaphysical and epistemological assumptions in design methods and processes. Although this, of course, is a somewhat overstated negative assessment of all the output that Mitcham describes in the various chapters about the domains of objects, knowledge, and processes, it is not unreasonable to say that the volition domain has had much more attention in the past than the other three domains. Clearly, most Continental philosophers did not see these domains as a priority in their reflections on technology compared to the culture-and-values issues that emerge in the volition domain. This challenge has now been picked up by analytical philosophers. In this chapter I discuss two research programs that are positioned in the analytical realm and aim at exploring the domains of technical artifacts and technological knowledge. Both are being carried out in the Netherlands. At Delft University of Technology there is the "Dual Nature of Technical Artifacts" research program, and at Eindhoven University of Technology we have the "Norms in Technological Knowledge" program. The two groups work closely together. Taken together the two philosophy-of-technology groups that work on these programs form probably the largest group in the philosophy of technology worldwide. I, however, do not confine my description of philosophical reflections on technical artifacts and technological knowledge to the work of these groups, but also draw from the work of other analytically oriented groups in other countries, mainly in the United States.

The Nature of Technical Artifacts

In the "Dual Nature of Technical Artifacts" program, technical artifacts are conceptualized according to what is seen as their two natures: a physical nature and a functional nature (Meijers, 2000). We recognise the physical nature when we describe the artifact in terms of its size, shape, number of parts, color, weight, smell, and all the other properties that the artifact possesses. Whatever we do with the artifact, it has that size, shape, number of parts, etc. Its physical nature is independent of what we know of it and what we do with it. One can say that it is non-relational, because it does not need a relationship with us to have those (physical, chemical, and mathematical) properties. Another way of saying more or less the same thing is that there is no intention involved in these properties. Intention means, loosely speaking, that someone has attention for it. Philosophers speak of intentional states of mind to indicate perception of something, knowledge about something, desire for something, etc. Another word for this can be "about-ness." Perception, knowledge, and desire are necessarily *about* something. One can say that the physical nature of a technical artifact does not depend on such an "about-ness." This, however, is different in the case of the functional nature. Functions are not intrinsic to the artifact. We, as users or designers, ascribe functions to artifacts. Functions do not exist without us ascribing them. Therefore the functional nature is a relational one, or, differently stated, one that requires intention (of a user or designer). Now let us study more closely how these intentions come in.

To see this, we first need to recognise that every artifact simultaneously has these two natures. The technical artifact has been constructed in such a way that it has certain physical properties that allow for certain functions to be realized. That is the result of the designer's work. The challenge for the designer was to find an appropriate physical nature (size, shape, number of parts, etc.) to enable the realization of a certain desired function. What determines the success or failure of the design is the extent to which the designer has been able to meet that challenge. The function that was intended by the designer (note: there was intention involved in the determination of the function) is commonly called the "proper" function. That is what the artifact is intended for by the designer. There are different ways in which the designer can express this "proper" function. What many designers nowadays think is best is to make the artifact express its own proper function, so that users will recognize what it is meant for. For instance, there are door handles that are designed in such a way that they almost seem to shout: "pull me!" The shape of the handle invites us to pull, and not to push. Thus the artifact communicates its proper function. In his book *Artifacts, Art Works and Agency*, Randall Dipert uses this phenomenon to distinguish between artifacts that do and artifacts that do not communicate what they are meant for (Dipert, 1993). Dipert uses the term "artifact" exclusively for the first type of object, and he calls the other type "instruments." His taxonomy of objects also contains "tools": these are the objects that have not even been modified to perform their function. Finally he uses the term "natural object" to indicate an object that neither has been modified nor is used for an intentional purpose. Although he distinguishes the four levels (natural objects, tools, instruments, and artifacts), his use of terms is confusing as it does not match the usual way in which we exploit those terms. Another option for the designer to express what he had defined as the proper function of the artifact is to add a manual to the artifact.

The designer, though, is not the only person who can ascribe functions to an artifact. Users also do this. They do that on the basis of beliefs. Users observe the object and try to appraise its physical nature. Then they reason from the perceived physical nature of the artifact to possible functions (in other words: they imagine what might be possible functional natures of the artifact). These beliefs can be either correct or incorrect. Correct beliefs will generally lead to good use of the artifact, but not necessarily the same use the designer had in mind. For example, a mug was intended (by the designer) to be used for holding liquids that people could then drink. But a secretary who sits in a room in which there is a draft that makes her papers fly away can place the same mug onto the papers and prevent them from flying away. Now the mug has been ascribed a function that is different from the proper function. We can call that function an "accidental" function. In this case the belief about the relationship between the physical nature of the artifact (in particular its weight) and the functional nature (as a device for holding paper) was correct, and the object fulfills the accidental function. In other cases this may not happen and the object may malfunction or even break down. In cases where it breaks down or malfunctions we still tend to say that it has kept its proper function, even though this function is no longer realized. A car that broke down and is in the garage now is still a car and not just a heap of metal.

Artifacts that malfunction are not, of course, appreciated. We usually assess the functioning of an artifact and then say either that it is good or bad. Evidently there is something normative about functions. Later we will come back to that point when we examine the nature of knowledge of functions. For now we focus on the fact that there are levels of "good" and "bad." We can say that this is a good hammer. In that case the predicate "good" refers to one particular hammer. We can also say that hammers of this brand are good hammers. Now the predicate refers to a whole set of hammers, namely all hammers of a certain brand. Furthermore we can say that hammers are good (for getting nails into pieces of wood). Now the predicate refers to all hammers. So we can distinguish at least the following levels: all hammers, all hammers of a particular brand (this is called "a type"), and one particular hammer of a certain brand (this is called "a token of that type").

What designers and users think and do with respect to artifacts can be described in terms of a plan (Houkes et al., 2002). Designers try to imagine what desires users may have, and they also have their own intentions. Designers have beliefs about what physical nature could be suitable for realizing a certain functional nature, and they also try to imagine what sorts of beliefs users might have with respect to that. Then they take action when they come up with possible physical realizations of the artifact, and users take action when they use the artifact. Both designers and users can be said to go through a sequence of actions in which their intentions, desires, and beliefs play a guiding role. We can therefore speak of two plans: a design plan and a user plan. Designers can also suggest user plans to the users in order to ensure that the artifact is used properly. One could therefore say that designers not only deliver an artifact, but also a user plan. This user plan can also be in the artifact itself, as we saw before (namely in the communicative properties of the artifact).

The conceptualization of an artifact as described so far is quite straightforward and simple, which is its strength and at the same time its weakness (Mitcham, 2002). Designing an artifact sounds pretty easy in this description, but every designer knows how complex it is in reality. In principle there are indeed only two natures to be taken into account (the physical and the functional), but in reality each of these natures has many aspects. Therefore it would be nice to have another conceptualization that does more justice to this complexity. Sarlemijn used six factors to describe the development of technical artifacts (Sarlemijn, 1993): scientific, technological, market, political, juridical, and aesthetic factors. For an even more detailed analysis we have to turn to the Dutch philosopher Herman Dooyeweerd, who has developed a view on reality in which its complexity plays a vital part. This view is based on his conviction that each entity (for instance an artifact) exists in different aspects of reality (he uses the term "modalities" to indicate those "modes of existence"). This conviction is based on his Christian background: the complexity of reality mirrors the manifold wisdom of he who created this reality (Dooyeweerd, 1969). Dooyeweerd defined fifteen modes of reality as follows (and I describe them by means of artifacts): each artifact exists

1. in a numerical way: it has a certain number of parts;
2. in a spatial way: it takes up a certain space;
3. in a kinematical way: it can move or be moved;
4. in a physical way: it can interact with other artifacts (e.g., hit them);

5. in a biotic way: it may be a living being itself or be used by living beings;
6. in a psychic way: it can be observed and experienced;
7. in a logical way: one can analyze it by distinguishing its properties;
8. in a developmental way: people have developed it;
9. in a symbolic way: it can be given a name and be represented in drawings or text;
10. in a social way: it can serve a purpose in the way people live and work together;
11. in an economic way: it can be bought and sold;
12. in an aesthetic way: it can be appraised for beauty (or detested for ugliness);
13. in a juridical way: it can be patented or be described in a law;
14. in an ethical way: it can be used in a good or a bad way; and
15. in a pistic (belief-related) way: it can be the object of trust and belief.

Note that in the aspects (1 through 4) the artifact can function as both subject and object (e.g., in the physical aspect: it can hit other artifacts or be hit by them), while in aspects (5 through 15) it can only serve as an object (e.g., in the economic aspect: it can be bought, but not buy). Note also that there is a certain sequence in the list, particularly for the lower aspects. Each aspect assumes the lower aspects. For example, an artifact can interact with other artifacts (physical aspect) because they can move (kinematical aspect); they can move only because there is space (spatial aspect); and we can only speak of three-dimensional space due to the fact that there are numbers (numerical aspect).

Dooyeweerd's idea is that there are certain laws for each of the aspects. For each aspect there are scientific disciplines that examine the laws of that particular aspect. For instance, physics examines laws in the physical aspect, psychology examines laws in the psychic aspect, and economics examines laws in the economic aspect. Some of these laws require obedience (for instance, the laws that are examined in the juridical aspect), other laws do not (for instance, the laws in the physical aspect). The consequence of this for designing artifacts is that the designer has to take into account all the laws that hold for the various aspects as far as the existence of the artifact is concerned. That means that designers have to take into account what amount of space is available, because no two things can be in the same place (spatial aspect); the designer has to examine what price people are willing to pay for it (economic aspect); the designer has to be concerned about possible abuse of the artifact (ethical aspect). For the pistic aspect it is striking that designers sometimes develop strong beliefs about their own artifacts and they need to be aware of that because otherwise they miss opportunities for better solutions. These are only examples, and extending the list will soon create the awareness that designing indeed is a very complex matter because of the enormous variety of laws in all those aspects. Of course it is impossible for a designer to catch them all, but it is good to try and catch as many as reasonably possible because missing out an essential one might lead to failure of the design. For setting priorities in the search for constraining laws, the designer can use another concept that Dooyeweerd defined as part of his ontology, namely the qualifying function of an entity. This function indicates in what aspect the entity, in our case an artifact, has to function primarily. For a banknote, the qualifying function is in the economic aspect: it has to be designed in such a way that at least it can be used as a means for buying and selling. That means, for instance, that its value has to be clear. Other aspects may be of interest too, but not as a first priority (for instance, it is nice when the banknote also functions well in the aesthetic aspect, i.e., when people appreciate its appearance, but this is not the primary concern for the designer). The qualifying function helps the designer to set priorities amid the enormous amount of law-related considerations.

In the description of what artifacts are, we have already met the idea of beliefs. Both designers and users have beliefs about artifacts. The concept of beliefs is closely related to the concept of knowledge. Therefore the domain of "technology as objects or artifacts" and the domain of "technology as knowledge" are related. In order to get a fuller understanding of how people deal with artifacts we have to move on to examining what technological knowledge is. That is the focus of the next section of this chapter.

The Nature of Technological Knowledge

The question "what is technological knowledge" raises the question "what is knowledge in general." In epistemology many debates circle around the question of whether or not the following description is adequate or can be improved to become adequate: knowledge is "justified true belief" (Audi, 1998). What does that mean? Well, in order for someone to be able to claim that the designer knows something, the designer first has to believe it (how can one know it without even believing it), the designer needs to have some sort of evidence or justification for believing it, and finally it has to be true. The content of the belief can be expressed in a proposition. For instance, when an engineer claims to know that material X has property Y, the designer has to believe it (i.e., believe the proposition: "material X has property Y"), have found justification for it (for example by looking it up in a handbook or by measuring it), and it has to be true (otherwise it can not be knowledge, but only a misunderstanding). In order for this knowledge to be called "scientific knowledge" there are more conditions, in particular for the way justification has been found. Already without even considering if this definition fits with technological knowledge, one can raise doubts about it. It may, for instance, be the case that the justification is not related to the truth of a fact (when my watch has stopped running at 3 o'clock, but I accidentally look at it when it is 3 o'clock again, I seem to have found justification for my belief that it is now 3 o'clock, but the fact that this is purely accidentally the real time makes us hesitate to call this "knowledge" of the right time). Examining the appropriateness of the definition for technological knowledge, however, raises even more questions.

Things get even more problematic with this definition when we question the idea that knowledge is belief-based. In the first place the knowledge in technology is of a different kind. A carpenter could say, "I know how to hammer a nail into a piece of wood." That kind of "knowing" is not proposition-based. It can be called knowing-how (Ryle, 1949). It is not the belief that hammering a nail into a piece of wood is a matter of first doing A, than doing B, and finally doing C. Even if asked to do so, the carpenter would have great difficulty making his knowledge of how to hammer a nail into a piece of wood explicit by describing such a sequence of action in such a way that it would really make clear why he always ends up with the nail going into the wood exactly as he intended. There is more in it than just the knowledge of what sequence of action to go through, and that part of his knowledge cannot be expressed in terms of propositions. Another question is whether all technological knowledge is belief-based. Beliefs are generally taken to be involuntary: you, reader, cannot decide whether or not you believe that what you have in your hand now is a book. Beliefs are a spontaneous result of perception, testimony, memory, or reasoning (these are generally seen as primary sources of beliefs). But when an engineer claims that he knows that for this piece of wood he needs such and such a nail, this is the outcome of a decision, and not a belief that was a spontaneous outcome of a perception or any other primary source of knowledge. That has to do with the normative dimension in that type of knowledge. Much knowledge about what should be—and many times, that is what engineers' knowledge is about—has a decision as a source and therefore is not involuntary like beliefs are.

Normativity plays an important part in what engineers, designers, and users know in various ways. We can see that by considering the kind of knowledge engineers can have of artifacts. Thereby we can refer to the two natures of artifacts. These two natures, the physical and the functional, give rise to the following types of technological knowledge (De Vries 2003):

1. knowledge of the physical nature of the artifact ("paper of type X has property Y");
2. knowledge of the functional nature of the artifact ("the function of a photocopier means that it ought to . . ."); and
3. knowledge of the relation between the physical and the functional nature of the artifact ("paper of type X is suitable for use in a photocopier").

Knowledge of the physical nature is about what is. There is no normativity in that. But the other two types of knowledge have a normative dimension. Let us first examine the knowledge of functions. Knowing that this machine is a photocopier means knowing that it ought to enable us to make a duplicate of a sheet of paper. There is an "ought to" in this knowledge, a normative dimension. It is this normative dimension that enables us to say "this is a good photocopier," or "photocopiers of this brand are good photocopiers," as explored in the previous section of this chapter. Now let us turn to the knowledge of relations between the physical nature and the functional nature of the artifact. This kind of knowledge can be expressed as such: I know that this type of paper is suitable for use in a photocopier. "Suitable" is a judgment. That too has a normative dimension. There is a second sort of this knowledge of relations between physical and functional nature: I know that paper with such and such properties is needed for use in photocopiers. This is not a judgment but a prescription. Prescriptions are normative too (they also have the "ought to" dimension that we saw in knowledge of functions). Note that this normative dimension makes technological knowledge different from scientific knowledge. Scientific knowledge does not have this "ought to" aspect. When a physicist studies a photo made in a bubble chamber, and says, "I know that this is an electron," (s)he does not mean to say that this is an object that "ought to . . . ," because there is no "ought to" to the behaviour of that object. It just does what it does, and there is no reason for us to prescribe anything to it, or assess whether or not we agree with its behaviour. Surely, there are norms for the acceptance of the knowledge of electrons (do we have enough evidence that it is an electron indeed?) but not in the content of that knowledge.

As in the previous section, we can get a more detailed impression of the content of technological knowledge by taking into account the (fifteen) aspects as defined by Dooyeweerd. The knowledge that is involved in designing artifacts contains knowledge of the numerical aspect, the spatial aspect, etc. As stated in the previous section, there are separate scientific disciplines for each of these aspects. That means that designers have to draw from various disciplines in order to gain all the knowledge that is necessary or useful in the design process (Ropohl, 1997). This makes designing a multidisciplinary affair. In the design process, all these knowledge elements blend together in the design. This can be called "integration of knowledge." That happens when the designer turns away from the abstract perspective of the artifact that is offered by the various scientific disciplines, to a comprehensive and concrete view on the artifact. Nowadays there is a second way of knowledge integration that is pursued, namely integration of knowledge at the abstract, scientific level. New interdisciplines are developed that seek for laws that transcend individual aspects. Examples of such disciplines are STS Studies (Science, Technology, and Society) and environmental studies. Such studies are closer to practical situations than the traditional disciplines are, and this was often the motive for developing them. Interdisciplinarity comes in degrees (Boden, 1997). It may start with scientists of different disciplines meeting now and then to get to know each other's work, to a daily close cooperation in which the disciplinary background of the participants is made manifest in their past achievements. Such degrees can also be found in the work of designers. Sometimes design work takes place by individual designers or by a group of designers, all of whom have the same disciplinary background. But in other cases design work takes place in groups of designers with quite different disciplinary backgrounds. In both cases knowledge of different aspects can be integrated, but in the second case there is of course a deeper knowledge of each of the aspects than in the first case. That is why there is a tendency nowadays to put together multidisciplinary design groups.

Consequences for Teaching about Technology

What does all this mean for teaching about technology? That is the question I address in this final section. It is important to note that most learners are much more aware of the artifacts dimension than of the knowledge dimension. When an average thirteen-year-old boy or girl is asked to say what comes into his/her mind when the word "technology" is mentioned, a whole list of artifacts (mainly of a "high-tech" character) is the result. The idea that technology also comprises knowledge, and that technology is something one can study, is much less obvious to them. When teaching about artifacts, the dual-nature concept can be used as an educational strategy to present the artifact in a very basic and concise way, so that the learner first gets to see the fundamentals of the artifact before going into any detail. To raise awareness of the complexity of the design process that led to the artifact, the concept of the modalities can be used, in combination with the idea of laws for the various aspects, and the qualifying function as a means for moving back to the basics. The awareness of these aspects also helps the teacher to seek useful relationships with other disciplines (in the case of tertiary education) or school subjects (in the case of primary and secondary education). When teaching, it is important to take into account the different nature of different types of knowledge (McCormick 1997). Knowledge that cannot be expressed in propositions probably must be taught with a different educational strategy from knowledge that can be expressed in propositions. In teaching about technology, the normative dimension should be taken into account. The learners should be well aware that knowledge in technology is often about what should be, not about what is. That means that knowledge in technology often is a matter of decisions and preferences. Values therefore often play an important part in technology, and discussions about that should not be avoided. Ethics and aesthetics (two fields in which values of good and bad, and of harmony or disharmony are concerned) should be involved in teaching about technology (in principle at all levels, although the practical elaboration of that will of course differ for different levels).

Thus philosophical reflections on artifacts and knowledge can be used for teaching about technology. In general one can say that the philosophy of technology is of great value for technology education. This book serves a purpose in that respect.

References

Audi, R. (1998). *Epistemology. A Contemporary Introduction to the Theory of Knowledge*. London and New York: Routledge.

Baird, D. (2004). *Thing Knowledge*. Chicago: Chicago University Press.

Boden, M. (1997). "What is interdisciplinarity?". In R. Cunningham (ed.), *Interdisciplinarity and the Organisation of Knowledge in Europe*. Euroscientia conference. Luxembourg: Office for the Official Publications of the European Communities: 13–26.

Dipert, R. (1993). *Artifacts, Art Works and Agency*. Philadelphia: Temple University Press.

Dooyeweerd, H. (1969). *A New Critique of Theoretical Thought, Vols I–IV* (transl. from Dutch by D. Freeman and W. Young). S.l.: The Presbyterian and Reformed Publishing Company.

Houkes, W., Vermaas, P. Dorst, H., and Vries, M.J. de (2002). Design and use as plans: an action-theoretical account. *Design Studies*, 23 (303–320).

Kroes, P. and Meijers, A. (2000). "Introduction: a discipline in search of its identity." In P. Kroes, and A. Meijers (eds.), *The Empirical Turn in the Philosophy of Technology*. Oxford: Elsevier Science, xvii–xxxv.

Laudan, R. (1984). "Introduction." In R. Laudan (ed.), *The Nature of Technological Knowledge. Are Models of Scientific Change Relevant?* Dordrecht: D. Reidel Publishing Company, 1–26.

Meijers, A. (2000). "The relational ontology of technical artifacts." In P. Kroes and A. Meijers (eds.), *The Empirical Turn in the Philosophy of Technology*. Oxford: Elsevier Science, 81–96.

McCormick, R. (1997). "Conceptual and procedural Knowledge." In M.J. de Vries and A. Tamir (eds), *Shaping Concepts of Technology. From Philosophical Perspectives to Mental Images*. Dordrecht: Kluwer Academic Publishers, 141–159.

Mitcham, C. (1994). *Thinking Through Technology. The Path between Engineering and Philosophy*. Chicago: University of Chicago Press.

Mitcham, C. (2002). "Do Artifacts Have Dual Natures? Two Points of Commentary on the Delft Project," *Techné*, 6: 2 (9–12).

Pitt, J. (2001). "What Engineers Know." *Techné*, 5: 3 (17–30).

Ropohl, G. (1997). "Knowledge Types in Technology." In M. de Vries, and A. Tamir (eds.), *Shaping Concepts of Technology: From Philosophical Perspectives to Mental Images*. Dordrecht: Kluwer Academic Publishers, 65–72.

Ryle, G. (1949). *The Concept of Mind*. Chicago: The University of Chicago Press.

Sarlemijn, A. (1993). "Designs are cultural alloys. STeMPJE in design methodology." In M. de Vries, N. Cross, and D. Grant (eds), *Design Methodology and Relationships with Science*. Dordrecht: Kluwer Academic Publishers, 191–248.

Scruton, R. (1996). *Modern Philosophy. An Introduction and Survey*. London: Penguin Books.

Vincenti, W. (1990). *What Engineers Know and How They Know It*. Baltimore: Johns Hopkins Press.

Vries, M.J. de (2003). "The nature of technological knowledge: extending empirically informed studies into what engineers know," *Techné*, 6: 3 (1–21).

Vries, M.J. de (2005a). *Teaching About Technology. An Introduction to the Philosophy of Technology for Non-philosophers*. Dordrecht: Springer. Kluwer Academic Publishers.

Vries, M.J. de (2005b). *80 Years of Research at Philips. The History of the Philips Natuurkundig Laboratorium, 1914–1994*. Amsterdam: Amsterdam University Press.

CHAPTER 3

Technology and Knowledge: Contributions from Learning Theories

Robert McCormick

Introduction

There is a tendency to see learning as a process that operates on the "content" of what is to be learned and that content is seen to be independent of *how* it is learned. Thus discussions of the nature of technological knowledge centre around philosophical arguments such as how science and technology might differ, or cultural analyses that try to relate knowledge to the nature of technological activity as found in industry and other contexts. These analyses are quite legitimate and important in order to clarify the nature of technological knowledge. However, these approaches tend to see knowledge as an object to be passed around and which will find its way into a learner's head. This is a legitimate view of how learning relates to knowledge, but it is only *one* view. It encapsulates a particular view of mind, and thus of the nature of knowledge. Another view, however, sees knowledge as closely related to the context in which it has been learned and used. Individuals who have come to understand ideas in different contexts will have different views of the knowledge they "possess." This view may still have a focus on the individual mind, but one that sees physical and perhaps even social aspects of knowledge intertwined with understanding.

Contemporary theories of learning contain elements of each of these individual and social views of mind, and each theory has important implications for how we see knowledge and how we structure and support student learning in the technology classroom. In this chapter, I explore the nature of these views of learning, what they have to say

about the nature of knowledge, and how that in turn relates to technological knowledge. With this kind of framework, it is then possible to
examine examples of technology classrooms through a different lens
than is often the case. Four such examples will be presented here. The
first relates to how knowledge learned in one context can be different to
that in another, even though some of the underlying ideas are the same.
One of the reasons for this is the role of tools in mediating thinking. The
second relates to how we might draw on and use knowledge from other
parts of the curriculum, and particularly from the science classroom.
The third draws on the ideas of knowledge learned in context, and the
way experts work, to argue that a qualitative approach to knowledge
might be more productive in technology education. The final example
explores the implications of social views of learning that give new
insights into collaborative activities.

Each of these examples contain some important implications for
viewing technology classrooms, and the richness they offer to both their
analysis and, more importantly, the kinds of student activities that are
planned and supported. The chapter ends with a plea for these kinds of
views to inform both research and pedagogy in technology education.

Contemporary Views of Learning: Two Approaches to Mind

These views can be characterized at one end of the spectrum as *symbol
processing* and at the other as *situated* views of the mind (Bredo, 1994).
The symbol-processing view, as the name suggests, sees the mind as a
manipulator of symbols. These symbols are learned and stored in memory; when confronted with a problem a person searches the memory for
symbols to represent the problem and then manipulates them to solve
the problem. This is the usual idea we have of applying the understanding of a concept to a new situation. The symbols are learned, through a
knowledge-construction process, that is, learners make meaning from
experiences.

The second view of mind is represented by a group of theories stemming from the sociocultural tradition. A common feature of this view
of learning is the role of others in creating and sharing meaning. The
construction in symbol processing has some social element in the construction process. For example, Piaget focused upon individual internalization of knowledge, but saw a role for peer interaction to produce
cognitive conflict that would result in a change in the thinking of the
individual, leading to the internalization of a concept or idea. The sociocultural view adds a concern for joint knowledge construction. This

latter approach to learning has been labeled as "situated," and is contrasted with a symbol processing view, with meaning being created through participating in social activity. In this sense, there is no individual notion of an idea or concept, but a distributed one.

Rather than seeing learning as a process of transfer of knowledge from the knowledgeable to the less knowledgeable, a situated view is concerned with engagement in culturally authentic activity. Such activity is part of a *community of practice* (Lave and Wenger, 1991). To learn to be a doctor is not just to learn the requisite physiology, anatomy etc., but to enter into the community of practice of doctors. A novice learner starts on the outside of the community and as understanding increases, moves towards a more central participation in that community of practice, eventually taking part in its transformation; what Lave and Wenger (1991) termed a movement from "legitimate peripheral participation" to central participation. Mutual understanding, or "intersubjectivity" comes through this participation (Rogoff, 1990), and with it a transformation of identity. Intersubjectivity between participants arises from the shared understanding based on a common focus of attention and some shared presuppositions that form the ground for communication.

From this view of situated learning comes a central focus on collaboration (between peers and others) and problem solving. Unlike the symbol-processing view, problem solving in a situated view is a shared activity even when it is undertaken with an expert; expert and novices jointly solving problems.

Another feature of situated learning is the notion of *enculturation and participation*. Learning is a process of enculturation into a domain, through participation in shared activities. So that when we learn, we learn to *become something*. It is not just a matter of mastering a body of knowledge. One reason for young people to learn technology is so that they can understand the nature of technologists and how they work; to allow them to participate in technological activity. (There is, however, no implication that this learning will result in them becoming technologists, just that they understand their domain.)

Participation, in the situated approach, means more than that learning is not simply "in the head," nor just that it takes place in a social *and* physical context, but that it is related to action. In contrast to the symbol-processing view, knowledge guides action, and action guides knowledge; the relationship between thinking and action is reciprocal. Knowledge is integrated with activity, along with the tools, sign systems, and skills associated with the activity. A study by Scribner (1985) illustrated this when she showed that dairy workers viewed their knowledge about dairy products in ways that depended on the nature of the activity they undertook and the kinds of paperwork and organization needed for that activity. Thus those who were warehouse workers differed in how they viewed their knowledge against that of delivery drivers. The tools (in this case "delivery notes") mediated their thinking.

Views of Learning and Knowledge

Viewing learning as transformation of identity and enculturation into communities of practice also requires a quite different conception of knowledge to that held by those who hold a symbol-processing view of mind. In symbol processing, "concepts" are objects to be internalized (stored in memory); in situated learning, "the activity in which knowledge is developed and deployed is not separable from or ancillary to learning and cognition" (Brown, Collins, and Duguid, 1989: 32). These two views will be explored.

Cognitive psychologists describe the structure of knowledge in terms of two types of knowledge, namely conceptual and procedural knowledge (Glaser, 1984). *Procedural knowledge* is simply "know-how-to-do-it" knowledge. *Conceptual knowledge*, on the other hand, is concerned with relationships among "items" of knowledge, such that when students can identify these links they are said to have "conceptual understanding." Thus, in the area of "gearing" in technology, we hope that students will see the relationships among "direction of rotation," "change of speed," and "torque." It is important to emphasize that conceptual knowledge is not simply factual knowledge, but consists of ideas that give some power to thinking about activity.

The idea of "situatedness" on the other hand means that context is crucially interwoven with knowledge, and that "decontextualized knowledge," the focus of educational institutions, is an unhelpful idea. Indeed Lave and Wenger (1991) reject the existence of such knowledge, arguing that the conditions of learning situate knowledge, and that schools themselves, for example, are very specific contexts. So, abstract and concrete knowledge are not distinct, but the former is simply disconnected from the activity of the community of practice. The implication of this is that, unlike the assumption in cognitive constructivism, a concept learned in, say, the science classroom will not necessarily be useable in the technology classroom, as I show later.

Theories of learning that see knowledge as "in the head" and those that see it "in action" value different kinds of knowledge. Each theory will have a different vision of what it is like to be an expert, which in various ways all learners are trying to be (or at least trying to develop their expertise). Cognitive constructivists are likely to favor a clear set of concepts that are well integrated in the expert's head, and that can be retrieved for use. (Later in the chapter I show how this is not quite so clear cut, as experts use context-specific knowledge.) Those who support a situated cognition view are likely to talk a different language, as their concern is rather with activity, practice and participation, and would see expertise in terms of the extent of participation in a community. Views of the nature of expertise will therefore depend on views of learning and knowledge.

Anna Sfard (1998) characterized the different positions on learning by pointing out that we all use metaphors that underlie our spontaneous everyday conceptions and our theorizing (e.g., about learning). She argues that two metaphors underlie theories of learning:

- the acquisition metaphor;
- the participation metaphor.

The acquisition metaphor (AM) is evident when we think about knowledge as a commodity (an object), that can be developed or constructed. For example, we talk of "concept development" with the concept as a basic unit of knowledge. Whether the knowledge-acquisition process is seen as either transmission or as a construction process, the individual accumulates it, like some kind of material. Typical words used that display this metaphor are: knowledge, concept, conception, idea, notion, misconception, meaning, sense, schema, fact, representation, material, and contents. There are also a number of processes that we use to describe how learners make knowledge their own: reception, acquisition, construction, internalization, appropriation, participatory appropriation, transmission, attainment, development, accumulation, and grasp. These processes may of course be different, but in the end, the knowledge becomes individual property that, once acquired, can be applied, transferred, and "given" to others.

The participation metaphor (PM) avoids referring to knowledge as an entity and replaces "knowledge" with "knowing," and "having knowledge" with "doing." Through the use of ideas of participation and discourse, "participation in activities" becomes important, not "possession of knowledge"; becoming a member of subject community replaces learning a subject.

Sfard (1998: 7) represents the way the metaphors map onto various aspects of theories in the form of a table (Table 3.1).

Table 3.1 The metaphorical mappings

Acquisition metaphor		Participation metaphor
Individual enrichment	Goal of learning	Community building
Acquisition of something	Learning	Becoming a participant
Recipient (consumer), (re)constructor	Student	Peripheral participant, apprentice
Provider, facilitator, mediator	Teacher	Expert participant, preserver of practice/discourse
Property, possession, commodity (individual, public)	Knowledge, concept	Aspect of practice/discourse/ activity
Having, possessing	Knowing	Belonging, participating, communicating

School Knowledge

Lave and Wenger (1991) draw attention to the problem, for say school technology, that those who work in schools are not part of the community of practice of technologists, but of "schooled adults." So, rather than a "master" [sic, "expert"] who is engaged in joint activity with the apprentice, we have a teacher who is trying to represent the community of practice of technologists. Learners, in contrast, engage in activity that draws its authenticity from the community of "schooling." Consequently, the knowledge that is the substance of the teaching and learning is related to this school community, and hence divorced from the world outside the educational institution. For the teacher or instructor who is not engaged in the situated activities of the community of practice (e.g., of production engineers), there is an obstacle, namely that this teacher is not necessarily a participant in that community. In many cases the teacher may never have been a member of the community in any sense outside of a school context, though of course some may have been designers or engineers and so forth, before coming into teaching. Teachers are thus participants in the community of practice of technology teachers, and with this comes associated *school* technology knowledge.

An example of the impact of school knowledge comes from Ireland where they teach technical drawing in schools, and within this, geometric drawing.[1] Students are given examination questions about mine shafts (as in coal mines) that ask them to make complex geometric constructions where they are given co-ordinates of planes and asked to show certain views to determine how the planes intersect. Students have to learn how to do these kinds of examination questions and teachers show them "rules of thumb" that allow them to enact procedures to carry out the constructions. In a sense they are almost examination tricks, and tricks that have little meaning outside the school context. Indeed when an expert draughtsperson from outside school tried one of these questions he took a long time to carry out the task (such that in the examination situation he would have failed because he did not complete enough of the question), simply because he did not know any of these rules of thumb. These were not rules of thumb that are derived from a community of practice of draughtspersons, but the "community of schooled adults," to use the Lave and Wenger phrase.

We now have developed the basic ideas of the relationships between at least two views of learning and their corresponding views of knowledge. Some of the consequences of these will be examined, with an emphasis on the situated view, which in my view provides the most insightful reflections on the technology classroom, and the associated knowledge issues.

Technological Knowledge in the Classroom

In this section, I examine four examples of where the implications of the ideas on learning are seen in action in the classroom. Viewing classroom activity using different perspectives on learning gives insights into the pedagogic issues for technology teachers, as well as setting agendas for research. The four examples concern knowledge in tools, knowledge for use, qualitative knowledge, and knowledge in collaborative activities. In the first example I explore the importance of the mediation of knowledge by the tools (both physical and symbolic) used in particular activities. This shows the findings of Scribner (1985), discussed earlier, operating in the school and makes the use of knowledge across the curriculum more problematic than may appear to those involved with the classroom. The second example extends this by illustrating how the context within which knowledge is learned shapes the nature of that knowledge, and limits the extent to which students can use the understanding gained in one school subject in another. The third example explores the nature of expert knowledge, seen as both context specific and qualitative, and shows how students and teachers already have access to such knowledge and should capitalize on it. Finally, the fourth example explores the implications for the social aspects of learning and how this throws new light on collaborative activity and how to understand the processes students carry out.

Example 1: Knowledge in Tools

In the days before computer-aided design, all those involved in drawing offices of factories used T-squares and set-squares. Such tools allowed horizontal, vertical, and angled lines (typically 60°, 30°, and 45°) to be drawn anywhere on the drawing board. Embedded in these tools were mathematical ideas (such as parallel and perpendicular lines), which in a sense are invisible to students. These ideas should be made visible. Evens and McCormick (1997) have shown how the language of a technology teacher teaching orthographic projection, and using T-squares and set-squares, is completely devoid of the underlying mathematical ideas. This is not because he does not know them, but because the ideas are embedded in the tools of this particular community of practice. It appears that the same may be true with computer-aided design packages, that contain knowledge built into the software features, and that similarly in mathematics dynamic geometry packages have different mathematical knowledge built in (see Davidson, Evens, and McCormick, 1998). Each package reflects its respective communities of practice.

The result of this is that, although students may learn ideas such as "reflection" in the mathematics class (as a concept), they may be unable to see this in orthographic drawing task where, for example, they will use a 45° line to "project" dimensions to a plan view from a side view. Our research on this has shown that a technology teacher may attach magical properties to the line, rather than explaining how the dimensions are consistently projected using this particular angle of line (Evens and McCormick, 1997). The line is produced using an appropriate set square, which has the angle of refection "embedded into it." Despite having learned about reflection in mathematics, few of the students may use the line to carry out the projection (e.g., measure the dimensions independently and transfer them to the new view). They may draw the line at the wrong angle (i.e., use the wrong set-square) and hence obtain the incorrect dimensions, or put the line in after all the views have been drawn, in which case it fulfils no function.

This example not only shows how the mathematics is embedded in the tools, but also the failure of mathematics classroom knowledge to transfer, because of not being learned in a form that can be used in the technology classroom. This insight, of the situated and mediated nature of knowledge, implies that teachers across the curriculum will need to explore the different ways their subjects view common concepts and ideas, and how the tools (symbolic and physical) they use frame their students' understanding of them.

Example 2: Knowledge for Use

Technology teachers are rightly concerned that students do not just acquire inert knowledge, but are able to use it in the process of designing and making. They also have to assume that knowledge from other areas of the curriculum is already understood by students, without which their task of teaching would become unmanageable. This is problematic, and underplays the difficulties for students in learning and using knowledge. The view from cognitive constructivism is that students should be able to use their ideas from, say, science (i.e., transfer them) because they will have learned them in a general form that is applicable anywhere. But, as I just illustrated in the first example, the situated view indicates that, if they have learned these ideas in a science classroom context, where say circuits are abstract and, for example, a resistance is represented by a coil of wires (both diagrammatically and in practical work), then when they are faced with an electronic circuit (with positive and negative "rails"), or a small ceramic resistor, they may not associate these with their equivalents in science.

An example of how technology teachers are likely to underplay the difficulties in teaching and learning the conceptual knowledge required in design and technology tasks is shown in the first lesson of an electronic badge project (with a simple LED and transistor switch), which my colleagues and I have researched (McCormick and Murphy, 1994). A teacher was trying to introduce and develop a number of terms and concepts "familiar" to students that would be used to differing degrees in the project. These terms and concepts, discussed during the first few minutes of the introductory part of the lesson, are shown in table 3.2, along with the ideas or terms used by students, indicating their prior knowledge. The number and difficulty of these electrics concepts are a demanding start to a project, and the answers given (by very few students in the class) indicate difficulties; we know from science education research that these concepts prove difficult for students throughout their secondary school career (Shipstone, 1985).

Although all this knowledge was the subject of specific teaching, later knowledge was invoked that would not have been available to most students. Thus, when the teacher did not have enough of the correct value resistor, he gave out two resistors the combined value of which (in series) was the same as the one he originally wanted, and he told students to solder them together. This implies that students understood the sum of resistors in series. In initially discussing resistance (Table 3.2: time 10.17), it is evident that student D has a "science-laboratory" view of resistors, that is, that they are made up of "lots of wires." How students can reconcile this with the small ceramic resistors they use is difficult to imagine, and requires a concept of conductivity not usually dealt with in the science lesson at this stage in secondary schooling.[2]

Table 3.2 Concepts and terms used in the first session of the electronic badge project; "B," "D," and "J" are students who can be identified during the interaction

Time	Concept or idea	Teacher's term or analogy	Students' term or idea (prior knowledge)
10:15	Circuit	Running track	D: goes in a complete circle . . . not a gap in it J: not broken
10:16	Battery	(accepts B's term) Provides the force	B: power source
10:16	Battery positive and negative	Starts at one point	
	Battery symbol and polarity	[visual] Cell is part of battery	D says it is a cell
10:15–10:16	Direction of flow (what 'flows' is unspecified)	It goes from . . . and goes to In fact he says this is not what happens [implying electron flow in opposite direction?]	D: from positive sign . . . to negative sign
10:17	Flow of electrons around circuit		
10:17	Control of flow of electrons	Implies a resistor by accepting D's response	Switch or a resistor
10:17	Resistor	Slows [electrons] down	Lots of little wires . . . it has to go further
	Volts	"v" as battery voltage	Volts
	Simple resistor	Restrict and direct flow of electrons	
	Light dependent resistor	[visual] LDR	Solar panel
	resistor color codes (being able to interpret)	Four colored bands give value: first number, second number, number of zero's	[new knowledge]
	resistor tolerance (final color band)	Amount [of resistors] above and below	[new knowledge]

Example 3: Qualitative Knowledge

It is already well understood in the field of, for example, physics problem-solving, that experts always start by thinking about solutions in qualitative terms (Glaser, 1984). This is in stark contrast to how we start novices off on learning how to do such problem solving, which is, invariably, with figures and equations; working without much overall understanding of what they are doing. Chris Dillon, in his account of qualitative approaches used by experts, characterizes them by the degree to which, on the one hand, they reflect the device (that is to be controlled or understood), and on the other, the mathematics (or science) model that could be used to represent the device's operation (Dillon, 1994). Psychologists who deal with real-world tasks also discuss knowledge in terms of the devices or systems to which they relate (Gott, 1988). For technologists this is important, because they deal with devices and systems (designing, making, and repairing them), and because their conceptual knowledge will be linked to them rather than only to abstract science concepts. In the area of "real-world" tasks it is the context-specific device knowledge that makes fault finding, for example, successful.

This contrasts with science, where the effort is to try to strip away the context to reveal the application of a scientific idea, law, or theory. Thus, tasks that are set in a context by science teachers are not necessarily taken seriously by them, and they expect the students to "look through" this context to the science "beneath" it. This can disadvantage girls who are likely to take the context seriously, as my colleague Patricia Murphy has shown (Murphy *et al.*, 1996). She gives an example of a teacher who sets a "dissolving-sugar" investigation in the context of tea drinking, and expects students to experiment with tea at a range of temperatures down to room temperature. The teacher may be surprised that a student (in this case a girl) resists this by saying "nobody drinks cold tea"; she sees no point in testing the solubility at temperatures much below that which makes the tea drinkable.

It is also true that many devices that students will come across in the technology classroom are too complex for them to understand in terms of their science understanding. A not-untypical technology project of a simple money-box, in which a coin dropped operates a pivoted beam, which in turn makes a bird rock, is likely to be beyond the science of an eleven-year-old student. The overall mechanism and each of the components (e.g., the falling coin, the beam, and pendulum) could be *understood* with science, and made to operate successfully. This could be done, for example, by:

- varying the distance of fall of the coin to allow enough momentum to be gained so that even a small coin would cause rocking;
- balancing the beam horizontally with an off-set pivot, such that it would move on impact;
- choosing the correct length pendulum to sustain rocking.

Not only is the science of this well beyond children aged around eleven years, even a professional engineer would be hard pushed to represent the operation of such a system as a whole through quantitative science and mathematics. Any engineer would use qualitative reasoning to ensure a working mechanism without resorting to the mathematics and physics. There may be some experimenting with the size of coins on a pivoted beam to determine the amount of fall necessary, and so on. It might look like trial and error, but in fact it would be qualitative reasoning supported by a qualitative knowledge of science.

The qualitative reasoning is not just a feature of the way an engineer might work, but also of two girls and their teacher in the above example. The girls had very little understanding of the science knowledge, but were able to use qualitative knowledge. The talk around this included making "the beam *slightly* longer." A second feature of the talk involved the device knowledge noted above. Just as experts talk about mechanisms, and even electronic circuits, not in the abstract but in the particulars of the device, so did the teacher and students, using these two features of qualitative knowledge. For example: "It depends how much money they put in, because if it's a 50p [a 50 pence piece is a large UK coin], its going to do "dong" like that, so it's going to go really far. Then if it's a 5p [a small UK coin] . . . it will still move only a bit."

In referring to the effect of the coins, the student says the big coin (50 pence) is going to go "dong," an illustration of device knowledge. The use of the phrase "to go really far" shows a qualitative idea, contrasting with the small coin (5 pence), which will only move it "only a bit." So they are starting to reason qualitatively about how the device works.

The teacher was similarly using qualitative knowledge in this way, but did not make this explicit. It is interesting to contrast the second example (of the badge) above, where the teacher felt obliged to explicitly teach or use electrical concepts from science, with this example of the mechanism where the teacher does not. Had the science ideas (at least about the pivoted beam) been invoked qualitatively, it is possible that the students would have been able to both use their science and see an important example of it. (In science at the students' level the beam is usually assumed to have no mass, and hence the concept of a counterweight to allow the off-set pivoted beam to balance, would be an extension of their ideas.)

Example 4: Knowledge in Collaborative Activities

Intersubjectivity is a central concept in collaboration in the sociocultural view of learning and, following on from the definition of it from Rogoff (1990) quoted earlier, she elaborates it:

- shared problem space;
- shared objects;
- shared or distributed cognition.

When students are collaborating, therefore, they need to establish shared thinking in these ways. For example, in a design project using computer-aided design (CAD), they would have to agree on the needs or problems they were trying to design for (this gives both shared goals and the basis for a "shared problem space"), and to share the ways that they express them. The computer screen can be seen as a shared object, to establish shared thinking, particularly when there is a drawing or text on the screen. Shared cognition is a more complex idea. The creation of an understanding in a discussion of a design can give rise to the pooling of ideas and the bringing of different kinds of expertise to bear on a design problem or need. But what is created is more than the sum of the thinking of those collaborating. Such thinking is not just working together and helping each other with the focus on the individual mind.

Such an example of collaboration using information communications technology (ICT) is well illustrated in desktop video-conferencing, involving two students from different schools who remotely collaborate on the design of a pen that can be manufactured from a series of plastic tubes.[3] The students had been working on this project prior to the lesson in which they collaborated. This was the first time they had ever used this communications software (though not the CAD), and prior to the lesson they had not communicated about what they would do. They started with a simple tube as the body of the pen, decided who would draw it, what color, then worked on the shape of the nib, and the pen top (shape and color).

During the interaction a number of statements were made by the students indicating collaborative thinking. The first concerned design decisions, which, although rudimentary at this initial stage, indicate how negotiation of shared understanding of the kind Rogoff (1990) indicated in her view of intersubjectivity. For example:

You're going to have the nib yellow? [indicating an implicit decision made by the other student]

It doesn't have to be round it can be square. [the student is checking that the other has considered this choice]

I'll do the clip red? [checking that this is ok]

Is that ok there, or is it a bit too big? [checking this size decision]

These design decisions are not yet very profound (color, shape and size), but as the students develop their work they could extend these in nature and range.

There were also statements that indicated students making thinking explicit, for example:

> I'm just going to draw it [*the pen top*] on it [*the body of the pen*] and then take it off. [This allows the student to get the size and proportions correct.]

This knowledge illustrates both the use of the software (to draw the pen in situ and then to move it to create it as a separate component) and the procedures involved in designing. Computer-supported collaborative activity lends itself to making thinking explicit, because the students have to explain their thinking to each other (this is the computer's "mediation" role).

Currently there is little classroom practice or research on this kind of activity, but we will need the insights of a situated view of learning, and hence collaboration, that will enable us to explore the conditions of intersubjectivity such that we can support students in the collaborative enterprise. After all, this collaboration is now a standard feature of the contemporary community of practice of professional designers (McCormick, 2004b).

Conclusion

Each of the above examples indicates to me the power of the understandings from taking views of learning as a starting point to understand the nature of knowledge as it is experienced both by technologists and those in schools trying to teach and learn in this important part of our culture. Taking a sociocultural view of learning does enrich this understanding, though it need not be taken as an exclusive perspective. In the first example I tried to illustrate the important insight from this view on the role of tools in mediating experience and understanding. Teachers need to be aware of this in the tools they use; one of our exercises in that research project was to put a technology teacher and a mathematics teacher side by side, give them a box to draw in three views and asked them to see how they each did it differently, using different symbolic and physical tools. This is the start of the kind of sharing across the curriculum that will enable teachers to understand the ways students see the knowledge differently as they move from class to class. Upon this sharing they can build a pedagogy that will help student to both see the differences and make the links in their understanding. A prerequisite, as I have indicated elsewhere (McCormick, 2004a), is a more substantial research base for teachers to draw upon.

The second example is another insight into this problem of linking understanding. Situated learning ideas indicate that knowledge is understood in the context within which it is learned. If a symbol-processing view of learning is taken, a teacher might assume that provided the concept of "electrical current" was understood in science lessons, it could be 'applied' in technology lessons. Two problems exist, first that even in the science context we know that students have quite different understanding of this concept (that reflect their everyday understanding rather than those taught in the science classroom). The second problem is that this concept as understood by students is not in an abstract generalizable form. Context is important and teachers need to take time to explore this. While we know a lot of the first problem from research, we have only just begun to work on the second one.

An extension of the context-specific nature of knowledge is seen in the third example, where experts (even viewed from the symbol process-ing perspective) operate with context-specific knowledge. They develop ways of working that stay close to the context they understand and formulate qualitative ideas that are powerful in thinking and acting. In technology education we might draw on this by stressing qualitative understanding. This does not deny the importance of quantitative knowledge, but it may be a better start to understanding and also bring some technological tasks (which involve relatively complex ideas) within the scope of school students. Here researchers in technology education, unlike those in technology outside school, have been particularly remiss. Though some of these ideas have been around for almost a decade (e.g., McCormick, 1997, 1999), little interest in them is yet evident in the technology-education-research literature.

The final example takes the social view of learning very seriously by interpreting collaborative activity as an attempt to jointly construct knowledge and understanding through the co-designing of artifacts. The new communication technologies bring this within the grasp of schools, and allow teachers to reflect the work of the communities of practice of designers in the world outside (McCormick, 2004b). Joint designing across geographically distant locations offers many possibili-ties to technology education, both to experience contemporary techno-logical activity and to develop a completely new view of collaborative learning. We know little about how to support this pedagogically, yet there is now sufficient theory and practice in other areas of learning and ICT education to enable us to begin to develop new approaches. Again, teachers need the support of empirical research that will allow them to translate the findings from the other areas into their practice.

Notes

1. I am obliged to Liam Bolger, for information from his research upon which we based this example (Bolger, 2001).
2. We have explored this kind of issue in Levinson, Murphy, and McCormick (1997).
3. The details of this are given in McCormick (2004b).

References

Bolger, W. (2001). *The Inter-relationship of Procedural and Conceptual Knowledge in Two- and Three-Dimensional Spatial Problem Solving of Technical Drawing Students*. Unpublished Ed.D. thesis. Milton Keynes: The Open University.

Bredo, E. (1994). "Reconstructing Educational Psychology: situated cognition and Deweyian pragmatism." *Educational Psychologist*, 29: 1 (23–35).

Brown, J. Collins, A., and Duguid, P. (1989). "Situated cognition and the culture of learning." *Educational Researcher*, 18: 1 (32–41).

Davidson, M., Evens, H., and McCormick, R. (1998). "Bridging the gap. The use of concepts from science and mathematics in design and technology at KS3." In J. Smith and E. Norman (eds.), *IDATER 98 International Conference on Design and Technology Educational Research and Curriculum Development*, 48–53. Loughborough: University of Loughborough.

Dillon, C. (1994). "Qualitative reasoning about physical systems—an overview." *Studies in Science Education*, 23 (39–57).

Evens, H. and McCormick, R. (1997). *Mathematics by Design: An Investigation at Key Stage 3*. Final Report for the Design Council. Milton Keynes: School of Education, The Open University.

Glaser, R. (1984). "Education and thinking: the role of knowledge." *American Psychologist*, 39: 2 (93–104).

Gott, S. (1988). "Apprenticeship instruction for real-world tasks: the coordination of procedures mental models and strategies." In E.Z. Rothkopf (ed.), *Review of Research in Education 15: 1988–89* (97–169). Washington DC: American Educational Research Association.

Lave, J. (1988). *Cognition in Practice: Mind, Mathematics and Culture in Everyday Life*. Cambridge: Cambridge University Press.

Lave, J. and Wenger, E. (1991). *Situated Learning: Legitimate Peripheral Participation*. Cambridge: Cambridge University Press.

Levinson, R., Murphy, P., and McCormick, R. (1997). "Science and technology concepts in a design and technology project: a pilot study." *Research in Science and Technological Education*, 15: 2 (235–255).

McCormick, R. (1994). "Learning through apprenticeship." In D. Blandow and M. Dyrenfurth (eds), *Technology Education in School and Industry*, 16–36. Dodrecht: Kluwer.

McCormick, R. (1997). "Conceptual and procedural knowledge." *International Journal of Technology and Design Education*, 7: 1–2 (141–159).

McCormick, R. (1999). "Capability lost and found?" *Journal of Design and Technology Education*, 4: 1 (5–14).

McCormick, R. (2004a). "Issues of learning and knowledge in technology education." *International Journal of Technology and Design*, 14: 1 (22–44).

McCormick, R. (2004b). "Collaboration: the challenge of ICT." *International Journal of Technology and Design Education* 14: 2 (159–76).

McCormick, R. and Murphy, P. (1994). *Learning the Processes in Technology*. Paper presented at the British Educational Research Association Annual Conference, Oxford University, England, September.

Murphy, P., Scanlon, E., and Issroff, K. with Hodgson, B. and Whitelegg, E. (1996). "Group work in Primary Science—emerging issues for learning and teaching." In K. Schnack (ed.), *Studies in Educational Theory and Curriculum*, Volume 14. Copenhagen: Danish School of Educational Studies.

Rogoff, B. (1990). *Apprenticeship in Thinking: Cognitive Development in a Social Context*. New York: Oxford University Press.

Scribner, S. (1985). "Knowledge at work." *Anthropology and Education Quarterly*, 16: 3 (199–206).

Sfard, A. (1998). "On two metaphors for learning and the dangers of choosing just one." *Educational Researcher*, 27: 2 (4–13).

Shipstone, D. (1985). "Electricity in simple circuits." In R. Driver, E. Guesne, and A. Tiberghien (eds), *Children's Ideas in Science*, 33–5. Buckingham: Open University Press.

CHAPTER 4

How to Understand Mundane Technology: New Ways of Thinking about Human–Technology Relations

Mike Michael

Introduction

In this chapter, I attempt to trace out some of the ways in which recent developments in the study of mundane technology might inform "technological literacy." As a subject taught in schools, "technology" (often twinned with design) makes certain assumptions about the nature of technology and the humans that engage with it. The design and production of technology is often conceptualized in terms of "fitness for function." However, the sociology of technology would problematize the very idea of "function" by showing how this is subject to all manner of negotiation. As we shall see, the malleability of "function" is something that is addressed in curricula, usually under a heading that addresses "context" (e.g., environmental or social effects). In contrast, latter-day sociology of science would seek to show how the functions of technologies emerge in the sociotechnical ensembles of which they are a part. In a sense, one can contrast the "assembling" of technology (by which is meant the assembling of skills, resources, and contexts to understand or make a technology) with the "ensembling" of technology, by which I mean the idea that technology emerges out of ensembles of heterogeneous entities in which there are various complex dynamics of ordering, disordering, and reordering. In this model of "ensembling," technologies are held to have an "influence" on people, often shaping them through their impacts upon their bodies. As such, humans are emergent too.

We also turn to more radical accounts of the relation between humans and technologies where it is not simply technologies and humans that are emergent, but the combination of these. Here, there is a shift of focus to the co-emergence of these—or rather, the production and reproduction of arrangements of humans-and-technologies, that is, of hybrids, or what I call co(a)gents. Here, the concern is with the role of such heterogeneous entities in the flow of everyday life.

In what follows, then, I begin by drawing a parallel between technological and scientific literacy in order to open up a discussion about some of the recent trends in the study of mundane technologies. I then return to the idea of technological literacy as it informs current educational practice and aspiration. I conclude by rereading "technological literacy" through the terms "ensembling," the "emergence of the human," and "co(a)gent" with a view to drawing out some implications for the teaching of technology, not least as this relates to citizenship.

Humans and Mundane Technologies:
From Understanding to Co(a)gency

What might be meant by "technological literacy?" In the multidisciplinary field of "public understanding of science" we find the cognate term "scientific literacy." This is a term that is commonly subjected to criticism because it assumes what has been called the "deficit model" of publics: publics are taken to be deficient in appropriate knowledge of science, and various attempts are made to measure and correct this deficit. Thus the Royal Society's (1985) report titled, "The Public Understanding of Science" laments the common failings in lay people's understanding of scientific knowledge and processes. If improved, scientific literacy, it is claimed, would lead, seemingly unproblematically, to greater practical competence in everyday life; increased capacity to make informed decisions; enhanced employability; enhanced ability to get involved in Western civilization and culture; a better-developed capacity to contribute to the democratic decision-making process with its increasingly prominent scientific content. However, against this model of the deficient public is counterposed a version of the lay local person who possesses local "folk" knowledges that are a crucial adjunct to expert knowledge. A classic example is Brian Wynne's (1996) case study of the contamination of the fells of Cumbria, a district in North-West England. As Wynne traces, in the immediate aftermath of the Chernobyl fallout, sheep farmers' local knowledge could have crucially supplemented the technical process whereby scientific measures of radiation were undertaken by government scientists. What Wynne identifies is not simply the importance of local knowledge, but also the relations between lay local publics and scientific institutions. In the Cumbrian case (as in many others), publics and their knowledges were deliberately marginalized: the "body language" (as Wynne calls it) of the institutions served to alienate those publics. At the crux of these relations, then, are matters of trust: does marginalization signal conspiracy? Does it signal incompetence? Here, we can trace an analytic movement from deficit, to local knowledge, to trust—a broadening out of the relation between science and the public. Further, as Irwin and Michael (2003) argue, this broadening can be extended to encompass the fact that publics are part of much wider—indeed, global—cultural and social processes, not least the pervasive cultures of consumption that are a core feature of late modern western societies (see Michael, 1998). Moreover, science itself is no less likely to be tied into these dynamics in that it is increasingly subject to the pressures of such consumers as environmental groups and user communities as well as multinationals and governments (e.g., Nowotny et al. 2001). To be "scientifically literate" in this context denotes the capacity to see science as embroiled in such dynamics—far beyond an understanding of scientific facts and procedures, it is to grasp the way that scientific institutions operate in the modern world (cf Durant, 1993).

Now the term "public understanding of science" clearly encompasses more than just laboratory science. The above example of Chernobyl includes within it technologies of various sorts, from the Chernobyl reactor itself to the Geiger counters of government scientists. Indeed, the emergence of novel technologies is deeply embroiled with these processes of "public understanding." Genetically modified organisms, xenotransplantation, nanotechnology, stem cells, smart identity cards, microchip implants—all these, and many more, are technologies that raise concerns in publics. In other words, these are sociotechnical ensembles that include social and technological actors—over and above the technologies themselves there are scientific institutions, regulatory bodies, commercial concerns, user groups—working more or less in concert. Lay people respond to these ensembles with displays of greater or lesser trust and skepticism. Thus, for example, in relation to xenotransplantation, lay respondents in focus groups were able to mobilize a number of reasons for being skeptical about this biotechnology, for example, lack of trust in scientists (seen to be motivated by hubris or money); concerns about animal welfare; worries over whether this innovation was the best way to deploy scarce resources; anxieties over the potential for cross-species viral infection (e.g., Michael and Brown, 2004). This skepticism might be said to be a sign of something like a "sociotechnical literacy."

However, notice that these technologies are "exotic" in the sense that they are ostensibly novel, are embroiled in controversy, and have meanings that are still flexible (see Bijker, 1995). They have yet to become the mundane technologies that, more or less invisibly, cohabit with us in our everyday lives. In a sense, exotic technologies are still in the process of being made, and it is relatively easy to pick our way through their embroilment in sociotechnical ensembles. When we turn to mundane technologies—shoes, Velcro, pens, TV remote controls, mattresses and so on—they are so well integrated into our daily routines that it is rather more of a chore to re-embed them within their sociotechnical ensembles. Of course, they are, of necessity, deeply embedded in such ensembles—one need only reflect on the vast apparatus of standardization that ensures that these mundane technologies "work." Ensuring that a "volt" is a "volt" or that the materials that make up mundane technologies are not poisonous (and remain so) is a continuing process that we, by and large, unreflectively and chronically trust to be properly conducted and governed (see Giddens, 1991). It is when things go wrong—when such and such a mundane technology is recalled by the manufacturer, for example—that what we might call the "ensembling" (as opposed to assembling) of mundane technologies becomes apparent.

Now, we do not need to keep these two discussions of "exotic" and "mundane" technologies so separate. Obviously, these categories are better situated on a scale rather than in opposition, and further, claims for ordinariness or novelty are part of the rhetorical arsenal by which technologies, new and old, are promoted or denigrated (Michael, 2003). More important in the present context is the way that exotic technologies have begun to illuminate the nature of our relation to technology per se. Bruno Latour (1991, 1992, 1993) has argued that technological nonhumans are necessarily present in all human encounters. Thus, "We are never faced with objects or social relations, we are faced with chains which are associations of humans (H) and nonhumans (NH). No-one has ever seen a social relation by itself . . . nor a technical relation . . . Instead we are always faced with chains which look like this H–NH–H–NH–H–NH . . ." (Latour, 1991: 110). Moreover, for Latour, both humans and nonhumans are to be conceptualized as effects, they emerge out of networks or assemblages of humans and nonhumans. This view of the embroilments of humans and technologies is something that we "Moderns" have lost sight of. "Premodern" societies were/are deeply concerned with the nature of these embroilments, making judgments about which combinations are valuable and which dangerous. By comparison, we moderns tend to deny such mixing in order to operate with such common "pure" dichotomous categories as humans and nonhumans, subjects and objects, culture and nature (and myriad others). Our recent ("amodern") sensitivity to these embroilments is an upshot of the proliferation of exotic mixtures of human and nonhuman, culture and nature that we come across in the media. Such examples as frozen embryos, sensory-equipped robots, gene synthesizers, and so on which straddle the divide between the cultural and the natural have alerted us to the fact that mundane technologies too are intrinsic to society—that is, that everyday life is mundanely heterogeneous made up of admixtures of the natural and cultural (also see Waldby, 2000).

There are two points, slightly at odds with one another, that can usefully be developed here. Firstly, this emergence of humans from their embroilments with technology suggests that mundane technological artifacts contribute to the shaping of human users. A classic example is that of the door-spring (or closer or groom). According to the strength of its spring and its tendency to slam the door, a door-groom requires certain capacities and skills on the part of human users: strength, quick reflexes, ease of movement, and so on. Latour (1992) makes this point as follows:

> [N]either my little nephews nor my grandmother could get in unaided because our groom needed the force of an able-bodied person to accumulate enough energy to close the door later . . . these doors discriminate against very little and very old persons. (234)

The action of the groom upon the human body can be said to shape and discipline the human actor—a process that Latour calls prescription (or proscription, or affordance, or allowance). As such, these technological artifacts can be thought in terms of acting as nonhuman moral agents—they embody a "local cultural condition" (Latour/Johnson, 1988: 301)—which, partly because they are so "ordinary," invisible even, to the human actors who interact with them, shape human comportment. On this score, such mundane technologies are more insidious than exotic ones the impact of which leads to such histrionic concerns about "post-humanity" or the nature of the "cyborg." Of course, there is nothing to say that any of these interactions between humans and technologies always proceeds smoothly or is not resisted (see Michael, 2000).

The second point shifts focus away from the (formative) action of mundane technology upon humans toward a new unit of analysis. These various embroilments of humans and nonhumans suggest that we should not keep them separate (indeed, Latour argues, the fact that we moderns have practiced "purification" of the human and nonhuman so assiduously has meant that these combinations have proliferated without our due consideration). For Latour and various others, the world should be seen to be populated by these mixtures—or hybrids. Let us consider an example. Contrary to the view that "it is guns that kill" or it is "people that kill," for Latour it is the "citizen-gun." Neither the "gun" nor the "citizen" have essences—they are not essentially good, or bad, or neutral, but are "relational": their qualities emerge as they enter new associations, accrue new goals, or are subject to new "translations." To enter into an association with a gun, both citizen and gun "translate" one another, becoming different. As Latour puts it, "The dual mistake of the materialists and of the sociologists is to start with essences, either those of subjects or those of objects . . . Either you give too much to the gun or too much to the gun-holder. Neither the subject, nor the object, nor their goals are fixed for ever. We have to shift our attention to this unknown X, this hybrid which can truly be said to act" (6). As such, as for "premoderns," it is the hybrid that should be the subject/object of judgment.

Taking this a step further, Michael (2000) has suggested the study of what he calls co(a)gents—discrete mixtures of an ostensibly limited number of humans and nonhumans. By co(a)gents Michael wants to connote two key things. On the one hand, he wants to emphasize the distributed agency or efficacy of the co(a)gent—it is a co-agent. On the other, he wants to stress that it is also an entity that can be considered unitary or singular—it is cogent. The unsightliness and evident artificiality of the linguistic unit "co(a)gent" also has the advantage of signaling the fact that co(a)gents are partial fabrications. They are heuristic analytic tools used to explore the heterogeneous processes of ordering and disordering that make up everyday life. That is to say, everyday life is conceived as a domain in which there are concurrent processes whereby arrangements of humans and nonhumans are reinforced, undermined, and reconfigured in various ways—it is made up of coexisting homeostatic, negentropic, and entropic dynamics. Mundane technologies play a part in these processes as parts of co(a)gents: they appear at regular intervals even as these are constantly "falling apart" in their interactions with other co(a)gents.

To abstract the key points, we can conceptualize mundane technology in terms of three aspects: "ensembling" or how it emerges from networks of heterogeneous (human and nonhuman) entities; its impact on the shaping of people; and as a component in co(a)gents. Having set out my intellectual stall, I now consider some of the implications of the foregoing for the idea of technological literacy.

Technological Literacy, Technically Speaking

I turn now to the teaching of technology in schools, and the role of technological literacy in this. In England and Wales, for example, the teaching of technology (under the rubric of Design and Technology) focuses centrally across the key stages on a number of themes:

- Developing, planning, and communicating ideas (at key stage 1 (KS1) this would include learning to develop ideas by shaping materials and putting together components);
- Working with tools, equipment, materials, and components to make quality products (e.g., at KS1 this would include learning to select tools, techniques, and materials for making a product from a range suggested by the teacher);
- Evaluating processes and products (e.g., at KS1 this would entail learning to identify what could be done differently or how work in the future could be improved);
- Knowledge and understanding of materials and component (e.g., at KS1 this would mean, for example, learning about the working characteristics of materials); and
- Breadth of study (e.g., at KS1 this would involve focused practical tasks that develop a range of techniques, skills, processes, and knowledge).

As pupils move through the key stages, these various themes of planning, practice, evaluation, understanding, and breadth become progressively more sophisticated. Most obviously, each curriculum aims to increase the skills and knowledge of the pupil, for instance, the use of ICTs in the design process, or the range of materials experienced by pupils, or the capacity to evaluate systematically the process of design and its products. So, by key stage 4, the nonstatutory guidelines include, under the heading of "Developing, planning and communicating ideas," the consideration of "issues that affect their planning [for example, the needs and values of a range of users; moral, economic, social, cultural, and environmental considerations; product maintenance; safety; the degree of accuracy needed in production]" as well as more technical and industrial concerns. Having noted this expansion of the curriculum, the main emphasis remains primarily upon the teaching of skills and knowledge.

The Design and Technology Association (DATA), which, in England and Wales and ever more so in Scotland, is "the recognized professional association which represents all those involved in design and technology education and associated subject areas" (http://web.data.org.uk/data/about_us/index.php) aims to transcend the National Curriculum's relatively narrow focus on those topics and skills that are open to assessment procedures. For DATA, design knowledge and practical skills in the making of quality products remain core, but this is allied to a view that young people also need to be prepared for citizenship in a "technological society" (http://web.data.org.uk/data/secondary/ks3_currplanning.php).

As it states on its website, for DATA, the teaching of Design and Technology should, amongst other things, "prepare young people to cope in a rapidly changing technological world; enable them to think and intervene creatively to improve that world; develop skills required to participate responsibly in home, school and community life (citizenship); help students to become discriminating consumers and users of products; help students to become autonomous, creative problem-solvers; . . . encourage the ability to consider critically the uses, effects and values dimension of design and technology (technological awareness or literacy)" (http://web.data.org.uk/data/secondary/ks3_currplanning. php).

Here, technological literacy moves beyond a mastery of technique or the assimilation of technical knowledge. Rather, it also embraces a concern with apparently substantive values. In actuality, these values are not set out explicitly; rather they are presented "formalistically" as, for instance, a commitment to discrimination, to improvement of the world, to criticism, creativity, and autonomy. Each of these is more or less uncontroversial because none says anything about content that would be addressed in such questions as what type of autonomy exactly? what limits are there to creativity? what can count as improvement? If technological literacy is aligned (correlated, even) with citizenship, then we might ask what sort of citizenship is being presupposed (after all, there are many models of citizenship and democracy—see Michael and Brown, 2000). I elaborate on this particular capacity to "do" citizenship in the conclusion. For the present, however, I am more interested in exploring a number of other features of this elaborated formulation of technology (and technological literacy) in relation to the three aspects of mundane technology identified above, namely, "ensembling," its impact on the shaping of people, and mundane technology as a component in co(a)gents.

Technological Literacy and Mundane Technology

"Ensembling" was contrasted to assembling in order to highlight the way that technology is, as it were, made "workable" by virtue of its embroilment in complex heterogeneous assemblages of entities. From the curricular outlines, we can see that the emphasis is very much upon "assembly"—the bringing together of more or less transparent resources, skills, knowledges, systems in order to allow for the design and production of a technological artifact. Of course, we should hardly be surprised by this in that within a traditional education system in which the assessment of the pupil is paramount, the student's capacity to marshal these various components in order to make technology is what is at stake. Of course, it is possible to extend this list indefinitely to include values, environment, culture—or rather a measurable sensitivity to these—in the assembly. We can illustrate more precisely what is meant by "ensembling" if we briefly consider a particular mundane technology. Michael (2000) traces how the TV remote control is embroiled in an ensemble of relations which it at once serves to reproduce, disrupt, and reorder. It is a technological artifact over which gender divides are played out ("Dad has control of it") or as Morley puts it, the remote control "is a highly visible symbol of condensed power relations" (147). At the same time it is liable routinely to go missing and much time and energy is expended on looking for it—as many of us know, this searching for the remote is never felt as routinized but rather as a disruption of routines. Moreover, these wanderings are facilitated accidentally by other technologies, such as the sofa. As Michael notes, there is a "technological coincidentalization" between the TV remote control and the "back of the sofa" (the space between the seat cushion and the back) such that the former neatly fits into the latter. Because of all these disruptions, other orderings are put in place to keep the remote control from wandering: new routines are developed (e.g., always place the remote on the mantle piece after use). With this familiar example, we illustrate the sorts of assumptions that are made in the design of a technology that become exposed often only when things go wrong. In this case, it is the most basic of assumptions about the hand that are being made: the remote needs to fit into the hand; the hand needs to get between sofa cushion and the back to remove the cushion.

In light of this example, to speak of "assembling" an artifact such that it fits in with its environment, with users' needs (both technical and aesthetic, functional and cultural) seems to me to miss the mark. Rather, the remote control enters into, and partly precipitates, a nexus of orderings, disorderings, and reorderings (both functional and cultural). We can draw a parallel here with a musical ensemble in which there are instruments that sometimes serially, sometimes concurrently, play melodically (routinized), or cacophonously (disordered), in concert or independently. The obvious implication for the teaching of technology (and technological literacy) are that such environments are complex and dynamic, at once transparent but full of hidden traps. More interestingly, one can point to the fact that pupils themselves are part of such ensembles: creativity, marshalling, design, invention entail mundane technologies (most obviously pen and paper), which themselves are folded into this "ensembling" process. Under such circumstances, it becomes difficult to assess product or process—or rather, what one is assessing is in actuality based on a "disensembling" of indiscrete dynamics (as opposed to a disassembling of discrete components). This is another way of making the same point as Bowker and Star (1999) who show how difficult it is to disaggregate the various component activities that go to make up something like "nursing health care" in order to audit them. The further irony is that the process of what I've called "disensembling" is itself subject to the same complexities; that is, the process of assessment (or audit) is the partial result of the mundane technologies of observations and recording (e.g., forms, or spreadsheets), with all the ordering and disordering that these entail.

Here, then, we see how our particular formulation of "mundane technology" serves to complicate (or, better still, "complexify") technological literacy on a number of levels: the conceptualization of the product-in-its-environment, the process of design and fabrication practice, the assessment procedure.

Now in all this, mundane technologies are involved in the "making" of people by impacting upon bodily capacities and skills. The entry of a technology into a context is thus not simply a matter of fit that can be rendered through the proper identification of the user. As we saw in Latour's example of the door-closer, users themselves must be partially re-formed (or configured, as Woolgar, 1991, puts it) by the technologies themselves. Bodies thus develop skills, forms of comportment, routines through which they accommodate to technologies. Even such "invisible" technologies as zips and Velcro require new routines (e.g., moving flesh out of the way of the zip teeth, removing lint from the Velcro's surfaces).

The implication here is that the "user" who informs the design process is an idealization. This is obvious enough, and part of technological literacy is no doubt the sensitivity to the multiplicity of potential users with their different capacities and contexts. However, the point is that the users are themselves partly constituted by the functions of the technology. The upshot is that technological literacy needs to grasp the complex (and partial) formative influence of technology. Moreover, the user who emerges in relation to a technology is highly variable. Returning to the example of the door-closer, the resistance this puts up to certain bodies generates the opportunity for the emergence of all sorts of strategies. For example, Latour's grandmother can recruit others (expand her bodily capacities through the social collective) to help her open the door—the door-closer becomes an opportunity for everyday sociality. Conversely, at the Ritz, the presence of a designated human door-opener is a mark of luxury—of conspicuous consumption. In other words, the functionality of technologies and the types of person (and human bodies) that become associated with it are contingent matters that reflect the "ensembling" of that technology. If there is a general moral to this account, it is that part of technological literacy is a sense of modesty—technologies will routinely outrun their putative functions: even as technologies "make" users, they are remade by those users. This co-emergence of user-and-technology brings us neatly to the notion of technology as a component in a co(a)gent.

Embedding technology in an ensemble—that is, ensembling—is potentially an endless process: the range of entities that can be seen to be a part of an ensemble is indefinite. The notion of co(a)gent allows for a heuristic combination of a relatively few components with which to interrogate, probe, or navigate through an ensemble in order to trace some of the usually hidden ordering and disordering patterns that make up everyday life (Michael, 2000). Some co(a)gents can be derived from popular culture. For instance, Michael situates the TV remote control within the co(a)gent of the couch potato in order to explore its role in the complex material and cultural dynamics entailed in the politics, morality, convenience, and health of television watching in particular, and consumption in general. Other co(a)gents can be explicitly "fabricated." For example, Michael develops the Cason (car-person) to trace some of the complexities of road rage; and the hudogledog (human-dog-doglead) to examine how it is that an entity, such as a human or dog or doglead, despite its routine entry into, and exit from, the hudogledog retains its identity—that is, remains identifiable as a particular singularity. In this latter case, each of the component entities moves in and out of co(a)gents: what is of interest is their apparent "unscathedness." Put another way, what work needs to be done to see—to accomplish the sense of—a technology that enters into, and falls out of, a series of co(a)gents, yet appears to remain singular and unchanged? Why does a pen stay a "pen" when, through its co(a)gency, it is variously a letter-writing implement, clutter, a probe, a child's graffiti tool of choice, and so on?

In a sense, this methodology of the co(a)gent is the obverse of the process of ensembling. Instead of situating a technology amongst the complex processes of ordering and disordering, it serves to unravel the work that goes into "extricating" a technology from its ensembles. In terms of technological literacy, one might ask why it is that even when technologies are designed to generate options—to be interactive (e.g., Barry, 2001)—they can be "closed down" in the sense that their multiple "functionalities" within ensembles are misrecognized or oversimplified. The co(a)gent is one possible concept for tracing out how this happens in ways that are commonsensical, but also in ways that are not immediately apparent.

In this section, I have attempted to unpick some implications of the present perspective on mundane technology for the notion of, and aspiration to, technological literacy. In the concluding section, I return to the link between literacy and citizenship.

Concluding Remarks: Technological Literacy and Citizenship

Above, I drew on the literature on the public understanding of science to examine the idea of technological literacy. In recent years, there is an evident shift from a concern with public understanding to an interest in "public engagement with science." Rather than educating the public so that they can take up their roles as scientific citizens, they are to be consulted, encouraged to participate, enabled to deliberate in the making of scientific decisions and policy (which, to reiterate, often concerns the development of particular technological innovations). Various techniques have been developed to allow the public to voice its views (e.g., citizens' juries, citizens' panels, consensus conferences, deliberative polling, focus groups—see Abelson et al., 2003, for a review of these techniques). Inevitably, many criticisms have been leveled at these "democratizing" initiatives. Key amongst these concerns the timing of such consultative events. As Wynne (2002) argues, the deliberation comes rather late in the day, a long way "downstream" in the innovation process when priorities and plans have been already been set. Wynne advocates a process whereby the deliberative process takes place far more "upstream." Citizenship here is no longer about having sufficient knowledge, or being asked to deliberate over a range of preset technological options; it is about having a say in the development of research programs, in agenda setting, in research funding, in prioritization of sociopolitical goals. Of course, such a version of public engagement and citizenship requires major reform of scientific institutions. In the absence of such public fora, laypeople have had recourse to other extra-governmental forms of citizenship, what Beck (1992) has called sub-politics.

In the context of Wynne's argument for citizenship to move politically, technologically, and, indeed, epistemologically upstream, this chapter advocates that we also move ontologically upstream. To be technologically literate, and thus a citizen, is therefore to perceive technology in the terms outlined above: as embroiled in a complex process of ensembling which, as the section on co(a)gents suggests, must be then rendered singular. As noted, this process of perception (or better still, to borrow from Whitehead, prehension—see Michael, 2002) is itself embroiled in the complex process of ensembling.

The pedagogic implications here are many, and range from recasting technological literacy to take into account the various political complexities Wynne identifies, through the teaching of case histories of technologies (possibly as sort of "co(a)gential phenomenology"), to a mode of "pedagogy" (if that is still the appropriate term) that sensitizes pupils to their own practical embroilment in ensembles (that is, their own status as co(a)gents). This is all, inevitably, much easier said than done, and like the radical implications of Wynne's analysis, the present argument also invites radical reform of pedagogic practice in relation to technology (and, indeed, all subjects given the universal presence of mundane technologies). Whatever the longer range implications, it is hoped that the present perspective has had the minimal effect of serving as a prompt to rethink the concept of technological literacy and the ways in which this might resource the "doing" of contemporary citizenship.

References

Abelson, J., Forest, P., Eyles J., Smith, P., Martin, E., and Gauvibin, F. (2003). "Deliberations about deliberation: Issues in the design and evaluation of public consultation processes." *Social Science and Medicine*, 57 (239–251).

Barry, A. (2001). *Political Machines*. London: Athlone.

Bijker, W.(1995). *Of Bicycles, Bakelite and Bulbs: Toward a Theory of Sociotechnical Change*. Cambridge, Mass.: The MIT Press.

62 • Mike Michael

Beck, U. (1992). *The Risk Society*. London: Sage.

Bowker, G. and Star, S. (1999). *Sorting Things Out: Classification and its Consequences*. Cambridge, Mass.: The MIT Press.

Callon, M. and Law, J. (1995)."Agency and the hybrid collectif." *The South Atlantic Quarterly*, 94 (481–507).

Durant, J. (1993). "What is scientific literacy?" In J.R. Durant and J. Gregory (eds)., *Science and Culture in Europe*, 129–137. London: Science Museum.

Giddens, A. (1991). *Modernity and Self-identity*, Cambridge: Polity.

International Technology Education Association (1996). *Technology for All Americans: A Rationale and Structure for the Study of Technology*. Reston, Viginia: International Technology Education Association.

Irwin, A. and Michael, M. (2003). *Science, Social Theory and Public Knowledge*. Maidenhead, Berks.: Open University Press/McGraw-Hill.

Lie, M. and Sorensen, K. (eds) (1996). *Making Technology Our Own? Domesticating Technologies into Everyday Life*. Oslo: Scandinavian University Press.

Latour, B. (1987). *Science in Action: How to Follow Engineers in Society*, Milton Keynes: Open University Press.

Latour, B. (1991). "Technology is society made durable." In J. Law (ed.), *A Sociology of Monsters*. London: Routledge.

Latour, B. (1992). "Where are the missing masses? A sociology of a few mundane artifacts." In W. Bijker and J. Law (eds), *Shaping Technology/Building Society*. Cambridge, Mass.: MIT Press.

Latour, B. (1993a). *We have Never been Modern*, Hemel Hempstead: Harvester Wheatsheaf.

Latour, B. (1993b). *On Technical Mediation: The Messenger Lectures on the Evolution of Civilization*. Cornell University, Institute of Economic Research: Working Papers Series.

Latour, B. and Johnson, J. (1988). "Mixing humans with non-humans? Sociology of a few mundane artifacts." *Social Problems*, 35 (298–310).

Michael, M. (1998). "Between citizen and consumer: multiplying the meanings of the public understanding of science." *Public Understanding of Science*, 7 (313–327).

Michael, M. (2000). *Reconnecting Culture, Technology and Nature: From Society to Heterogeneity*. London: Routledge.

Michael, M. (2002). "Comprehension, apprehension, and prehension: heterogeneity and the public understanding of science." *Science, Technology and Human Values*, 27: 3 (357–370).

Michael, M. (2003). "Between the mundane and the exotic: time for a different sociotechnical stuff." *Time and Society*, 12: 1 (127–143).

Michael, M. and Brown, N. (2000). "From the representation of publics to the performance of 'lay political science'." *Social Epistemology*, 14: 1 (3–19).

Michael, M. and Brown, N. (2004). "The meat of the matter: grasping and judging xenotransplantation." *Public Understanding of Science*, 13 (379–397).

Miller, D. (ed.) (1998). *Material Cultures: Why Some Things Matter.* London: UCL Press.

Nowotny, H., Scott, P., and Gibbons, M. (2001). *Re-Thinking Science: Knowledge and the Public in an Age of Uncertainty.* Cambridge: Polity.

Royal Society of London (1985). *The Public Understanding of Science.* London: The Royal Society.

Waldby, C. (2000). *The Visible Human Project: Informatic Bodies and Posthuman Medicine.* London: Routledge.

Whitehead, A. (1929). *Process and Reality.* Cambridge: Cambridge University Press.

Woolgar, S. (1991). "Configuring the user: the case of usability trials." In J. Law, (ed.), *A Sociology of Monsters.* London: Routledge.

Wynne, B. (1996). "May the sheep safely graze? A reflexive view of the expert-lay divide." In S. Lash, B. Szerszynski, and B. Wynne (eds), *Risk, Environment and Modernity* (44–83). London: Sage.

Wynne, B. (2002). "Risk and environment as legitimatory discourses of technology: reflexivity inside out?" *Current Sociology*, 50: 3 (459–477).

CHAPTER 5

Walking the Plank: Meditations on a Process of Skill

Tim Ingold

Was there ever a bookcase that gave a fraction of the satisfaction as the one fashioned by your own hands?

The editor, *The Handyman and Home Mechanic*

On Sawing a Plank

I am making a bookcase from wooden planks. Each shelf has to be cut to the right length. Marking the distance along the plank with a tape measure, I use a pencil and set-square to draw a straight line across it. After these preliminaries, I set the plank on a trestle, lift my left leg, and kneel with as much of my weight as I can upon it, while keeping my balance on the ground with my right foot. The line to be cut slightly overhangs the right end of the trestle. Then, stooping, I place the palm of my left hand on the plank just to the left of the line, grasping it around the edge by the fingers. Taking up a saw with my right hand, I wrap my fingers around the handle—all, that is, except the index finger, which is extended along the flat of the handle, enabling me to fine-tune the direction of the blade.

Now, as I press down with a rigid arm on the left hand, I engage the teeth of the saw with the edge, at the point where it meets my drawn line, and gently nick the edge with two or three short up-strokes. To guide the saw at this critical juncture, I bend the thumb of my left hand, so that the hard surface of the joint juts out to touch the blade of the saw just above the teeth. Once the slot in the edge is long enough that there is no further risk of the saw jumping out and lacerating my thumb, I can begin to work it with downward strokes. At this point, I have to attend more to the alignment of the blade than to the precise positioning of the teeth, in order to ensure that the evolving cut proceeds in exactly the right direction. To do this, I have to position my head so that it is directly above the tool, looking down. From this angle, the blade appears as a straight line and I can see the wood on either side of the cut.

The first strokes are crucial, since the further the cut goes, the less room there is for manoeuvre. After a while, however, I can relax my gaze and settle down to a rhythmic up-and-down movement with long, smooth, and even strokes. Though delivered to the saw through the right hand and forearm, the movement is actually felt throughout my entire body in the oscillating balance of forces in my knees, legs, hands, arms, and back. The groove I have already cut now serves as a jig that prevents the saw from veering off the straight line. Because of the way the saw's teeth are cut, they slice the wood on the downward stroke, whereas the upward stroke is restorative, returning the body–saw–plank system to a position from which the next cycle can be launched. However, a good saw requires little or no pressure on the down-stroke, and works under its own weight.

Although a confident, regular movement ensures an even cut, no two strokes are ever precisely the same. With each stroke, I have to adjust my posture ever so slightly to allow for the advancing groove, and for possible irregularities in the grain of the wood. Moreover, I still have to watch to make sure I keep to the line, since even though the saw is constrained to slide within the existing groove, the groove itself is slightly wider than the blade, allowing for some slight axial torque. This is where the index finger of my right hand, stretched along the handle of the saw, comes into play. In effect, I use it to steer within the tight margins afforded by the groove. The actual width of the groove is determined by the setting of the saw's teeth, which are bent outwards, alternately to one side and the other of the blade. The point of this is that it allows clearance for the blade to slide within the groove. It would otherwise become jammed.

As I approach the end of the line a marked drop in the pitch of the sound created by my sawing, caused by a loss of tensile strength in the plank, serves as an audible warning to slow down. Once again, I have to concentrate on the cutting edge. For a clean finish, the last few strokes are as critical as the first. To prevent the free end from breaking off under its own weight, leaving a cracked or splintered edge, I must shift my left hand to the right of the groove, no longer pressing down on the plank but supporting it. At the same time I saw ever more slowly and lightly until, eventually, the cut end comes free in my left hand and I allow it to drop to the ground.

This description of a quite elementary episode of tool use might seem unnecessarily elaborate. It serves, however, to illustrate three themes of fundamental significance for the proper understanding of technical skill. These themes concern (a) the processional quality of tool use, (b) the synergy of practitioner, tool and material, and (c) the coupling of perception and action. In the following sections I elaborate on each theme in turn, using the example of sawing a plank for purposes of illustration. I conclude with some remarks on the fate of skill in a world increasingly engineered to the specifications of technology.

The Processional Quality of Tool-Use

The use of a tool is commonly understood as a discrete step in an operational sequence, a *chaîne opératoire*, one of a number of such steps that together comprise a schedule for the assembly of a complete object like a bookcase. It does not take just one step, however, to saw a plank. It takes many steps; moreover these steps are no more discrete or discontinuous than those of a walker. That is to say, they do not follow one another in succession, like beads on a string. Their order is processional rather than successional. In walking, every step is a development of the one before and a preparation for the one following. The same is true of every stroke of the saw. Like going for a walk, sawing a plank has the character of a journey that proceeds from place to place, through a movement that— though rhythmic and repetitive—is never strictly monotonous.

The journey does have recognizable phases—of getting ready, setting out, carrying on, and finishing off—and these lend a certain temporal shape to the overall movement. These phases are not, however, sharply demarcated. When, leaving the front door of my house, I turn the corner into the street, I alter my pace and gait, and lift my sights from the immediate vicinity of the doorstep to the longer vista of the pavement. The movement, nevertheless, is continuous. It is the same with sawing. Like turning a corner, the initial nicking of the edge of the plank leads into the smooth downward strokes of the cut through an unbroken transition. Only when I look back on the ground covered can I say that one phase of the process is finished, and another has begun. The same is true of the process as a whole. When do I begin to saw? Is it when I mark the line, when I rest my knee and hand on the plank, when I nick the edge, or when I commence the downward strokes? And when do I cease? Perhaps, having cut through the plank, I lay down the saw, but this may only be to pick up the next piece to be cut. In sawing as in walking, movement always overshoots its destinations.

Let us take a closer look at the four phases of the process, beginning with "getting ready." Even before setting out, I need to have arrived at some overall conception of the task to be performed—of what is to be done, how to do it, and the tools and materials required. This conception covers an assortment of factors that are only loosely connected, and serves to guide the work rather than strictly to determine its course. Charles Keller aptly calls it an "umbrella plan," an idiosyncratic constellation—peculiar to each practitioner—of stylistic, functional, procedural, and economic considerations assembled specifically for the task at hand (Keller, 2001: 35). Though the composition of the umbrella plan calls for forethought, such thinking is itself a mundane practical activity, set in the context of the workplace, rather than a purely intellectual, "inside-the-head" exercise (Leudar and Costall, 1996: 164). It includes, for example, "sizing up" the planks, deciding which to select for the shelf I want to cut and which to reserve for other purposes, so as to minimize the waste from off-cuts. It also includes the retrieval of the saw and trestle from where I last put them, so that I have them to hand for when the cutting is to begin. Even drawing the line across the plank, with pencil and set-square, can be understood as part of the planning process, a "measuring out" that is done not in advance of engagement with the material but directly, at full scale, on the material itself. Crucially, the pencil line can be erased. Although inscribed *on* the material, it is not, like the subsequent cut, indelibly incised *into* it. Evidently, then, the umbrella plan is in no sense confined within the mind of the practitioner. On the contrary, it is laid out over the workplace itself: in the marking up of the materials and in their disposition in relation to the body of the practitioner, and the tools that he will bring to bear on them.

There is a critical moment, in implementing any task, when getting ready gives way to setting out. This is the moment at which rehearsal ends and performance begins. From that point on there is no turning back. Pencil marks can be rubbed out, but an incision made with the blade of a saw cannot be contrived to disappear. The skilled practitioner chooses his moment with care, knowing that to set out before one is ready, or alternatively to allow the right moment to pass unnoticed, could jeopardize the entire project. The Ancient Greeks had a word for this moment, namely *kairos*. Jean-Pierre Vernant explains:

> In intervening with his tools, the artisan must recognize and wait for the moment when the time is ripe and be able to adapt himself entirely to the circumstances. He must never desert his post, . . . for if he does the *kairos* might pass and the work be spoiled. (1983: 291–292)

This moment of setting out, however, is also marked by a switch of perspective, from the encompassing view of the umbrella plan to a narrow focus on the initial point of contact between tool and material. Thus my attention, in setting out to saw a plank, is fixed on that constricted space between where the teeth of the saw meet the edge of the plank, where the edge of the plank is gripped by the fingers of my left hand, and where the joint of my left thumb guides the blade of the saw. For that brief interval while I nick the edge with a series of short, upward strokes, my overall conception of the work fades into the background as I concentrate on the precise details of the emergent cut. There is a certain tension in these initial movements—each is like a gasp, a sudden intake of breath, that runs counter to the direction in which the saw is disposed to run, and in which the wood is disposed to receive it. The wood resists, and seems to want to expel the saw by causing it to jump out.

It is when I reverse the rhythm, cutting with down-strokes rather than up-strokes, that setting out gives way to carrying on. The reversal is somewhat analogous to what happens when I set out with a rowboat from the shore, turning from the initial and rather awkward pushing of the oars in backstroke to the more comfortable and efficient movement of pulling once a sufficient depth of water has been reached. In sawing as in rowing, from that moment on it seems that I am working *with* the instruments and materials at my disposal rather than *against* them. Although I am of course cutting the plank against the grain, the wood nevertheless "takes in" or accommodates the saw along the line that I have already cut, and yields to its movement rather than repelling it. In duration the phase of carrying on is generally the longest, and it can call for considerable strength and endurance. But it is also the most relaxed, flowing in a smooth legato rhythm that contrasts markedly with the abrupt staccato passage of setting out. At the same time, my focus also shifts, from the point where the drawn line meets the edge to its entire length, and from the detail of the saw's teeth to the alignment of the blade as a whole. So it continues, until I reach the phase of finishing off. There is no precise moment when carrying on ends and finishing off begins, but rather a point of inflection from which the movement is gradually retarded and its amplitude diminished. Simultaneously, my attention begins to shift from the line of the cut to its destination, where it intersects the trailing edge of the plank.

It is commonly supposed that each stage in the process of making an artifact is completed at the point when the material outcome precisely matches the maker's initial intention. Holding an image of the intended outcome at the forefront of his mind, the maker is said to measure his progress against the extent to which it has been realized and to cease once he has achieved a result congruent with the image. In practice, however, it is not the image of the end product that governs the phase of finishing off. By the time this phase is reached, any deviations from the initial plan will have been either accepted or corrected (Keller, 2001: 40). If I have kept my saw to the drawn line, then I need have no further concern that it might deviate from it; if I have not, then it is far too late for remedial action. Yet the judgment of when and how to finish can be just as crucial as choosing the moment to set out. To reach this judgment the practitioner must once again focus down on the finer details of the work. Keller's examples are drawn from the crafts of the weaver and the silversmith. The weaver has to decide at what point no more weft strands can be added; the silversmith how many more hammer-blows the metal will take without cracking. Likewise in sawing a plank, to obtain a clean cut the final strokes must be finely judged such that one reaches the edge without actually sawing through it. Thus, the end of the line is approached as an asymptote: the closer I come to it, the gentler and more delicate my strokes, and the more my attention is focused on the finishing point, until eventually, the free end comes loose in my hand.

Finally, journey completed, I put away my saw and place the plank, now cut to the right length, where it will next be needed. Yet, this placement of tools and materials is already part of the formation of the umbrella plan for the next operation. Putting things away in the right places is a way of getting ready. Thus in the use of tools, every ending is a new beginning.

The Synergy of Practitioner, Tool, and Material

What does it mean to say that in carrying out some task, a tool is used? We might suppose that use is what happens when an object, endowed with a certain function, is placed at the disposal of an agent, intent on a certain purpose. I want to cut a plank, and I have a saw. So I use the saw to cut the plank. However from the account I have already presented it is clear that I need more than the saw to cut wood. I need the trestle to provide support, I need my hands and knees respectively to grip the saw and to hold the plank in place, I need every muscle of my body to deliver the force that drives the saw and to maintain my balance as I work, I need my eyes and ears to monitor progress. Even the plank itself becomes part of the equipment for cutting, in that the evolving groove helps to guide the work. Cutting wood, then, is an effect not of the saw alone but of the entire system of forces and relations set up by the intimate engagement of the saw, the trestle, the work-piece, and my own body. What then becomes of our concept of use? To answer this question we need to consider three things. First, what does it take for an object of some kind, such as the saw or trestle, to count as a tool? Second, how does the instrumentality of the tool compare with that of the human body with which it is conjoined? And third, can this conjunction be considered apart from the gestural movements in which it is set to work?

No object considered purely in and for itself, in terms of its intrinsic attributes alone, can be a tool. To describe a thing as a tool is to place it in *relation* to other things within a field of activity in which it can exert a certain effect. Indeed, we tend to name our tools by the activities in which they are characteristically or normatively engaged, or by the effects they have in them. Thus to call an object a saw is to position it within the context of a story such as the one I have just told, of cutting a plank. To name the tool is to invoke the story. It follows that for an object to count as a tool it must be endowed with a story, which the practitioner should know and understand in order to recognize it as such and use it appropriately. Considered as tools, objects *are* their stories. We are of course more accustomed to think of tools as having certain functions. My point, however, is that the functions of things are not attributes but narratives. They are the stories we tell about them. This point, I believe, resolves a paradox that has long bedeviled discussions of the concept of function. The dictionary defines function as "the special kind of activity proper to anything; the mode of action by which it fulfils its purpose." Thus the function of the saw is to cut wood: this is the activity traditionally deemed "proper" to it, and for which it has been expressly designed. Yet as David Pye has observed, nothing we design is ever truly fit for purpose. A saw that really worked would not produce quantities of sawdust. The best we can say of its function is that it is "what someone has provisionally decided that [it] may reasonably be expected to do at present" (Pye, 1978: 11–14). So, if we were to decide that the saw should be used, in a quite different context, as a musical instrument, that should count just as well. How can the idea that every tool has a proper function be reconciled with the fact that in practice, nothing ever works except as a component of a system constituted in the present moment (Preston, 2000)?

The parallel between tool-use and storytelling suggests an answer, for the meanings of stories do not come ready-made from the past, embedded in a static, closed tradition. Nor however are they constructed de novo, moment by moment, to accord with the ever-changing conditions of the present. They are rather discovered only retrospectively, often long after the telling, when listeners—faced with circumstances similar to those recounted in a particular story—find in its unfolding guidance on how to proceed. Now just as stories do not carry their meanings ready-made into the world, likewise the ways in which tools are to be used do not come prepackaged with the tools themselves. But neither are the uses of tools simply invented on the spot, without regard to any history of past practice. Rather, they are revealed to practitioners when, faced with a recurrent task in which the same devices were known previously to have been employed, they are perceived to afford the wherewithal for its accomplishment. Thus the functions of tools, like the meanings of stories, are recognized through the alignment of present circumstances with the conjunctions of the past. Once recognized, these functions provide the practitioner with the means to keep on going. Every use of a tool, in short, is a remembering of how to use it, that at once picks up the strands of past practice and carries them forward in current contexts. The skilled practitioner is like an accomplished story-teller whose tales are told in the practice of his craft rather than in words. Thus considered as tools, things have the same processional character as the activities they make possible. As we have seen, the activity of cutting a plank is more a walk than a step. Similarly the function of the saw lies more in a story, or perhaps a series of stories, than in a set of attributes. Functionality and narrativity are two sides of the same coin.

Yet, although the saw, both in its construction and in its patterns of wear and tear, embodies a history of past use, it remembers nothing of this history. Indeed, it remembers nothing at all. And this suggests an answer to our second question. We have already seen that to cut wood, a saw is not enough. At the very least, the saw is gripped by hand and watched by eye. How, then, does the use of these bodily organs compare with the use of extra-somatic equipment such as the saw? In his celebrated essay on techniques of the body, Marcel Mauss declared that the body is "man's first and most natural technical object, and at the same time technical means" (Mauss, 1979: 104). But if using the hands to grip and the eyes to watch, and even the brain to think, is tantamount to converting them into objects of my will, then where am *I* the subject, the user of these bodily means? Should we, like Mauss, follow Plato in supposing that the entire body, and not just the tools that serve to extend the range and effectivity of its actions, is the instrument of an intelligence that is necessarily disembodied, and that stands aloof from the world in which it intervenes? Or should we rather find an alternative way of thinking about use that does not presuppose an initial separation between the user and the used, between subject and object? Perhaps it would be better to say that in an activity like cutting wood, my hand is not so much used as brought into use, in the sense that it is guided in its movements by the remembered traces of past performance, already inscribed in an accustomed—that is, *usual*—pattern of dexterous activity (Ingold, 2000: 352). But if the hand, as it drives the saw, remembers how to move, the saw it grips does not. For *only the body remembers*. Thus in the relation between hand and saw there lies a fundamental asymmetry. The hand can bring itself into use, and in its practiced movements can tell the story of its own life. But the saw relies on the hand for its story to be told. Or more generally, while extra-somatic tools have biographies, the body is both biographer and autobiographer.

If an object such as a saw, however, becomes a tool only through being placed within a field of effective action, then the same goes for the organs of the body. As André Leroi-Gourhan has observed, it is in what it makes or does, not in what it is, that the human hand comes into its own (Leroi-Gourhan, 1993: 240). Where the tool has its stories, the hand has its gestures. Considered in purely anatomical terms, of course, the hand is merely a complex arrangement of bone and muscle tissue. But the hands I use in sawing are more than that. They are skilled. Concentrated in them are capacities of movement and feeling that have been developed through a life-history of past practice. What is a hand if not a compendium of such capacities, particular to the manifold tasks in which it is brought into use, and the gestures they entail? Thus while hands make gestures, gestures also make hands. And of course they make tools too. It follows that gesture is foundational to both tool-making and tool use. The point would be obvious were it not for a certain conceptual blindness that causes us to see both bodies and tools out of context, as things-in-themselves (Sigaut, 1993: 387). But "bringing into use" is not a matter of attaching an object with certain attributes to a body with certain anatomical features; it is rather a matter of joining a story to the appropriate gestures. The tool, as the epitome of the story, selects from the compendium of the hand the gestures proper to its re-enactment. Yet, the tool has its story only because it is set in a context that includes the trestle, the wood, and all the other paraphernalia of the workshop. And the hand has its gestures only because it has grown and developed within the organic synergy of practitioner, tool, and material. The practice of sawing issues as much from the trestle and plank as from the saw, as much from the saw as from the carpenter, as much from the carpenter's eyes and ears as from his hands, as much from his ears and hands as from his mind. You only get sawing when all these things, and more, are bound together and work in unison.

The Coupling of Perception and Action

Close examination of a carpenter at work reveals an apparent paradox. In sawing, as I have already observed, no two strokes are precisely the same. In its oscillations the right hand—alternately driving the saw down and pulling it back up—never follows an identical trajectory, The force, amplitude, speed, and torque of the manual gesture vary, albeit almost imperceptibly, from stroke to stroke. So also does the posture of the body, and the muscular–skeletal configurations of tension and compression that keep it in balance. Yet, the outcome, in skilled hands, is a perfectly clean, straight cut. How can the regularity of the cut be reconciled with this variability of posture and gesture, given that the body alone imparts movement to the blade of the saw? In a now-classic study, the Russian neuroscientist Nicholai Bernstein was confronted with an identical paradox. Bernstein observed the gestures of a skilled blacksmith, hitting the iron on the anvil over and over again with a hammer. He found that although the smith consistently brought the hammer down to exactly the same spot on the anvil, the trajectories of individual arm joints varied from stroke to stroke. How, he wondered, can the motion of the hammer be so reliably reproduced, when it is only by way of the inconstant arm that the hammer is contrived to move (Latash, 1996: 286)? His answer was that the essence of the smith's dexterity lay not in the constancy of his movements, but in the "*tuning of the movements to an emergent task*" (Bernstein, 1996: 23, original emphasis). For the novice every stroke is the same, so that the slightest irregularity throws him irretrievably off course. For the accomplished blacksmith or carpenter, by contrast, every stroke is different. The fine-tuning or "sensory correction" of the craftsman's movement depends, however, on an intimate coupling of perception and action. Thus in sawing, the visual monitoring of the evolving cut, through eyes positioned above to see the wood on either side, continually corrects the alignment of the blade through subtle adjustments of the index finger along the handle of the saw. Likewise, the right hand responds in its oscillations to the sound and feel of the saw as it bites into the grain. This multisensory coupling establishes the dexterity and control that are the hallmarks of skilled practice.

Dexterity is a necessary accompaniment to what David Pye (1968: 4–5) has called the "workmanship of risk." In such workmanship, the quality of the outcome depends at every moment on the care and judgment with which the task proceeds. Thus when working with a saw, as with any other hand-held tool, the result is never a foregone conclusion; rather there is an ever-present danger, throughout the work, that it may go awry. The greatest risk is undoubtedly in the phases of setting out, when the first indelible marks are cut in the edge of the plank, and in finishing off, where careless work could lead to splintering. Of course, there are ways to reduce risk, as when the carpenter initially steadies the blade against the joint of the thumb. And the phase of carrying on, when the groove is well advanced and helps to guide the saw, is much less risky than those of setting out and finishing off. As Pye notes, the workmanship of risk is hardly ever seen in a pure form, but is rather combined in various ways with what he calls the "workmanship of certainty." If, in the workmanship of risk, the result is always in doubt, in the workmanship of certainty it is already predetermined and unalterable from outset. For example, in my use of the set-square to draw a line across the plank, prior to cutting, the trajectory of the pencil point is preset by the straight edge of the square. All I have to do is run my pencil along it, which I can do at speed. But just as every craftsman engaged in the workmanship of risk will seek to reduce it through the use of jigs and templates, so conversely, a degree of risk invariably creeps into the apparently most predetermined of operations. Thus even when the saw is guided by its own groove, maintaining the uniformity of the line calls for continuous attention and correction.

Earlier I compared sawing a plank to going for a walk. As with the walk, the task has a beginning and an ending. Every ending, however, is potentially a new beginning, marking not a terminus but a pause for rest in an otherwise continuous journey. The carpenter, a workman of risk, is like the wayfarer who travels from place to place, sustaining himself both perceptually and materially through a continual engagement with the field of practice, or what I have elsewhere called the "taskscape" (Ingold, 2000: 194–200), that opens up along his path. In this respect, he is the complete opposite of the machine operative, a workman of certainty, whose activity is constrained by the parameters of a determining system. Here, "the product is made by a planned series of operations, each of which has to be started and stopped by the operative, but with the result of each one predetermined and outside his control" (Pye, 1968: 6). Starting and stopping, as this passage reveals, is not the same as beginning and ending. Between beginning and ending, the practitioner's movements are continually and subtly responsive to the ever-changing conditions of the task as it unfolds. Between starting and stopping, by contrast, he has nothing to do but to leave the system to run its course, according to settings determined in advance. Thus whereas for the craftsman the intervals between ending and beginning again are pauses for rest, for the machine operative those between stopping and restarting are when all the significant action takes place: when plans are laid, instruments reset and materials assembled. Like a traveler who goes everywhere by transport rather than on foot, it is only when he reaches successive destinations that the operative gets down to business. His journey is more like a series of interconnected terminals than a walk. The intimate coupling between movement and perception that governs the work of the craftsman is broken.

Now in any episode of tool use, some gestures are performed just once or a few times, others are repeated over and over again. The former typically occur while getting ready, setting out, and finishing off; the latter during the intermediate phase of carrying on. In our case of sawing a plank, drawing the line, kneeling down, nicking the edge, and shifting the left hand to hold the cut end exemplify the first, while the regular strokes of the saw exemplify the second. When we speak of the activity of sawing, it is usually these *recurrent* movements that we have in mind, rather than the "one-off" or *occurrent* movements with which they open and close. In this sense, sawing is one of a suite of commonplace tool-assisted activities, including also hammering, pounding, and scraping, that all involve the repetition of manual gesture. Indeed this kind of back-and-forth or "reciprocating" movement comes naturally to the living body. In a fluent performance, it has a rhythmic quality (Leroi-Gourhan, 1993: 309–310). This quality does not, however, lie in the repetitiveness of the movement itself. For there to be rhythm, movement must be *felt*. And feeling lies in the coupling of movement and perception that, as we have seen, is the key to skilled practice. As Leroi-Gourhan clearly recognized, technical activity is conducted not against a static background but in a world the manifold constituents of which undergo their own particular cycles. By way of perception, the practitioner's own rhythmic gestures are attuned to the multiple rhythms of the environment. Thus any task, itself a movement, unfolds within the "network of movements" in which the existence of every living being, animal or human, is suspended (1993: 282). An operation like sawing a plank, for example, comprises not one movement but an ensemble of concurrent movements, both within and without the body. The carpenter who has a feel for what he is doing is one who can bring these several movements more or less into phase with one another, so that they resonate or are "in tune."

Rhythm, then, is not a movement but a relation between movements. Every such relation is a specific resonance, and the synergy of practitioner, tool, and raw material establishes an entire field of such resonances. But this field is not monotonous, for every cycle is set not within fixed parameters but within a framework that is itself suspended in movement, in an environment where nothing is quite the same from moment to moment. As Henri Lefebvre argues, there is no rhythm in the mechanical oscillations of a determining system that periodically returns to its exact starting point. Rhythmicity implies not just repetition but *differences within repetition* (Lefebvre, 2004: 90). It is precisely because no two strokes of the saw are identical that sawing is rhythmic rather than mechanical. Or to put it another way, fluent performance is rhythmic only because imperfections in the system call for continual correction. This is why, as Willeke Wendrich observes in her choreography of Egyptian basketry, "working rhythm goes hand in hand with concentration." In her study, skilled basket-makers were distinguished by a steady working rhythm, intense concentration, and a regular appearance of the product. Inexperienced practitioners, by contrast, could not maintain a rhythm, they were easily distracted, and their work was irregular in appearance (Wendrich, 1999: 390–391). The same, I am sure, applies in the field of carpentry. An arrhythmic and distracted performance with the saw is unlikely to lead to a regular line.

I emphasize this point in order to correct the widespread misapprehension that the training of the body through repetitive exercise—or what Lefebvre (2004: 38–45) calls *dressage*—leads to a progressive loss of conscious awareness or concentration in the task. Paul Connerton, for example, remarks that the repetition of certain operations leads to their bodily execution becoming increasingly automatic, to the point that "awareness retreats [and] the movement flows involuntarily" (Connerton, 1989: 94). In this view, awareness intervenes only to interrupt the otherwise automatic and involuntary flow of habitual action. I have shown, to the contrary, that the skilled handling of tools is anything but automatic, but is rather rhythmically responsive to ever-changing environmental conditions (see also Ingold, 1999: 437). In this responsiveness there lies a form of awareness that does not so much retreat as grow in intensity with the fluency of action. This is not the awareness of a mind that holds itself aloof from the messy, hands-on business of work. It is rather immanent in practical, perceptual activity, reaching out into its surroundings along multiple pathways of sensory participation (Farnell, 2000: 409). The retreat of awareness that Connerton takes to be an effect of enskilment in fact results from the very opposite process of deskilling—that is, from the *dissolution* of the link between perception and action that underwrites the skill of the practitioner. Only in the operation of a perfect, determining system can concentration be thus banished from practice, so as to intervene solely in the intervals between stopping and starting. The conjunction of rhythmicity and concentration is characteristic of the workmanship of risk. It is in the workmanship of certainty—in the operation of a perfectly determining system—that concentration lapses, movement becomes automatic, and rhythm gives way to mechanism.

Conclusion

Throughout history, at least in the Western world, the project of technology has been to capture the skills of the craftsman or artisan, and to reconfigure their practice as the application of rational principles the specification of which has no regard for human experience and sensibility. "At the core of technology," as Carl Mitcham succinctly puts it, "there seems to be a desire to transform the heuristics of technique into algorithms of practice" (1978: 252). Where once he had been guided on his way through the taskscape by stories of past use, the practitioner now becomes bound to the execution of a step-by-step sequence of determinate operations already built into the design and construction of his equipment. Thus the flow of action is broken up into discrete operational steps. Though each operation may differ from the one preceding and the one following, the operation itself is perfectly monotonous and its repetitive motion—no longer reciprocal but rotary—is underwritten by sameness rather than difference. The effect is to replace the rhythmic pulse of dexterous activity, governed by the coupling of perception and action, with the metronomic oscillations of a mechanically determining system.

As inhabitants of modern metropolitan societies, contemporary practitioners find themselves in an environment in which the technological project appears to have triumphed, sweeping all else before it. The appearance, however, is deceptive. As François Sigaut has shown through what he calls the "law of the irreducibility of skills," the project has been chasing an ever-receding goal. "The entire history of technics," he writes, "might be interpreted as a constantly renewed attempt to build skills into machines by means of algorithms, an attempt constantly foiled because other skills always tend to develop around the new machines" (Sigaut, 1994: 446). Or to put it another way, as fast as narratives of use are converted by technology into algorithmic structures, those structures are themselves put to use within the ongoing activities of inhabitants, and through the stories of this use they are reincorporated into the field of effective action within which all life is lived. In short, the advance of technology does not augur the end of skill. To the contrary, the essence of skill has come to lie in the improvisational ability of practitioners to disassemble the constructions of technology, and creatively to incorporate the pieces into their own walks of life.

References

Bernstein, N. (1996). "On dexterity and its development." In M. Latash and M. Turvey (eds), *Dexterity and its Development*, 3–244. Mahwah, NJ: Lawrence Erlbaum Associates.

Connerton, P. (1989). *How Societies Remember*. Cambridge: Cambridge University Press.

Farnell, B. (2000). "Getting out of the habitus: an alternative model of dynamically embodied social action." *Journal of the Royal Anthropological Institute* (N.S.) 6 (397–418).

Ingold, T. (1999). "'Tools for the hand, language for the face': an appreciation of Leroi-Gourhan's *Gesture and Speech*." *Studies in the History and Philosophy of Biological and Biomedical Science* 30 (411–453).

Ingold, T. (2000). *The Perception of the Environment: Essays on Livelihood, Dwelling and Skill*. London: Routledge.

Keller, C. (2001). "Thought and production: insights of the practitioner." In M.B. Schiffer (ed.), *Anthropological Perspectives on Technology*, 33–45. Albuquerque: University of New Mexico Press.

Latash, M. (1996). "The Bernstein problem: how does the central nervous system make its choices?" In M. Latash and M.T. Turvey (eds), *Dexterity and its Development*, 277–303. Mahwah, NJ: Lawrence Erlbaum Associates.

Lefebvre, H. (2004). *Rhythmanalysis: Space, Time and Everyday Life*. London: Continuum.

Leroi-Gourhan, A. (1993). *Gesture and Speech* (trans. A. Bostock Berger, intr. R. White). Cambridge, MA and London: MIT Press.

Leudar, I. and Costall, A. (1996). "Situating action IV: planning as Situated Action." *Ecological Psychology* 8 (153–170).

Mauss, M. (1979). "Body techniques." In *Sociology and Psychology: Essays*, 97–123. London: Routledge and Kegan Paul.

Mitcham, C. (1978). "Types of technology." In *Research in Philosophy and Technology* Vol 1, 229–294. Greenwich. Connecticut: JAI Press.

Preston, B. (2000). "The functions of things: a philosophical perspective on material culture." In P. Graves-Brown (ed.), *Matter, Materiality and Modern Culture*, 22–49. London: Routledge.

Pye, D. (1968). *The Nature and Art of Workmanship*. Cambridge: Cambridge University Press.

Pye, D. (1978). *The Nature and Aesthetics of Design*. London: Herbert Press.

Sigaut, F. (1993). "How can we analyze and describe technical actions?" In A. Berthelet and J. Chavaillon (eds), *The Use of Tools by Humans and Non-Human Primates*, 381–397. Oxford: Clarendon Press.

Sigaut, F. (1994). "Technology." In T. Ingold (ed.), *Companion Encyclopedia of Anthropology: Humanity, Culture and Social Life*, 420–459. London: Routledge.

Vernant, J. (1983). *Myth and Thought Among the Greeks*. London: Routledge and Kegan Paul.

Wendrich, W. (1999). *The World According to Basketry: An Ethno-Archaeological Interpretation of Basketry Production in Egypt*. University of Leiden: CNWS.

CHAPTER 6

Ethical Technological Literacy as Democratic Curriculum Keystone

Steve Keirl

I would like to set the scene for this chapter by making four inter-related points. First, I take as a premise that something called "democracy" is a desirable form of social and political organization for our local and global harmonious coexistence. I see such a democracy as an ethically defensible system of politics and government. I also take as a premise that something called education is essential to healthy democratic practice—in at least a twofold sense. This education must, in ethically defensible ways, both educate for democracy and be conducted democratically.

Second, however, we live in times of considerable curriculum contestation. Competing stakeholder interests, policy shifts, and pushes for curriculum-as-cure for societal problems interact with traditional forms of knowledge organization and pedagogy. Despite (or because of) this climate, I argue that something called technological literacy ought to be a component of twenty-first-century education for *any* society in this globalizing world. Furthermore, I argue for such a component to be a keystone (something that is critical to the integrity) of the avowed democratic curriculum.

In the contested and crowded curriculum, there is only room for so much. But the argument of this chapter is that, since technology constitutes such a pervasive and hegemonic part of life on the planet, it is unacceptable that technology education currently constitutes such a minor part of the curriculum—especially as that which does exist mostly takes on mere instrumental and/or atomized forms.

Third, I recognize that there are greatly varying interpretations of what might be meant by technological literacy since both literacy and technology are politically and educationally contested terms. Unsurprisingly perhaps, I also argue for an ethically defensible technological literacy (rather than one constructed differently). This is seen as the appropriate technological literacy for an ethically defensible form of political organization for intra- and inter-species coexistence.

Fourth, there is perhaps a distinctly idealistic flavor to what has been said. But, taking "democracy" as an example, it is the continuous striving for the ideal, never its attainment, that is the nature of things. By definition, the ideal remains unattainable, as it requires continuous re-visioning. Certainly, all the principal terms used—ethics, democracy, technology, education, curriculum, literacy—are of their nature contestable, if not contentious. But that is the challenge. For a species incapable of adequately defining itself without reference to the technologies that pervade every moment of its existence, it seems remarkable that those technologies and their related constructs are largely taken for granted, remain unquestioned, and are seen as unproblematic. Thus, I argue that, in general, what is happening in the name of education is merely maintenance of a status quo that is no longer defensible.

Adopting Critical Approaches

To the great benefit (hopefully) of the planet, and to the credit of those who have led the way, we now have an ever-strengthening sense of a philosophy of technology. With its foundations only a century and a quarter ago and after a tentative start, we can now draw on deeper discourses and debates (e.g., Mumford, 1934; Ihde, 1993; Mitcham, 1994; Ferre, 1995; Feenberg, 1999). However, no philosophy or educational, political, or ethical enquiry can "be" without a critical dynamic. Critical enquiry and critique are the very oxygen of any "philosophy of . . . ."

Thus, to explore the ideas under review, a critical approach is not only a necessary tool, but must also be a "way of being" in engaging the problem. It is an inadequate proposal that we just *apply the tool* of critical enquiry *to* technology, or *to* ethics, or *to* democracy. It is easy to attend the debating club and go home when the hypothetical is over. It is something different to live and practise the critique.

Because we actually live these phenomena as part of our existence, it can be argued that we need a *critical consciousness* across the population at all times. This may seem an unrealistic proposition—not because anyone of the population is incapable of critique at some level. Rather, this is because the status quo is one of materialism, consumerism, and impotence in matters regarding technologies. Education is a part—even an instrument—of that status quo and it is a reflection of today's education systems that critical consciousness is not celebrated systemically.

To put into practice what has just been said, the following subheading warrants interrogation.

The World We Have Created

The use of the pronoun "we," and the concepts "created" and "world," must be seen as problematic. I, for one, deny having created, or having had any part in creating, the technological world. It must have been somebody else—not me.

I also refute the implication in the "we." I did not join with others in creating this world. And so we distance ourselves from, absolve ourselves of, any responsibility for technologies. The "we," of course, is comfortably ambiguous—all-embracing yet anonymity-guaranteeing. It is the species, not me. "Include me out" of any part in the decision-making.

The action of *creating* has religious meaning for some. It can also imply human potency, control, design, and/or making. Its use in this sub-heading suggests human agency. Talk of "the world" must be deconstructed too. There is the world as planet. There is the world as altered by human action—planet-plus and, of course, planet-minus. There is an implicit sense here of what we commonly call "environment"—an altogether slippery term but helpfully clarified by Franklin (2004) who distinguishes between "the built and constructed environment, which is truly a product of technology; [and]. . . *nature* which is not. . . . we [must] get away from the egocentric and technocentric mindset that regards nature as an infrastructure to be adjusted and used like all other infrastructures" (Franklin, 2004: 118).

I would like to present seven sets of random snapshots—impressions—of "the world we have created" today. They are necessarily brief. The point is to forefront, as a part of our "technological being," what is usually in the background of our lives. They should be read not for the explicit technologies but for the implicit issues and contexts, which accompany them.

One: Where Would We (Could We) Be Without Them— Three "Must-Have" Things?

In 1876 a Western Union executive said, "The telephone has too many shortcomings to be seriously considered as a means of communication" (Kurzweil, 1999: 169).

As a model of an oxymoronic "smart technology," the phone is a keen contender. Today, we can phone someone in the full knowledge that our location, duration of use, and whom we contacted are readily logged. Our call may be monitored, trawled, or tapped. Employers can tell us when to have the (mobile) phone switched on (the phone as dog lead). Answering machines and caller identification let us screen callers—including friends and relatives—before we speak with them. Phoning call-centers lets us use menus, join queues, and listen to music. Researchers and marketers contact us without invitation. We cannot avoid the unwanted call signals and conversations of others in public places.

We defend the mobile phone as a safeguard against negative situations in which we or our families might find ourselves—without considering more appropriate technological or social solutions to the initial problems. We even create rationales for the product beyond those originally conceived for it. We still await definitive scientific data about the associated radiation issues of either the phones or their towers. Meanwhile, aesthetically, we are happy with the towers so long as they are NIMBY — not in my back yard.

Well might we say that the telephone has too many shortcomings to be seriously considered as a means of communication.

Let's consider a second necessity. I have something with which I can kill people instantly and violently. Alternatively, I can use it for years and passively contribute to deaths and ill health—while also corrupting the environment. It's expensive, quickly obsolete, energy-inefficient, and antisocial. Its existence necessitates whole bureaucracies, its own insurance industry, multi-billion-dollar infrastructure costs, and a swathe of police resources. As lynchpin of oil-based economies or alternative lounge-room, we must have our cars.

Thirdly, isn't the computer wonderful? Yet, do we question the advance of computer-based systems as time-consumptive (recalling the decades-old prediction of the leisure time that would be created)? Do we question their designed rapid obsolescence, the massive increase of associated paper consumption, their roles as props, with their associated peripherals of telecommunications, scanning and copying technologies, for a tired economic system? Do we question their role as backbone of personal, corporate, and state surveillance systems, their role in labor displacement, their capacity for depersonalization at home and in the workplace? Do we question their limits as tools of learning—as themselves being incapable of distinguishing among fact, fiction, opinion, belief, wisdom, knowledge, or information; their role as crux of a digital economy to provide the taxation framework to replace an oil-based economy? Do we question the ways they shape our personal identities and community interactions, or, do we question them as another technology of dependence?

Two: Being Human Beings
We like to think we are human beings—that is our tag, our species. But emergent technologies make things somewhat unclear now.

We genetically design animals to grow organs for humans. As with human reproductive cloning, xenotransplantation raises issues related to our sense of identity. The integrity of who each of us *is* comes under challenge (Somerville, 1999).

Meanwhile, we develop toy "pets" that are very basic robots. The merging of biotechnologies with robotics presents the prospect of manufacturing toys or animals with myriad design variables to fulfill our perceived needs. Is this merely a socialization towards our own redesign as we become more artificial and our robots become more human?

Our decades-old pursuit of artificial intelligence (AI) continues, yet the question of consciousness remains central—as both technological challenge and ethical minefield. Sigman (2001) sees these changes as "far stranger than the genome, the internet or cloning. They are the greatest offensive ever against humanity. They threaten to topple us into post-humanity."

The potential—for good and otherwise—of nanotechnologies is huge (see, for example, Scientific American, 2001). Drexler (1996: 80) points out that a "designer" may be human *or* AI and will build, at a molecular level, nanocircuits and nanomachines.

The aggregation of these four human-shaping technologies could presage the trans-human or post-human period. Vinge talks of the aggregation as "technological Singularity" and Broderick "The Spike" (Broderick, 2001). We might once have been pre-human but our time as humans (in the sense that we have known it) may be up. We cannot be so sure about being human beings any longer.

Three: Jeans, Genes, or Geans?
"I think I'll wear my jeans today." We drop the word "jeans" into a sentence and that is that—it is a lot easier to say "jeans" than to say:

> [B]rass rivets from Namibian copper and Australian zinc; zip teeth from Japan; zip tape from France; thread made from petroleum in Japan and subsequently spun in Ireland; synthetic indigo dye which when discarded

cuts out light in water and so kills fish and plants; labor, carried out in Tunisia, paying about $A1.50 per hour; and, cotton probably grown in a Majority World country using large amounts of water and probably a genetically modified seed. (adapted from Sinclair, 2001)

Ten years ago, Penenberg reported that the U.S. government had granted itself exclusive rights over the genes of a Papua New Guinean tribe, which protested: "First they stole our land. Then they took the animals, the trees and the minerals from beneath the soil. Now they're back again. This time they want our minds and our bodies." By 1996 "the US Patent and Trademark Office had patented human cells, cell lines, genes, seven animals, and numerous altered plants and microorganisms. That year, there were patents pending for over 200 other genetically engineered animals" (Penenberg, 1996).

Four: Watching
In any public (and, increasingly, any nonpublic) place—whether you are traveling by public transport, driving, buying, selling, trading, transacting, phoning, hiring, hostelling, motelling, subscribing, computing, globally positioning, shopping, using any form of swipe card, having medical treatment—data will have been gathered and your "identity" may be scanned, profiled, or even stolen. "The Pentagon calls it Total Information Awareness" (New Internationalist [NI], 2005: 12).

One proposal for a "cyber-fairness symposium" canvassed such workplace surveillance issues as privacy in performance monitoring, online snooping, and cyber-slacking, and free speech and censorship online. Increasingly too, "management by software" is a matter of concern.

Cameras are pervasive, whether in restaurants, pubs, shopping malls, or built into the many satellites around the planet. The latter, some with a 100 mm resolution, serve the purposes of defense, meteorology, surveying, or surveillance (Riviere, 1999). NI (2005) reports China's plans for 100 satellites by 2020.

Combine the decreasingly personal "PC," interpersonal telephone surveillance, the technology of biometrics, and the push for "national" (actually, personal) identity cards, and the basis for totalitarian government is laid. In less than twenty years, we have passively accepted this situation.

Five: Grand Designs?
Today we design babies. In the minority world, the how, when, and where of bringing babies into being is increasingly a matter of

technology and design—whether it is the technology of contraception, of fertilization, of genetic makeup or of birth-method. Meanwhile a recent United Nations report (UNICEF, 2005) informs us that one in twelve children worldwide die before their fifth birthday, that is, 83 per 1000.

Then, we design our lives—or, our lives (lifestyles) are designed for us. Multiple new identities are available through drug technologies, ownership of products, and virtual realities. Markets, through their technologies, mold us.

And we design endings. If there is one thing that we do superbly well with technologies it is kill each other. Today, we design wars. Meanwhile human stem-cell research pursues the gene that will simply "switch off." "Programmed cell death research will allow us to choose exactly when, if ever, we die" (ABC, 2001). The implication is that the choice will be ours. Why so? Who gets to live? For how long? Will the choice be available to everyone on the planet? Imagine looking forward to our deathdays after lots of birthdays.

Six: Whose Technological Knowledge for What End?
In the United Kingdom, almost a third of public spending on research is funded by the Ministry of Defense (Radford, 2005).

One of Monsanto's directors announced their aim to become the Microsoft of global agri-business with farmers and even governments licensed to the company and its products—a range of chemicals and genetically modified organisms (GMOs). Attendant outcomes include an end of diversification in farming practices, the control of farmers, "special arrangements" with governments and, as-yet-unseen environmental consequences.

Syngenta market "golden rice"—a Swiss "invention"—and call it a "pharma-food" as it is enriched with Vitamin A. When Greenpeace pointed out that a child would have to eat 3.7 kilos of this rice to get a daily dose of Vitamin A, the "inventor" described Greenpeace as "guilty of crimes against humanity" (Sinai, 2001: 9).

Not only is almost all technological research and development funded for profit, but it is also vulnerable to secrecy, patent control, and suppression. Altruism is compelled to play a secondary role to markets, and public participation in the development of any technology is subject to tight control if not total repression. The regular suppression of alternative technologies is described by Sclove (1995) as "elite Luddism." (see, for example, Cannon, 1987; Sclove, 1995; Eisen, 1999; Feenberg, 1999; Keirl, 2001; Schlosser, 2002; Tutt, 2003).

One of the greatest features of the Internet is its potential as a tool for a different globalization—global democracy. Such a concept is anathema to governments which, through the World Intellectual Property Organization (WIPO) and the World Trade Organization (WTO) are collaborating to "govern" intellectual transactions and determine their "ownership" as "property." The key to this is the *licensing* of broadband servers—by which what may be communicated is controlled by governments at the "guidance" of vested interest (Uaeuq, 2001).

Seven: How Much Is Enough?

I collect brushes, mops, and scourers used for utensil cleaning in the kitchen sink. I have approximately 540—all different—and just one case of consumer choice gone mad—but only for those who actually have sinks, plates, taps, and even water.

Today, most products are created for profit—not to fulfill a genuine need. No matter the desirability, ethically or otherwise, the product must be generated and sold. The Kraft global "food" company budgeted $800m in two years for the marketing of 100 new products—all of which, I suspect, we could live without. Gillette's Venus razor "for women" cost $300m in research, development, and manufacturing and $150m for advertising in 29 countries. Coca-Cola's global television (alone) advertising ran to at least 20,000 adverts over the last 50 years— one a day for the period (Schiller, 2001). In 2004, Australian company Dairy Farmers had a range of 800 dairy-product variations (Sinclair, 2004).

In 1960, Packard cautioned:

> [T]he environment for a satisfying style of life is being undermined by all the emphasis on ever-greater productivity and consumption. As a result, the nation faces the hazard of developing a healthy economy within the confines of a psychologically sick and psychologically impoverished society. (Packard, 1960: 293).

Since then, two generations have been born to such conditions. A more recent analysis from a clinical psychologist argues that:

> [H]igh degrees of materialism have a toxic effect on psychological and social wellbeing. A strong materialist orientation has been associated with diminished life satisfaction, impaired self-esteem, dissatisfaction with friendships and leisure activities, and a pre-disposition to depression . . . (a) worrying rash of "consumption disorders" such as compulsive shopping, consumer vertigo and kleptomania . . .

Hyper-materialism also features predominantly in the emerging plague of "existential disorders" such as chronic boredom, ennui, jadedness, purposelessness, meaninglessness and alienation." (Schumaker, 2001: 35)

Technologies' Attributes

Having presented these seven sets of snapshots, what can be said of technologies? Technology *is* a complex phenomenon and we must eschew the one-line definition. Disciplines such as economics, sociology, anthropology and politics offer perspectives but fail to locate (rather, they dislocate) potential for real understandings of technology. Technology's complexity does not make the phenomenon of technology impenetrable. It is possible to identify some key attributes of technology. For example, technologies are *integral* to our lives and cultures. We can hardly define our existence without reference to them yet they remain *outside* of common critical discourse. All technologies have contested values. No technology is neutral or universally good. All technologies are created by a manufacturing or enabling process resulting from human intention and design. A technology cannot "be" in any functional sense without a relational human engagement.

This may well be less the case in the future. Technologies often undergo "function creep"—uses other than those originally intended. Technologies converge and gain greater technological efficacy than the sum of the parts. The post-human condition or era is emerging, where the balance between our human identity as we have known it and the engineered human is shifting.

Technologies almost always emerge faster than the necessary associated ethical and legal considerations. Personal and collective identities are shaped by the technologies with which we interact; and, as the raison d'être of technology, power and empowerment are subject to attribution, distribution and ownership—in equitable or inequitable ways.

Ethics and the Life of Technologies

When posed the fundamental ethical question, "How should we live?" we tend not to think first of technologies. Since ethical questions usually emerge after the technology has arrived, the question becomes, "How should we live *with* (this or that) technology?" This cart-before-the-horse issue is a major one for humanity (and, thus, for education and politics).

One relatively simple approach in critiquing ethics–technology relations is to see the life of any technology as a continuum of four. It must be noted that "life" here is taken to begin at the germinative stage of an idea or thought and not when the technology actually joins us in "our world." The phases are given below:

- *intention*—the point of intent, the point of conception (not of the detail of the technology's form but of the perceived outcome), or, in the sense of volition, the intention to act;
- *design*—the activity that articulates the intention in a way that can be made real;
- *manifestation*—the making, reification, or bringing-into-being of the design; and,
- *application*—the uses and consequences resulting from a technology's being in the world. Importantly, "uses and consequences" may well differ from those of the original intention.

The current situation is that ethical critique, if applied at all, is applied most readily during the fourth phase (after-the-fact), least so at the first phase, and with varying degrees in the middle phases of a technology's life. The ever-powerful interrogatory "Why?" applied to the *intention* is the necessary beginning for ethical questioning and one outcome could be that the intention is unacceptable and further developments unnecessary.

Such interrogation may have various origins. For example, a single criterion may dismiss the *need* for yet another washing-up brush or dairy product. A different approach might apply communal or spiritual principles (such as those of Amish culture) and conduct an analysis of the effects a technology might have on shared values (Sclove, 1995; Ihde, 2002). Alternatively, one might draw on sophisticated sets of design or sustainability principles (e.g., Mayall, 1979).

However, it is not enough to say we should simply *apply* some ethics at the intention stage and all will be well. Matters are more complex than this. As Ihde (2002) argues, "all technologies display ambiguous, multistable possibilities" (Ihde, 2002: 106) and the idea that a technology's take-up or its effects are predictable is untenable. Thus, I argue, that what is called for is a critical ethical consciousness, articulated through a rich technological literacy which enables societies and their members to critique *all* phases of technologies' lives. Such a proposal cannot be some kind of technology audit or checklist but must, itself, be integral to our praxis, to our being-with the world.

It is precisely through the recognition of the existential nature of technology and "technology as phenomenon" that space can be made for ethics–technology relations. To perceive technology as phenomenon is to recognize human complexity and richness. Our "being" and our "being-with" are so shaped. Embedded in, rather than peripheral to, technology-as-phenomenon are ethical matters.

Both ethics and technology enjoy intimate, yet curiously different, relationships with our very human "being." (It is recognized that ours is not the only technological species.) While the quality of our *existence* is intertwined with our technologies, so the quality of our *coexistence* is intertwined with our ethics. Ethics, as a human construct, cannot "be" without reference to other persons (and species). Human beings are ethical animals and we are technological animals.

Despite the significance of the two phenomena to humanity, they have received different kinds of attention over the ages. Technology has been a matter of practical action, tangible, indisputable in its reality, and little valued by the academy. By contrast, ethics has enjoyed thousands of years of academic debate. So far as philosophy is concerned, ethics is a major field of enquiry while the philosophy of technology is a mere infant. One misconceived deduction has been that ethics is a matter of theory while technology is a matter of practice.

Yet, both technology and ethics are contestable fields begging rational discourses, both are values-rich; both share interests with democratic theory; both have an interest in matters of determinism and free will; both beg sophisticated understandings about "choice"; and, neither is an explicit or properly understood educational reality.

Both Singer (1995) and Warnock (1978, 1998) refute the assertion that ethics may be out of touch with the day-to-day world. As Singer argues, "in the advancement of ethics lies the possibility of a new and more hopeful turn in world history" (Singer, 1995: 20). It is impossible here to articulate the huge field of moral philosophy but useful summaries abound (e.g., Singer, 1993; Warnock, 1998; Blackburn, 2001). Slote (1995: 591–595) contends that perhaps the "major problem . . . of moral philosophy . . . is coming up with a rationally defensible theory of right and wrong action." Virtue ethics invites consideration of how we should "be" by drawing on inner traits rather than referencing against some external rule system. Meanwhile axiological ethics focuses on *values* and explores something of our relationship with things—so offers a tangible connection with discussions of the material and technological world. Dent (1995) says:

> Philosophical concern with value has focused on three connected issues:
> first, on what sort of property or characteristic of something its "having

value" or "being of value" is; second, on whether having value is an objective or subjective matter, whether value reposes in the object or is a matter of how we feel towards it; third, on trying to say what things have value, are valuable. These concerns closely parallel concerns with the nature of good, from which value is seldom carefully distinguished in philosophical discussion, though the terms are clearly not synonymous. (Dent, 1995: 895)

Frankena (1973) is one who discusses ways in which "good" can be applied, and offers a practical analysis of values which distinguishes between "moral" values (those we may contend to be good on moral grounds) and "non-moral" values. Such value-analysis can be well applied to each of technology's four life-phases. He says:

[O]ne may commend a thing or say it is good on various grounds. If the thing is a person, motive, intention, deed, or trait of character, one may commend it on moral grounds; then, one is using "good" in the moral sense . . . One may also commend something on nonmoral grounds, and then one may apply the term "good" to all sorts of things, not just to persons and their acts or dispositions. (Frankena, 1973: 81)

Central to Singer's (1995) text is a discussion of the notion of self-interest. "Self-interested acts must be shown to be compatible with more broadly based ethical principles if they are to be ethically defensible, for the notion of ethics carries with it the idea of something bigger than the individual. If I am to defend my conduct on ethical grounds, I cannot point only to the benefits it brings me. I must address myself to a larger audience" (Singer, 1995: 10). This last comment reminds us of the potential cultural specificity of ethical discourse (and of technological distribution). There are dangers in seeking universal ethical principles and then applying them from one culture or race with disregard to another. It is not insignificant that there are races and religions whose ethical (and/or) technological perspectives are significantly different from our own (see, for example, Ferre, 1995; Diamond, 1998). Here, the matter of our global coexistence is paramount.

Democracy, Technology, and Ethics

Warnock (1996) points to the common interest held by existentialist philosophers in human freedom. "They are all of them interested in the world considered as the environment of man [sic] . . . because of his power to choose his own courses of action" (Warnock, 1996: 1). Her postscript, some twenty-five years on, places existentialism "with other decision-making moral theories" (Warnock, 1996: 141). Freedom and, its sometime reciprocal, control are ethical concerns for both democracy and technology. Ihde (1993) points to the (mis)perception of our ability to control technologies (well encapsulated in the teasing ambiguity of Thompson's (1991) text title—*Controlling Technology*). The intertwined nature of technologies and our lives is reflected in our political systems and orders. Matters of power emerge when one asks who actually controls technologies or whether it controls us. Here there is resonance with the Enlightenment period witnessed in Mumford's (1934) critique of "progress" and throughout Postman's (2000) text. Rybczynski, (1983), Palmer (1994), Sclove, (1995), Winner (1977, 1995), and Feenberg (1999), all write lucidly of technology-politics relations. Sclove (1995) discusses technology as both enabler and disabler of democracy and democratic process and points to the seeming impotence of the individual to influence technological development. He posits:

> [I]t is possible to evolve societies in which people live in greater freedom, exert greater influence on their circumstances, and experience greater dignity, self-esteem, purpose, and well-being. The route to such a society must include struggles toward democratic institutions for evolving a more democratic technological order. Is it realistic to envision a democratics of technology? Isn't it unrealistic not to? (Sclove, 1995: 244)

To achieve such ends as "democratic institutions" and "a democratics of technology" presupposes ethical engagements with justice, welfare and futures. The question arises, what choice, if any, have we over the use of the technologies of surveillance, genetic engineering and xeno-transplantation, nanotechnology, waste, and the post-human future? Compound such questions with reference to the inequitable distribution of technologies within and across cultures and nations, and the confluence of ethics, politics, and technology becomes transparent.

Determinism, Free Will, and Choice

The view that we *have* choices is countered by determinist arguments. The broad thesis is that all events in the world are the effects of earlier events "that all our choices, decisions, intentions, other mental events, and our actions are no more than effects of other equally necessitated events" (Weatherford, 1995: 194). Are we truly free to choose—either within our cultural, social, and political contexts or given the level of information we may hold? Have we a free will to exercise? The determinists would say not.

Such a position is anathema to "practical" ethics, democracy and, hopefully, education alike. Warnock (1996, 1998) argues that ethics implies choice and is thus apparently incompatible with determinism or, conversely, that "choice" is illusory for determinists. Underpinning ethics, democracy and technology is some sense of the right to, and the exercise of, free will which, in turn, implies choice-making. However, there is something of a conundrum when we consider technology as many of us would deny that we played any part in the decision-making and development concerning the technologies in our lives. Whilst we might refute technological determinism (something Winner [1977: 74] calls a "potential swamp of intellectual muddles") we are not currently best positioned to say that we willed our technologies into existence—or that we can will them out of existence. Here our sense of individual and collective *dis*empowerment emerges. It is hardly surprising that populist views on technology hold sway. "That's the way things are going"—"You can't stop progress"—"It's all inevitable." To yield to such views is to deny a capability to act which, of course, is both to deny the existence of choices and to deny the point of choosing to reject, adopt or adapt to technologies.

The phenomenon of technologies as pervasive-yet-invisible is well documented (Winner, 1977; Palmer, 1994; Sclove, 1995). Meanwhile, Packard (1960), Van (1998), and Schumaker (2001) all link our personal and social psychological well-being (or ill-being) to the material world of production and what we are led to *believe* are choices. With any technology there are foreseen and unforeseen consequences and the quality of knowledge and understanding we hold will directly influence the quality of our decision-making. Invariably the situation will be imperfect and we can only do our best. However, when obsolescence, over-production, low quality, high energy-use, non-recyclability, and harm to the well-being of people are transparent there seems to be no rational explanation for our "choice" in continuing to design, manufacture, use and discard a mass of technologies. This is not an ethical practice.

Knowledge is a part of the matter but an equally important issue concerns the very act of choosing to choose—namely the matter of will. Will—as design or intention—is part of the act of conception of a technology. Yet when it comes to our take-up of technologies we seem unable to apply a will guided by any particular principles. Thus, there are two prerequisites of choice to consider: first, being equipped with a critical and emancipatory technological knowledge on which to base a choice; and, second, having the personal and collective political will to make the choice.

Education Climates for Ethical Technological Literacy

Before commenting on technology education (in some jurisdictions, importantly and increasingly, know as design and technology education), four contextual points must be made. First, education is ideological and, therefore, contested (Apple, 1979, 2001). As Apple (2001) argues, the dominant Western ideology of today valorizes a particular economic model:

> The idea of the "consumer" is crucial . . . For neoliberals, the world in essence is a vast supermarket. "Consumer choice" is the guarantor of democracy. In effect, education is seen as one more product like bread, cars, and television . . . Thus, democracy is turned into consumption practices . . . the ideal of the citizen is that of purchaser. The ideological effects of this position are momentous. Rather than democracy being a *political* concept, it is transformed into a wholly *economic* one. (Apple, 2001: 39)

The shaping of curriculum as purveyor of ideology in England and Wales was well documented by Simon (1985, 1988). More recently, Smith (1999) comments "The official 'mood' of school education in contemporary western society is dominated by a 'specify, measure and report' approach" (Smith, 1999: 172). In other words, the ideology is instrumentally delivered under a guise of standards, performance and efficiency. Fortunately, such ideology holds no guarantee of permanence.

Second, if democracy is the ideal, ethically based, form of political organization then so must be the education systems on which it is based and for which it exists. In her cogent exploration of education, democracy, and the public Interest, White (1973) comes, inter alia, to two conclusions. She comments that "[t]here is at least *one* policy which *must* be in the public interest in a democracy. This (policy) is an appropriate education for a democracy" (White, 1973: 237). Thus education is the keystone for the well-being of the democracy and for the well-being of its participants. White also argues that the determination of what might constitute that "appropriate education" cannot be left to "experts." She contends that moral judgments are central to the determination of the core policy (i.e., education) of a democracy.

Third, increasing calls for citizenship education must be critiqued for the kind of ideology or democracy it may serve.

Talk of a thinking citizenry, rights issues, control of knowledge, ability to participate in democracy, empowerment to shape preferred futures, commitment to justice and equity—in all, ethical action—must come from a curriculum of empowerment not one of servility. Preparing the individual as servant of the state or tool of the economy is not what an education for democracy is about (Keirl, 2001b: 15).

Finally, a field such as (design and) technology education has, apart from its own *special* educational contribution, a role to play in the *general* education of all students. "General education" means both that education which is compulsory to all students of a certain age and that which is general in nature (e.g., literacy, numeracy, citizenship, technological literacy, ethics). It is articulated through all subjects and activities.

(Design and) Technology Curriculum

"Curriculum" here is not taken in a technicist sense to mean some sort of narrow prescription of what is to be taught in schools or of how it is to be taught. Rather, curriculum is seen as "all those discursive practices, which affect what and how students learn, and what and how teachers teach" (Reid and Johnson, 1999). This approach is necessary if curriculum-as-ideology is to be engaged—as a field for contestation and as a space for holistic, dynamic, and ethical interpretations of technological literacy.

Traditional technology education has been constrained to a primary function of skilling. However, a quality technology education is not about just skills at the kitchen worktop, computer keyboard, or workshop bench. Skills *education* is a part of any quality education. Uncritical skill replication is not. Skilling taught as empowerment, as part of personal potential or cultural heritage, skilling explored as a part of one's being, skilling as exploration of mind-body and self-environment relations, skilling as community asset—these are some understandings of *skill as education*. Skilling "to get a job" is simply not enough.

What, then, are the essences of a technology curriculum that will be democratic in nature, democracy-serving, and will articulate matters of ethics, technological literacy, and choice? It is argued that a quality technology education must be grounded by five major considerations.

First, it must be understood as a prime device for students' *personal knowledge creation*. How knowledge is constructed is a matter for the student as much as anyone else. Transformative learning must be valorized over transmissive learning. Second, values and ethics must emerge and be central, not marginal, to technology education practice. Third, the personal and species' relationships with technologies must emerge—the existential warrants introduction. Fourth, the choice issues—both the instrumental capacity to choose as well as the will to act—should emerge. Finally, the pedagogical implications of these four must be understood and articulated.

Quality curriculum design is of the essence. No longer can technology education be prescribed by populist orthodoxies which portray technology as things, as neutral, as computers, as applied science or as vocational education (Keirl, 1999). No longer can technology education be dominated by limited interests of stakeholder groups such as economic instrumentalists or select professions (Layton, 1994). It must be viewed politically (Petrina, 2000) and holistically too (Seemann, 2003).

Critical and emancipatory curriculum designs are needed if global democratic interests are to be valued *and* served. One recent iteration (DETE, 2001; Keirl, 2002, 2004), which is grounded in a three-dimensional articulation of technological literacy, has perhaps taken a step in the right direction.

Technological literacy can be viewed as having three dimensions, all of which are equally valid and important. All students benefit from all dimensions of technological literacy and must not be constrained in their learning to one aspect alone. The three dimensions are:

- *the operational*, through which students develop skills and competencies at a technical level to use materials and equipment in order to make products and systems (they learn to use and do);
- *the cultural*, through which students contextualize their learning in the world of designed and made products, processes and systems. They recognize the interdependence of technologies with people . . . and they apply their technical learning in practical ways to realize designs and solve practical problems (they learn through technology); and,
- *the critical*, through which students are empowered to take a full and critical role as autonomous citizens in technological societies. They are able to make refined judgments about the worth of the intentions and consequences of technological products, processes and systems on themselves and others (they learn about, and to be with, technology) (DETE, 2001).

By *interweaving* the operational, cultural, and critical-emancipatory dimensions, holistic, critical, ethical and dynamic understandings of technology can be facilitated. Much technology curriculum today addresses only the operational dimension. In fact, in so valorizing, it creates a hidden curriculum (Apple, 1979) of debarring alternative, richer understandings and so reinforces the populist orthodoxies and the status quo discussed above.

This three-dimensioned technological literacy is articulated through three strands—critiquing, designing, and making—and, again, it is their interplay that matters.

In such a curriculum, to design is to work with intention. It is, thus, by any definition, not about accident. Design is about making choices and weighing up competing variables. It is values-rich and not values-neutral. It is not about right answers. It is about uncertainties and working with inadequate information. It is a form of knowledge creation. Design (whether noun or verb) is legitimately open to advocacy, defense and contestation. For all of these reasons, taught well, it sits most uncomfortably with orthodox education as well as with orthodox technology education. Design education calls for student-centered learning and organization, a curbing of transmissive teaching, the creation of classrooms of uncertainty, the valorization of healthy doubt, skepticism, and critique.

In such a curriculum, critiquing can be seen as a way of acting as well as a way of thinking. "Critical thinkers critique in order to redesign, remodel, and make better" (Paul, 1995: 526). Critiquing is taking things apart in purposeful ways. The disassembly, dismantling, deconstruction, or analysis of something must achieve more than an identification of all the components. The judgments made when critiquing can expose the intentions behind designs, the unanticipated applications of technologies and the relationships between people and technologies. Through critiquing, new meanings and knowledge emerge for the critic. This offers other ways of seeing, judging, and living in the designed world.

Around the world, very real progress is being made in quality technology curriculum development but this is largely localized rather than systemic. Debate over vision and ideology remains thin yet perspective is all-important.

It is the case today that we have enough aggregated knowledge and the philosophical tools to address what are serious issues for humanity's existence, for the harmonious coexistence of its members, and for humanity's harmonious coexistence with other species and the planet. These issues are technological. We live with, through, and because of technologies and as they are integral to our lives and existences, we can be passive acceptors/recipients of them or we can be active critics/rejecters of them—albeit that, for now, outright rejection may be problematic. There is no compelling reason why we should accept any technology as fait accompli.

It is indeed time for ethical technological literacy to be articulated *and* practised. Holistic approaches to technology education can interweave and valorize key issues and counter narrow materialism, instrumentalism, and reductionism. Developing critical interrogations of the technological world while continuously fore-fronting the ethical question "How should we live?" will serve to loosen the currently stagnant status quo. Such an education not only skills but also offers democratic societies a new critical technological consciousness—one which can become a shared way-of-being.

An ethical technological literacy offers students real possibilities of: exposing technological-deterministic fallacies; interrogating design intentions; understanding technological knowledge formulations and distributions; maintaining-as-norm a skepticism towards technologies; understanding the political nature of technologies and seeing their potential to strengthen or erode democratic life.

What has been offered here amounts to an exploration of existence and our capacities to shape it. Integral to these is our technological praxis. Our shared futures—that of humanity—ultimately depend on key ethical questions and the technologies we choose to create. Both the way we live and the way we bring technologies to being must be democratic, that is, ethical. If this is to be our common goal for a common good then the keystone must be an ethically defensible technological literacy.

References

ABC (Australian Broadcasting Corporation) (2001). *Aftershock*. URL: http://abc.net.au/aftershock/guide.htm

Apple, M. (1979). *Ideology and Curriculum*. London: Routledge and Kegan Paul.

Apple, M. (2001). *Educating the "Right" Way: Markets, Standards, God and Inequality*. New York: Routledge Falmer.

Blackburn, S. (2001). *Ethics: A Very Short Introduction*. Oxford: Oxford University Press.

Broderick, D. (2001). *The Spike: How Our Lives are Being Transformed by Rapidly Advancing Technologies*. New York: Forge.

Cannon, G. (1987). *The Politics of Food*. London: Century Hutchinson.

Dent, N. (1995). "Value." In T. Honderich (ed.), *The Oxford Companion to Philosophy*. Oxford: Oxford University Press.

Department of Education, Training, and Employment (DETE) (2001). South Australian Curriculum Standards and Accountability Framework (SACSA), URL: http://www.sacsa.sa.edu.au

Diamond, J. (1998). *Guns, Germs and Steel: A Short History of Everybody for the Last 13000 Years*. London: Vintage.

Drexler, K. (1990). *Engines of Creation*. London: Fourth Estate.

Eisen, J. (1999). *Suppressed Inventions and other Discoveries*. New York: Avery.

Feenberg, A.(1999). *Questioning Technology*. London: Routledge.

Ferré, F. (1995). *Philosophy of Technology*. Athens, Georgia: The University of Georgia Press.

Frankena, W. (1973). *Ethics*. Englewood Cliffs, N.J: Prentice-Hall.

Franklin, U. (2004). *The Real World of Technology*. Toronto: Anansi.

Ihde, D. (1993). *Philosophy of Technology: An Introduction*. New York: Paragon House.

Ihde, D. (2002). *Bodies in Technology*. Minneapolis: University of Minnesota Press.

Keirl, S. (1999). "Determining technology education: knowing the orthodox, the interests, and the potential." In B. Johnson and A. Reid (eds), *Contesting the Curriculum*. Sydney: Social Science Press.

Keirl, S. (2001). As if Democracy Mattered . . . design, technology and citizenship or "Living with the temperamental elephant." In E. Norman and P. Roberts (eds), *Design and Technology Educational Research and Curriculum Development: The Emerging International Research Agenda*. Loughborough, UK: Loughborough University.

Keirl, S. (2002). "A moment in Design and Technology curriculum development as a component of educational reform." In M. Pavlova, M. and M. Gurevich (eds), *Proceedings of 1ˢᵗ Biennial International Conference on Technology Education*–10–13 July 2002, Nizhny Novgorod, Russia.

Keirl, S. (2004). "Critiquing and designing as keys of technological literacy: matters arising from the meeting." In H. Middleton, M. Pavlova, and D. Roebuck (eds), *Learning for Innovation in Technology Education: Proceedings of the 3ʳᵈ Biennial International Conference on Technology Education Research*, Surfers Paradise, Australia, 9–11, December 2004.

Kurzweil, R. (1999). *The Age of Spiritual Machines: When computers Exceed Human Intelligence*. St Leonards, N.S.W: Allen & Unwin.

Layton, D. (ed.) (1994). *Innovations in Science and Technology Education*, Vol. V. Paris: UNESCO.

Mayall, W. (1979). *Principles in Design*. London: Design Council.

Mitcham, C. (1994). *Thinking Through Technology: The Path between Engineering and Philosophy:* Chicago: University of Chicago Press.

Mumford, L. (1934). *Technics and Civilization*. London: Routledge & Kegan Paul.

(NI) *New Internationalist* (2005). "They are watching you," No. 376, March 2005, 12–13.

Packard, V. (1960). *The Waste Makers*. Harmondsworth: Pelican.

Palmer, L. (1994). "Regulating Technology." In L. Green and R. Guinery (eds), *Framing Technology: Society, Choice and Change*. St Leonards: Allen & Unwin.

Paul, R. (1995). *Critical Thinking: How to Prepare Students for a Rapidly Changing World*. Cheltenham, Vic: Hawker Brownlow Education.

Penenberg, A. (1996). "Gene piracy." In *21.C Scanning the Future* no. 2: 1996: 44–50.

Petrina, S. (2000). "The politics of technological literacy." *International Journal of Technology and Design Education*, 10 (181–206).

Postman, N. (2000). *Building a Bridge to the Eighteenth Century: How the Past can Improve our Future*. Carlton North, Vic: Scribe Publications.

Reid, A. and Johnson, B. (eds), (1999). *Contesting the Curriculum*. Katoomba: Social Science Press.

Riviere, P. (1999). "How the United States spies on us all." *Le Monde Diplomatique*. January 1999.

Robotham, J. (1995). "Weaving the tangled web." *Sydney Morning Herald*, December 16, 1995.

Rybczynski, W. (1985). *Taming the Tiger: The Struggle to Control Technology*. Harmondsworth: Penguin.

Schiller, D. (2001). "Globe with a logo—The big sell: the world takeover." *Le Monde Diplomatique*, May 2001: 15.

Schlosser E. (2002). *Fast Food Nation: What the All-American Meal is Doing to the World*. London: Penguin.

Schumaker, J. (2001). "Dead zone." *New Internationalist*, 336: July (34–35).

Scientific American, (2001), Special Edition: Nanotechnology. 285: 3, September.

Sclove, R. (1995). *Democracy and Technology*. New York: The Guilford Press.

Seemann, K. (2003). "Basic principles in holistic technology education." *Journal of Technology Education*, 14: 2.

Sigman, M. (2001). "Goodbye to human identity." *Le Monde Diplomatique*, August 2001 (16).

Simon, B. (1985). *Does Education Matter?* London: Lawrence and Wishart.

Simon, B. (1988). *Bending the Rules: The Baker "reform" of education*. London: Lawrence and Wishart.

Sinai, A. (2001). "Seeds of irreversible change." *Le Monde Diplomatique*, July.

Sinclair, L. (2004). "Shake-up for milk giant." *The Australian*, Nov. 25th.

Sinclair, R.(2001). "Jeans: The other side of denim." *Modus*, 05 (7–9). Wellesbourne, UK: Design and Technology Association.

Singer, P. (1993). *Practical Ethics*. Cambridge: Cambridge University Press.

Singer, P. (1995). *How are We to Live? Ethics in an Age of Self-Interest*. Port Melbourne: Mandarin.

Slote, M. (1995). "Problems of moral philosophy." In T. Honderich (ed.), *The Oxford Companion to Philosophy*. Oxford: Oxford University Press.

Smith, R. (1999). "Education for sustainable lives: education for sustainability lives!" In A. Reid and B. Johnson (eds), *Contesting the Curriculum*. Katoomba: Social Science Press.

Somerville, M. (2000). *The Ethical Canary: Science, Society and the Human Spirit*. Harmondsworth: Viking/Penguin.

Thompson, W. (ed.) (1991). *Controlling Technology*. Buffalo: Prometheus Books.

Tutt, K. (2003). *The Scientist, the Madman, the Thief and their Lightbulb*. London: Pocket Books.

Uaeuq, P. (2001). "I'm a cybercriminal. So jail me." *Le Monde Diplomatique*, July (16).

(UNICEF) United Nations Children's Fund (2005). *Children Under Threat–The State of the World's Children*. URL: http://www.unicef.org/sowc05/english/fullreport.html

Van, J. (1998). "User Abusers." *The Weekend Australian*. 4–5 April.

Warnock, M. (1978). *Ethics Since 1900*. Oxford: Oxford University Press.

Warnock, M. (1996). *Existentialism*. Oxford: Oxford University Press.

Warnock, M. (1998). *An Intelligent Person's Guide to Ethics*. London: Duckworth.

Weatherford, R. (1995). "Choosing and deciding." In T. Honderich (ed.), *The Oxford Companion to Philosophy*. Oxford: Oxford University Press.

White, P. (1973). "Education, democracy, and the public interest." In R. Peters (ed.), The *Philosophy of Education*. London: Oxford University Press.

Winner, L. (1977). *Autonomous Technology: Technics-Out-of-Control as a Theme in Political Thought*. Cambridge: Massachusetts Institute of Technology.

Winner, L. (1995). "Political ergonomics." In R. Buchanan and V. Margolin (eds), *Discovering Design: Explorations in Design Studies*. Chicago: University of Chicago Press.

PART 2

Considering Aspects of Design in Developing Technological Literacy

CHAPTER 7

Understanding Technological Design

Carl Mitcham and J. Britt Holbrook

> The proper study of mankind [*sic*] is the science of design.
> Herbert A. Simon (1968: 83)

In *Science and the Modern World* (1925), philosopher Alfred North Whitehead identified "the invention of invention" as the greatest invention of the late nineteenth century. Invention ceased to be an accidental or rare event and became a methodologically pursued and economically promoted process. In *American Genesis* (1989), historian Thomas P. Hughes even went so far as to compare the achievements of such inventors as Thomas Edison and Henry Ford to those of Renaissance artists. During the late twentieth century something similar happened with technological design, a human activity much more directly related to the Renaissance. According to the lead story in an early twenty-first-century issue of *Business Week*:

> When people talked about innovation in the '90s, they invariably meant technology. When people speak about innovation today, it is more than likely they mean design. Consumers, who are choking on choice, look at design as the new differentiator. In a sea of look-alike products and services, design creates the "Wow!" factor. Managers, facing fierce global competition, look to design for the kind of innovation that generates organic growth, new revenues, and wider profit margins. (Nussbaum, 2005: 62)

Beyond its possible economic ramifications, we now speak of designing things as diverse as paintings and engineering products, processes, and systems; suburban residential communities, cities, and the environment;

the layouts of magazines, newspapers, and computer web pages; and political, military, and advertising campaigns. Jeans, drugs—and even babies—have all been (or conceivably could be) designed. Clearly, any comprehensive education for technological literacy must include an extended appreciation of the essence and implications of contemporary technological design.

The Etymology of "Design"

Design is not as simple a notion as it might initially appear. Surprisingly, there is no word in classical Hebrew or Greek that directly translates as "design." This etymological fact immediately reinforces the idea that there is indeed something peculiarly modern about design.

The term "design" has roots in the Latin *designare*, meaning to mark out, trace, denote, or devise, with cognates in Italian (*disegno*, drawing) and French (*dessein*, plan or purpose; and *dessin*, drawing or sketch). The English "design" can function as either verb (meaning to mark out, nominate, appoint; to plan, propose, intend; and to sketch, draw) or noun (mental plan and artistic shape). In these senses it first appears in the mid-to-late sixteenth and early seventeenth centuries.

Attentive philosophers and theologians might object, contending that the notion of design has been central to an argument for the existence of God since at least the Middle Ages, though some may wish to go back as far as Cicero. (See *De natura deorum* ii, 34, for Cicero's description of providence in nature by means of a contrast between art and chance.) But the so-called argument from design for the existence of God does not actually use the word "design" until the eighteenth century. In Thomas Aquinas's famous fifth way (*Summa theologiae* I, q.2, a.3) the argument is from the "governance of the world" to a governor, more a political than a technological image. The fifth way is more properly described as an argument toward teleology than an argument from design. Even Issac Newton, undoubtedly the most influential advocate of order in nature and a proponent of the idea that such order can only be accounted for by God, refers to the "counsel and dominion" of God rather than any design capabilities (*Principia Mathematica*, Book III, "General Scholium"). It was Bernard Nieuwentyt and, most famously, William Paley, who during the early Industrial Revolution turned teleology into design by describing many things in nature if not the world as a whole as like a watch (a machine) that has to have had a watchmaker (a designer). It is not by chance that the heyday of the argument from design coincided with the rise of mechanistic science. It is this idea of design in nature—design that presupposes a (divine) designer—against which David Hume argued in his *Dialogues Concerning Natural Religion*; and it is this idea of design for which Charles Darwin sought to offer an alternative account, design by natural selection or unintentional design—a view often used by classical economists to explain as well the source of order in the market.

Since the late scientific and early industrial revolutions the verb "design" has developed progressive associations with modern engineering and technology. As denoting "the act of conceiving and planning the structure and parameter values of a system, device, process, or work of art" (*McGraw-Hill Dictionary of Scientific and Technical Terms*) or any such conception and plan, it has also come to be applied to an increasingly diverse range of human experiences. For the artist and architect, design is fundamentally an activity honoring tradition and aesthetic principles, and thus not something readily transferred to the world at large. For engineers, design is simply conscious if not rationalized construction, something much more generalizable. Engineers design structures, devices, processes, and systems. Adopting this sense, even artists can be described in a new way as designers of paintings and statues. Industrial designers likewise design consumer products, graphic designers advertisements and displays, and entrepreneurs business strategies. Musicians design their compositions, poets and novelists their works of literature. Scientists design hypotheses and how to test them. Physicians design treatments for their patients. Teachers design new curricula, parents how to raise their children. The United States and the United Kingdom attempt to design a new, democratic Iraq (a designer country) to take its proper place in a redesigned Middle East.

Unlike aesthetic design, engineering design has been extended from mechanical structure across economic and political affairs into psychology and biology. There are designer drugs and designer organisms (genes)—all mass produced (thus annulling particularity) and planned out beforehand (in an attempt to escape uncertainty if not concern and worry). In the arena of sports, athletes design strategies for improving their games: some undertake specific drug-regimens designed both to enhance their performance and to avoid detection; some rely on improved equipment design (e.g., in golf, where design improvements have in turn made it necessary to redesign certain golf courses). For many, not just for professional athletes, nutritionists design meal plans, and personal trainers design workouts.

People today design their lives—that is, they try to think out in advance how to go about doing something, and in the process to bring to bear as much scientific information and technical competence as possible. For group behaviors, designs take the form of policies. In what are now the most characteristic design and policy constructing activities they use computers to assemble and organize this information, to render it in graphic form, and thus to test out alternative courses of action before actually undertaking them. Test is no longer by lived experience but by modeling and simulation. People construct in miniature, on the screen, in virtual form, their actions—in order, they say, to live those lives more effectively, more fully, more responsibly.

In essence, design thus turns making (not to say living) into thinking—a thinking beforehand about how to make (or how to live). Is this simply an unqualified good? Or is it as problematic as that more here-and-now making (and living) that it progressively replaces?

Technological Design History

Technological design has a history, and a specifically modern history—which may be briefly summarized as follows. Prior to the rise of modern technology, design was hidden or embedded in the craft of making as a characteristic activity of human beings. Artisans in their particularities of body, place, and history were at one and the same time those who conceived or imagined artifacts and then worked to fabricate them. Aboriginally, they were also the users. Artisans in wooded geographies worked with wood, wood growing there (not elsewhere); artisans living in rock-rich landscapes worked with stone, stone quarried there (not elsewhere). They worked also with the strength and skills of their own bodies, and within the traditions of their peoples or cultures; they used and lived with what they made. Each artifact so fabricated itself had its unique body, place, and history—which guided and circumscribed its human engagements. There were no generalized things or devices. Tools were task specific and gendered (see, for example, Illich, 1983). Even when particularities were exchanged in trade they remained specific in fact. All things had a natural particularity that is today at once highly prized and difficult to understand.

The historical impetus behind the rise of technological design as a new and specialized activity was the industrial mode of mass production. Prior to mechanical industrialization, the artisan was at once designer and worker—yet neither. Artisans, as it were, designed artifacts in the course of constructing them, so that making seldom involved anything like a separate moment of thinking out or planning beforehand, but proceeded instead as intuitive cut-and-try fabrication, letting oneself be guided by materials and tradition, and even by personal relationships in the community. Testing took place continuously right in the making and then again in the using.

The design process was disembedded from this rich, intimate context by the demands of mechanization and its increasing divisions of labor. Coordinate with the replacement of human power with coal and steam-driven prime movers, and the gearing of power into repetitive motions in order to mass produce identical products, two things happened. Design historian Penny Sparke summarizes these in *An Introduction to Design and Culture in the Twentieth Century* (1986):

> [F]irst came the need for a designer as pattern maker for artifacts that could be mass produced; second came the need for designer as form giver for artifacts that could be mass marketed. Mass marketing in turn may be read as a turning of users into consumers in much the same way as mass production turns workers into laborers, repetitive shopping serving as an echo of the repetitive mechanical motions required of industrial laborers. Now niche mass marketing asks designers to try to re-create the feel of particularities—something that nevertheless often feels, when designed, artificial or false.

In Sparke's words, "design is characterized by a dual alliance with both mass production and mass consumption."

> Like Janus, design looks in two directions at the same time: as a silent quality of all mass-produced goods it plays a generally unacknowledged but vital role in all our lives; as named concept within the mass media it is, however, much more visible and generally recognized . . . [But] design as an adjunct of marketing has grown out of design as an aspect of mass production. (Sparke, 1986: xix–xx)

It is difficult for us not to read back into craft work some primitive form of design. But this is as great a mistake as thinking of the hand-copied book (literally, a manuscript) as a primitive form of the book that rolled off Gutenberg's press. Instead, design is properly seen as both a response to and a promotion of industrial production. To quote Sparke again, "Changes in production and in design . . . advanced in leaps and bounds and made otherwise complex tasks simple." Textile production provides an oft-cited exemplar. The Spinning Jenny and the Jacquard loom fundamentally transformed

> the way textiles were both conceived and made and intensified the changes in the process of design that the division of labor had already instigated. No longer could the [artisan] make spontaneous decisions about the

appearance of the final product during its manufacture but . . . the desired pattern had to be fully planned and broken down into its component parts before manufacture began. This method of designing prior to production was echoed in fabric printing with the use of the mechanical roller, and in ceramics production where molds were used increasingly in the mass-production sector. The effects of these organizational changes in production methods were felt both in the appearance of the final products . . . and in the structure of labor patterns within the factory, with the emergence of a new breed of "art-workers" who translated the ideas of fine artists into mass production. (Sparke 1986: 4)

The effects were felt as well in the new breed of "engineering-workers" who thought out the internal structure of products at the mechanical, chemical, and eventually electronic, molecular, and even genetic levels. This structural design was complemented by design of the mechanical, chemical, and other processes by which such products could be produced.

Technological Design as the Turning of Making into Thinking

Technological design connotes consciousness, intention, in making, using, or acting. But making remains fundamental. The consciousness at issue in making can, as already indicated, be of (a) the surface, the shape, the look or feel of the object (industrial and/or graphic design), and/or of (b) that which is beneath or behind the surface (engineering design). These two senses of technological design have engendered two quite different literatures on design. With regard to industrial- or graphic-design literature, the focus is on aesthetics and communication, especially in the context of competitive markets (advertising). (A leading effort to bridge this hiatus in the worlds of design is the work of Margolin and Buchanan, 1995.) With regard to engineering-design literature, the focus is on making and making processes, especially the methodologies for thinking or conceiving such processes with greater efficiency (see, for example, Cross, 1989).

Engineering design thus constitutes a distinctive way of turning making into thinking, engendering not only a special kind of making but also a unique way of thinking. The attempt comprehensively to explicate engineering-design thinking and making was first undertaken by the Dutch engineer and philosopher Hendrick van Riessen in his book *Filosofie en techniek* (1949).

Taking off from van Riessen, one may describe modern technology as a whole as distinguished from premodern or traditional technology insofar as artifacts are designed and produced from what he termed "neutral" elements. "Neutral" here means isolated, decontextualized, disembedded, standardized, and interchangeable or replaceable. Such neutral elements (processes as well as material parts), precisely because of their disembedded character, are largely deprived of qualitative value.

Reduction in contextual or qualitative value means in turn that, in the course of being integrated into a design, these neutral elements may be subjected to quantitative assessment—that is, numbered, measured, weighed in relation to eventual production and use. The design process itself is thus commonly described as composed of two basic moments: analysis (breaking down, identifying, and assessing the parts) and synthesis (bringing together or integrating the parts).

Take, for example, the designing of some machine. The machine is first defined in broad terms, commonly with regard to inputs, outputs, and operational specifications. The design engineer, thinking in frameworks provided by the technological sciences (mechanics, thermodynamics, strength of materials, etc.), decides on the general or global character of the design (whether the machine is to incorporate a heat engine, electric motor, etc.). Within such parameters a dialogue then begins between the analysis of more detailed functions and parts, available technological building blocks (as summarized in engineering handbooks on parts, materials, and processes), and their synthesis into a functioning unit to meet the original specifications.

The engineering design is a modular product composed of neutral elements, elements that mean nothing until they are integrated into some product, process, or system. The same elements may be integrated into many different machines, and their integration is always contingent or with little reference to larger inherited contexts. Furthermore, the design process itself has been progressively modularized. What was in the nineteenth century originally manifest in calculation and mechanical (that is, modularized) drawing is increasingly computerized, the computer process being composed of numerous modular subroutines and bits of information.

Engineering design is to traditional making as composing complex computer graphics with clip art is to freehand drawing. The difference between engineering design and clip-art composition is that in engineering design the aesthetic eye tends to be blinded by technical standards and calculations founded again in the technological sciences: formulas for determining the bearing load of a beam, the reduction of friction in a mechanical assembly, energy consumption efficiency, and more. It is as if various options in clip-art composition were to be tested by calculations of minimal area covered with maximum number of pieces used or some other such mathematical determination.

As a consequence of this new state of affairs, design engineers, although not deprived of creativity, are called upon to exercise their creativity in what may be termed calculative ingenuity. The same engineer is also increasingly alienated or separated from actual fabrication. Making is preceded by a calculative thinking-out in advance. Early on in the emergence of engineering design there remained numerous opportunities for feedback from the actual construction or making that would take place in the shop or in the factory. Insofar as this calculative thinking-out in advance increasingly and effectively analyzes or modularizes parts and processes, there is less and less opportunity or need for such feedback. Indeed, making may even be described as itself reduced to a thinking-out, insofar as engineers are able fully to prepare in their minds and on their computer screens artifacts and production processes. This trajectory in engineering design is illustrated in Karl Sabbagh's *21st-Century Jet: The Making and Marketing of the Boeing 777* (1996), a narrative account of the first wide-body passenger jet designed completely with computers, for which no prototype or test model was ever constructed.

The Problematics of Technological Design

In an essay stimulated by van Riessen, the Dutch aerospace engineer Ad Vlot has reflected on the problematics of this new way of thinking before making. Vlot writes:

> In the traditional form of technology the same craftsperson is the designer and the maker, and the parts of a product are unique for that specific product. Standardized bolts, rivets, switches, transistors, filters, etc. are typical of modern technology. In this way the technological design method that isolates the different disciplines corresponding to the various neutral elements becomes a powerful tool used by the engineer in combination with automation to control the designed artifact before it becomes operational. [But] this systematic design method does not correspond with reality, in which every thing is unique, variable, and embedded in relationships. Therefore the art of engineering involves the "feeling of the engineer" for dealing with frictions between the result of theoretical optimization and reality such as variations, wear, environmental influences and, above all, human freedom that may disturb the process or functioning of the artifacts. (Vlot, 2000: 210)

For Vlot there thus exists the possibility that thought-out products may not be sufficiently thought out. In conjunction with the professional engineering obligation "to hold paramount the safety, health, and welfare of the public" (as it is termed, for instance, in the U.S. National Society of Professional Engineers 1993 Code of Ethics, Fundamental Canons, 1) this implies a practical responsibility to think harder and more broadly than might otherwise be the case. Design engineers have what Carl Mitcham (1994b) has called a duty *plus respicere*, that is, a professional obligation to expand design thinking in order to take more aspects of reality into account.

Yet as Vlot acknowledges, the issue of human freedom—in contrast to the issues of variations, wear, and environmental influences—presents special challenges for any duty *plus respicere*. Human freedom includes the freedom to use improperly (to fail to follow directions for use), to misuse (to employ as means for some unintended or socially disapproved end), or to abuse (to treat in such a manner as to degrade or destroy more rapidly than planned). From one perspective—for instance, that of Michel de Certeau (1984)—misuse may actually manifest human freedom and creativity in a way that should not be abridged. Technical-function theorists, especially those influenced by the concept of proper functions in biology, have a tendency to read the use plan of a designer as a moral prescription (Franssen, 2005). But what is wrong with using a screwdriver as a chisel?

Bart Kemper (2004), however, argues that at least some artifacts ought to be designed taking into account possibilities for "evil intent." Kemper focuses in particular on otherwise benign artifacts that might be turned into weapons of mass destruction: vans and fertilizer (e.g., in the case of the Oklahoma City car-bomb attack carried out by Timothy McVeigh) or airplanes and skyscrapers (e.g., in the case of the 9/11 attacks on the World Trade Center). Vans and fertilizers and planes and skyscrapers can all be improperly used or misused in various relatively benign ways (as when a van is turned into living quarters or so much fertilizer is put on plants that they die). Although such designer-unintended uses might be worth modest attention in the design process, the stakes are raised dramatically when evil intent is able to employ such products in ways that can kill hundreds or thousands of people. In such cases, Kemper argues, engineers have an obligation to try to design them so as to make misuse difficult. The principle would be a simple extension of that manifested in designs such the safety shields to keep workers from harming themselves with large punch-press machines or passive restraints in automobiles to strap in the driver and passengers whether they like it or not. Nitrogen fertilizers could be so diluted as to make them more difficult to use in powerful explosives; airplanes can be equipped with stronger cockpit doors and tall buildings with structures that better withstand planes crashing into them.

Objections to Any Duty *Plus Respicere*

It may be objected that an engineering duty *plus respicere* to take such aspects of human behavior and reality into account—especially the potential evil intent of terrorists—is unreasonable on at least two counts: (a) such considerations are outside the scope of engineering knowledge and practice, and (b) no one, especially not an engineer, can predict all aspects of the future.

First, what is the character of engineering such that engineers might be called on to consider apparently nonengineering issues like the intentions of terrorists? In the popular mind engineering is commonly taken to be focused on making matter or energy useful to human beings in the most efficient manner. Engineering students certainly often enroll in their programs of study expecting to be able to rely on their mathematical, scientific, and computer aptitudes and to avoid developing interpersonal or communication skills. As such, engineering is reduced to quantitative calculations of inputs and outputs aimed at maximizing an output/input ratio defined as efficiency—and it seems unfair to ask persons with such technical abilities to consider the many possibilities of misuse.

Engineers do not, however, simply aim at some abstract ideal of efficiency; they aim at specific instances of efficiency as determined by particular situations. Sometimes what is important in designing a bridge is that it will be durable and last a long time; other times what is important is that it can be constructed as quickly as possible. The value of efficiency is formal and contextual, given substance by other values external to the design process. Engineering as the pursuit of efficiency is subordinate to whatever external specifications define the relevant inputs and outputs. At the same time, external specifications are almost always negotiated with the engineers to whom they are given. Engineering clients seldom know for sure how to specify what they want; indeed, they often have to learn from the engineers they hire that some of their desired specifications are at odds—that there are tradeoffs between cost and quality, for instance—while others are impossible. No engineer will take a job that makes unrealistic demands on a budget while requiring previously unattainable levels of safety and reliability or that specifies a system with a perpetual-motion machine as its prime mover.

Even more does the understanding of engineering as design call for such engineering–client negotiation. To some extent design rests on natural science (physics, chemistry, and biology) and on engineering science (mechanics, thermodynamics, electronics), but the design of products, processes, and systems also requires appreciation of human needs and how the social world works. Engineered artifacts must ultimately find a home in human experience and make their way in the marketplaces of money and ideas or find themselves relegated to what one author has described as "inventions necessity is not the mother of" (Jones 1973). Engineering-design failures can be as much social as technical. The most effective engineers are those who either have a sense of public need or interest or know how to enter into dialogue with the public to assess in advance how designs might be used. It is thus not unreasonable to ask them to consider as well how their designs might be misused—perhaps by unparticipating interlocutors and unanticipated users.

Moreover, the extensive technical work that engineers do to guard against technical failure provides preparation for parallel analyses to avoid social misuse. Robert Charles Metzger's *Debugging by Thinking* (2003) argues for a multidisciplinary deployment of logic, mathematics, psychology, safety analysis, computer science, and engineering in order to avoid and correct software errors. This is virtually an operationalization of the duty *plus respicere*. From Metzger's perspective there is something professionally irresponsible about the too common release of software programs that have been insufficiently tested for multiple weaknesses. But such interdisciplinary skills exercised at the technical level readily blend into the exercise of related analyses at the social level. Indeed, just as earlier complaints about the difficulties of taking into account multiple possibilities for unintended consequences in the environmental area have led to the development of methods for environmental-impact assessment, so it seems reasonable to postulate the formulation of methods for misuse-and-evil-intent possibility assessments.

This last point also suggests an initial response to the second objection, that no engineer can be expected to be able to predict all aspects of the future. The future, and the future consequences of designs, can be studied. Futurology is the most general effort to undertake such a study, and has generally not been directed toward assessing the results of particular design projects. Indeed, often it seeks to predict or to call for the emergence of various designs. But the proliferation of scientific, sociological, and other efforts to develop technology-assessment methods and to analyze and empirically examine unintended consequences, uncertainty, and risk all point toward a rich variety of possible theoretical and practical responses to the general challenge set forth in the second objection. (In this regard see, for example, Averill, 2005.) To accept the objection at face value is simply to make an excuse or to refuse to acknowledge the work being done to advance knowledge of unintended consequences. The unintended consequences of design may be difficult to predict or not fully predictable, but they are certainly able to be assessed more fully than is often done.

The Metaphysics of Technological Design

There is nevertheless a deeper sense in which the future may be described as unpredictable—a sense that deserves consideration and exhibits, as it were, an ontological tension with the very idea of technological design. Design and designing constitute an attempt to prefigure the future that sees the future as open to indefinite manipulation. The design stance (to reinterpret what is for Daniel Dennett, 1987, an epistemological term) involves a conception of the human as both a subject and object of design, planning, thinking-out, and the further activities of making, remaking, and transforming. As such it opposes a traditional understanding of the human as fundamentally rooted or particularized, although in ways that are open to the more-than-human.

The traditional or premodern view of the world is that it constitutes a reality that ultimately calls for acceptance. The world may be tinkered with around the margins, but the human condition is one that human beings do not have the option of escaping. The metaphysical basis of engineering design was, for one philosophical observer, dramatically disclosed in a common reaction to the 1957 launch of Sputnik as simply the first step toward an escape from human imprisonment to the Earth. According to Hannah Arendt, "The banality [of such a view] should not make us overlook how extraordinary in fact it was; for although Christians have spoken of the earth as a vale of tears and philosophers have looked upon their body as a prison of mind or soul, nobody in the history of mankind has ever conceived of the earth as a prison for men's bodies or shown such eagerness to go literally from here to the moon" (Arendt, 1958: 2). The engineered achievement of space flight represents the apogee of a historico-philosophical trajectory that began with early modern arguments for a "conquest of nature" (Francis Bacon) that would enable humans to become its "masters and possessors" (René Descartes). At its deepest level technological design aims to enlarge human freedom to world-transformational levels.

The paradox of the designed world, which refuses to accept the given-ness of the human condition, is that it nevertheless creates a world to which even the designer is to some degree forced to submit. In the first instance this does not appear to be submission at all. The designed world is, after all, a world of human creation. Yet all designed products, processes, and systems also have some, however marginal or residual, undesigned consequences. This is as true of engineering as of other types of design (including artistic or graphic design). Just as philosophers of science have argued that all scientific theories are underdetermined by the evidence, so are designs underdetermined by the intentions and analyses of their designers. Just as the world is susceptible to design, it is also in its contingencies and complexities always resistant to design. As design takes hold and its consequences (intended and unintended) pro-liferate, the need or demand for more design multiplies. More and more thinking and planning and designing seems to be required just to live with the designs that have been created. What other solution to design shortcomings is there than simply more design? There appears to be less and less space, even in a radically pluralist culture, for anyone who would live the undesigned life.

Nowhere is the demand for more and more design (and its limitations) more apparent than in relation to the issue of sustainability. Despite the claims of those who deploy the argument from design to postulate from the intricacies of nature the reality of a creator (or designer) God, the real reason the multiple parts of nature function together as they do both in organisms and across ecosystems is that they have not been consciously designed. Nature works as well as it does because it has taken form slowly over periods of time that are quite beyond human scale not by conscious design but by trial-and-error selection. As humans introduce new changes into nature of a speed and character that is non-natural, these changes interfere with existing relationships and introduce pertubations that design must work increasingly hard to comprehend and control. Environmental sustainability and sustainable development demand increasingly more research and conscious planning. The disciplines of environmental science and engineering point projects for Earth-systems engineering and dreams for managing the planet (U.S. National Academy of Engineering, 2002). (Extended, such dreams take on prospects for redesigning Mars and other planets through terraforming.)

Yet even among engineers there are recognitions of the fact that dreams repeatedly bump up against the complexities of nature—and the consequent difficulties of design. The very fact that design seems to demand more and more design points to an inherent resistance to design. This resistance to design is a limitation that designers (and users) ultimately have an obligation to acknowledge in both theory and practice.

Authenticity in Technological Design

If the world is both susceptible and at the same time to resistant to design, how ought human beings respond? One extreme would be to emphasize susceptibility and ignore resistance. Maybe resistance can be overcome by better or deeper or more thoroughgoing design (nanotechnological design)—overwhelmed by more and more design. Another extreme would be to emphasize resistance and argue that susceptibility is at best illusory and at worst harmful. Unable to design completely, humans ought not to design at all.

Precisely because they seek to ignore one aspect of the complex ambivalence that is the reality of the experience of technological design, both extremes exhibit a kind of inauthenticity. Adapting yet redesigning a notion of authenticity found in Søren Kierkegaard, perhaps it would be possible to confront the dialectic of susceptibility and resistance to design by acknowledging the dialectic. As has been argued in another context,

> The human world is a complex of both finitude and infinitude, necessity and possibility, determination and freedom. Authenticity consists in accepting in proper proportions both my freedom and my un-freedom; inauthenticity consists in failing to accept some aspect of either or both. In the world of traditional making it may be suggested that the most common temptation to inauthenticity was to deny all freedom (what Kierkegaard called the "despair of necessity"). In the world of design, the most common temptation to inauthenticity may be instead to deny all determination (Kierkegaard's "despair of possibility"). (Mitcham, 2001: 34)

On the one hand, to reject opportunities for design (susceptibility to design) is to fall inauthentically into "the despair of necessity." On the other, to design while denying necessity (resistance to design) is to fall inauthentically into "the despair of possibility." Authenticity entails recognizing a obligation to design with an openness to the limits of design—that is, recognizing in engineering design a duty *plus respicere*, a professional obligation to expand design thinking in order to try to take more, including now the limits of design, into account.

Patrick Feng (2000), in a related argument, raises the issue of a reaction to technology that he suggests is a "barrier to ethical design." According to Feng,

> For many people, the idea that technology is moving faster than we can adapt seems commonsensical. When a 1995 opinion poll asked American consumers whether they agreed with the statement "technology has almost gotten out of control," an astounding 63 percent of respondents said yes. Media reports reinforce this belief: with few exceptions, the press in America tends to talk about technology as if it were an external force beyond human control. (209)

Such a fatalism with regard to technology, along with its flip-side, the blind faith in technological progress, is inauthentic. A more authentic attitude toward technology would be characterized by Feng's claim that "*technology both shapes and is shaped by its social context*" (212, author's emphasis). Such an authentic attitude "opens the door to including ethical discussions in the actual *design* of artifacts" (212, author's emphasis). At the root of a possible ethics of design there will thus rest a recognition that no matter how good or sophisticated the technological design, to some degree results can always transcend intentions—and the recurring presence of such results are phenomena that human designers, even in their attempts to design around them, must accept. Further recognition that such acceptance may imply a limitation not just *in* design but *on* design may be suggested as the beginning of wisdom for design.

References

Arendt, H. (1958). *The Human Condition*. Chicago: University of Chicago Press.

Averill, Marilyn. (2005). "Unintended Consequences." In Carl Mitcham (ed.), *Encyclopedia of Science, Technology, and Ethics* (Detroit: Macmillan Reference), vol. 4, 1995–1999.

Certeau, Michel de. (1984). *The Practice of Everyday Life*. Trans. Steven Rendall. Berkeley, CA: University of California Press.

Cross, Nigel. (1989). *Engineering Design Methods*. New York: John Wiley.

Dennett, Daniel. (1987). *The Intentional Stance*. Cambridge, MA: MIT Press.

Feng, Patrick. (2000). "Rethinking technology, revitalizing ethics: overcoming barriers to ethical design," *Science and Engineering Ethics*, vol. 6, no. 2, 207–220.

Franssen, M. (2005). "Technical functions." In Carl Mitcham (ed.), *Encyclopedia of Science, Technology, and Ethics* (Detroit: Macmillan Reference), vol. 4, 1887–1890.

Hughes, Thomas P. (1989). *American Genesis: A Century of Invention and Technological Enthusiasm, 1870–1970*. New York: Viking.

Illich, Ivan. (1983). *Gender*. New York: Pantheon.

Jones, Stacy V. (1973). *Inventions Necessity Is Not the Mother of.* New York: Quadrangle.

Kemper, B. (2004). "Evil intent and design responsibility," *Science and Engineering Ethics*, vol. 10, no. 2, 303–309.

Margolin, V. and Richard Buchanan (eds) (1995). *The Idea of Design*. Cambridge, MA: MIT Press.

McGraw-Hill Dictionary of Scientific and Technical Terms. (1994). 5th ed. New York: McGraw-Hill.

Mentzger, R.C. (2003). *Debugging by Thinking: A Multidisciplinary Approach*. Boston: Digital Press.

Mitcham, C. (1994a). *Thinking through Technology: The Path between Engineering and Philosophy* (Chicago: University of Chicago Press).

Mitcham, C. (1994b). "Engineering Design Research and Social Responsibility." In S. Kristin and Shrader-Frechette (eds), *Ethics of Scientific Research* (Lanham, MD: Rowman and Littlefield), 153–168.

Mitcham, C. (2001). "Dasein versus design: the problematics of turning making into thinking," *International Journal of Technology and Design Education*, vol. 11, no. 1, 27–36.

Nussbaum, B. (2005). "Annual design awards 2005," *Business Week* (July 4, 2005), 62–63.

Riessen, H. van. (1949). *Filosofie en techniek [Philosophy and technology]*. Kampen: J.H. Kok.

Sabbagh, K. (1996). *21st-Century Jet: The Making and Marketing of the Boeing 777*. New York: Scribners.

Simon, Herbert A. (1968). *The Sciences of the Artificial*. Cambridge, MA: MIT Press. 2nd ed., 1981; 3rd ed., 1996.

Sparke, P. (1986). *An Introduction to Design and Culture in the Twentieth Century*. London: Allen and Unwin.

U.S. National Academy of Engineering. (2002). *Engineering and Environmental Challenges: Technical Symposium on Earth Systems Engineering*. Washington, DC: National Academy Press.

Vlot, Ad. (2000). "Toward a juridical turn for the ethics of technology? An aerospace case." In Peter Kroes and Anthonie Meijers (eds), *The Empirical Turn in the Philosophy of Technology, Research in Philosophy and Technology*, vol. 20, 207–218.

Whitehead, A.N. (1925). *Science and the Modern World*. New York: Macmillan.

CHAPTER 8

The Designer Fallacy and Technological Imagination

Don Ihde

Earlier in the twentieth century, literary theorists developed the notion of an "intentional fallacy." This was the notion that the meaning of a text lay with the author's intentions: if these could be uncovered, then the meaning of the text was established. One can easily see how, if this is the only true way to establish meaning, there could be difficulties. What if the author was long dead? Or, even if the author was living, how could one tell that he or she was telling the truth? What of unintended meanings, or meanings that fit but were not thought of in advance? Thus, the intentional fallacy recognizes such difficulties and cannot be considered an adequate account of interpretation.

I hold that there is a parallel "fallacy" which is at least implicit in the history of technology design. In simple form, the "designer fallacy," as I shall call it, is the notion that a designer can design into a technology, its purposes and uses. In turn, this fallacy implies some degree of material neutrality or plasticity in the object, over which the designer has control. In short, the designer fallacy is "deistic" in its eighteenth-century sense, that the designer-god, working with plastic material, creates a machine or artifact that seems "intelligent" by design—and performs in its designed way. Instead, I hold, the design process operates in very different ways, ways that imply a much more complex set of interrelations between any designer, the materials that make the technology possible, and the uses to which any technology may be put.

First, some examples of simple designer fallacies: Thomas Edison, the great late-nineteenth–early-twentieth-century American inventor, was among the first to design and invent a machine to reproduce sounds—the phonograph. The machine, at first, was a mechanical device that consisted of a speaking tube into which someone would speak; this was attached to a sensitive diaphragm that would reverberate with the sound waves coming into the tube, and the diaphragm, in turn, was connected to a crystal needle that would trace the wave patterns onto a rotating roll covered with tinfoil. As the crank was turned, the speaker sounding into the tube, a "record" was made on the foil. The same machine, played back, would reverse the process and one could hear well enough to understand and recognize the sounds, originally inscribed on the roller—"Mary had a little lamb . . ." (Nyre, 2003: 89–90).

Here, the designer intent was to reproduce sounds. But the intent, at this stage, remained ambiguous, and the primary possible use of this machine was drawn from the resultant capacities that emerged, more than from any preplanned single use. It could be a rather primitive dictation machine. Clearly, it would have restricted use since the number of play-backs was very limited due to the softness of the foil: only a time or two could the play-back remain intelligible. But, in spite of this, the machine was advertised in the typically glowing rhetoric of technological promise of the late nineteenth century. It was advertised as "the miracle of the 19th Century," a machine that speaks:

> It will Talk, Sing, Laugh, Crow, Whistle, Repeat cornet solos, imitating the Human Voice, enunciating and pronouncing every word perfectly, IN EVERY KNOWN LANGUAGE." (Nyre, 2003: 89)

If one, with the anachronistic insight of knowing anything about the subsequent history of recordings, would then read back to Edison's early machines, one might have predicted that one early dominant use of recording devices would quickly evolve into music recording, which in turn, also transformed a number of musical practices. For example, early recording-devices could record for only three and a half to four minutes of time—thus the music played must be three and a half to four minutes long, a tradition for the "popular song" that persisted well past the time of early recording devices. The new machine calls for new practices, but in this case not "intended" ones.

The phonograph actually was invented later than the telephone, which was invented at least once by Alexander Graham Bell. Here the designer intent was for an amplifying device capable of transmitting a voice over distance, thus intended as a prosthetic technology for the hard-of-hearing (e.g., Bell's mother). The telephone was the early antecedent of "chat" on the internet, but the party line on which all the neighbors "chatted" was not foreseen, let alone the subsequent telephone wiring of early-twentieth century America.

Even the typewriter was first designed as a prosthetic technology: an aid for blind or myopic people to be able to produce clear script. Instead, as Friedrich Kittler has pointed out, the typewriter become, dominantly, a business machine and one which transformed the secretariat of the late nineteenth century from male to female (male secretaries often refused to adapt to this "machine" which they thought deskilled their handwork, but young women seeking both a public role and pre-skilled with keyboard or piano skills, easily found a new role) (Kittler, 1990).

The designer fallacy also plays a role in Langdon Winner's best-known article "Do artifacts have politics?" This article traces the history of Robert Moses' designs of the bridges over the parkways of Long Island. Winner claims that Moses' ulterior intention was to keep the lower classes and races out of pristine Long Island's growing suburbs. Thus he deliberately designed low bridges that would prevent large trucks and double-decker buses from the parkways. In one sense, there was some success with this material strategy if one looks at the demographics of the early twentieth century, but a counter-strategy defeated whatever politics were first employed. The Eisenhower Interstate development of the 1950s called for all interstate highways to have high bridges so that trucks—including those carrying ballistic missiles for the cold war—could clear them, thus opening the way for what we Long Islanders call our "longest parking lots" of multi-laned highways. The cold war trumps suburban protection.

The language and notion of "intent," while still dominant, is inverted by Edward Tenner in his well-known book *Why Things Bite Back: Technology and the Revenge of Unintended Consequences* (Knopf, 1996). Tenner catalogues and classifies an enormous number of technologies, presumably designed for certain uses, that end up having disastrous or contrary unintended consequences. He spoofs Toffler's notion of the paperless society, where, "making paper copies of anything is a primitive use of [electronic word-processing] machines and violates their very spirit (quoted Toffler, 1970: ix), in light of the higher-papered society of today" (Tenner, 1996: ix) Or, something as simple as a home-security system, designed to increase security, he contends, subverts security by producing false alarms and overwhelming police ability to respond. "In Philadelphia, on 3,000 of 157,000 calls from automatic security systems over three years were real; by diverting the full-time equivalent of fifty-eight police officers for useless calls, the systems may have promoted crime elsewhere" (Tenner, 1996: 7). Tenner's examples are of *unintended,* but also of *unpredictable*, effects. The patterns traced here apply equally to simple and complex technologies. I, myself, have lived through the long-term claim to virtually infinite free energy to be produced from nuclear sources, through the Three Mile Island near-melt-down situation, to the closing of Long Island's Shoreham nuclear plant, designed as part of this trajectory of designer intent, but to end as a colossal, four-billion-dollar "technology museum" which to date has no use at all.

From the comparatively simple examples above, one can note that designer intent may be subverted, become a minor use, or not result in uses in line with intended ends at all. In addition, with unintended consequences the theme becomes the unpredictability of the uses of technologies. But, there remains a persistence of the designer fallacy, that in some way "intent" determines, however successfully or unsuccessfully, outcomes. My argument is directed *against* this framing and description of the design project. What I hope to establish is a description that recognizes much more complex relations between designers, technologies, and the ultimate uses of technologies in variable social and cultural situations. My approach is descriptivist in a sense parallel to those in science studies and the history of science which eschew end results over the examination of development in process (Kuhn, Latour, Pickering). I will open the way to my counter-thesis by looking at several variations upon technologies and the embedded ways in which these function.

First, I want to show something about how technologies are differently *embedded* in different cultural contexts. My first example is the windmill—a device that, like a pinwheel, turns with the wind. The most ancient example, according to Lynn White, Jr., is to be found in India, a wind-driven prayer wheel or "automated praying device." (White, 1971). There were, and continue to be, hand-driven prayer wheels, rotating drums on a hand-held handle, which can have written prayers on the surfaces, which are then spun with the prayers presumably being sent outwards. The "automated" prayer wheel of the wind-driven device lets "nature" do the work. Later, in Mesopotamia, larger versions of the windmill occurred in the ninth century. These devices actually powered applications such as milling. Moving, finally, to Europe, "windmill fields" developed to help pump out the lowlands of Holland in the ninth century in an early "technological revolution" of larger-scale power use. Finally, today, we are now moving into the argument phase of wind-generated energy, well accepted and in place in Denmark, which produces nearly twenty percent of its energy with windmill farms. In England and the United States, such windmill farms, proposed for offshore or mountain-ridge sites, are undergoing technology assessment battles along NIMBY (not-in-my-back-yard) lines.

Abstractly, one can argue that these are all the "same" technology, wind-driven devices to supply different powers, but each example is differently culturally embedded. The need to have relatively constant praying is quite different from the need to have renewable energy, and to call each a different "use" is to abstract from the complexity of the cultural background. The "same" technology is embedded differently in the different historical-cultural settings. But this is also to say that the "same" technology can fit into different contexts and is *field located*.

A closer look, however, also shows that what I have called the "same" technology is also materially different in each context. The Indian wind-driven prayer wheel is a relatively small device, whereas the Danish and contemporary high-tech windmill is up to a 100 meters tall; and the former responds to the speed of the wind with faster or slower revolutions, whereas the latter turns at the same speed through self-governing blade adjustment. Both entail what Andrew Pickering (1995: 102) calls a process of "tuning" and a "dance of agency" in the development process.

In design, the "tuning" and "dance of agency" can often turn around "designer intent." Bruno Latour has made the familiar Post-It example famous in *Science in Action*. The designer, experimenting with the material properties of various glues, accidentally as it were, produced a glue that would stick only temporarily—thus seemingly a failure in terms of "designed glues." But, instead of simply casting off the new-propertied invention, the designer began to think of possible new uses and chanced upon page marks for hymn books (Latour, 1987: 140). Thus, a new use, both unintended and unplanned, led to what today is a massive market for Post-It products. One could say, were one to adopt Latourean language, that the nonhuman here transformed the human (designer) with its actant, material behavior. I have frequently employed a similar example from the million-year-old "hand-axe," the chipped tool from pre-modern hominids that is usually thought to be a scraper and butchering tool (although no one knows the possible uses, which could be many), but from which evolved the small, sharp, earlier-thought-to-be-detrius chips, now recognized to have been used for cutting and even, possibly, surgery—an archaic version of the Post-It story.

Allow a quick pause with respect to the designer-intent model of technological development: It should appear by now that the "designer fallacy" may well be the rule rather than the exception. Although it may be the case that some technologies have come into being and performed as "intended" by their designers (I admit, I can think of none that have served solely in this way), there would seem to be none that could not be subverted to other, to unintended, or unsuspected uses and results. Moreover, whether simple or complex, the same indeterminacy seems to apply. As artifactual, technologies seem to potentially contain *multiple uses or trajectories of development*—If even the simplest artifact, an Acheulean hand-axe, could be used for multiple purposes, it differs little in outcome from the purposely designed multitask tool, the Swiss Army Knife. Indeed, multitasking may be an emergent pattern for contemporary technologies. Some have begun to hold that the trajectory of multitasking for information technologies is toward a single big and a single small multitasking instrument. The mobile technology, like the Swiss Army Knife, is a cell phone, digital camera, bar-code reader, email device, etc. is the single small multitasking technology, while the large home entertainment system (TV, DVD, computer screen, etc.) connected to the economic, entertainment, communications dimensions of life, is the big multitasking instrument. Although much of this remains technofantasy, it is plausible technofantasy.

Fantasy, however, is one type of *imagination* that also plays a role in, behind, and through design activity. I think a case can be made that in the High Middle Ages, a form of technofantasy began to emerge that, at first slowly, but with acceleration, began to shape the form of culture in Europe, which in turn pointed towards the saturated technological culture of today. Lynn White, Jr. has argued that there was something of a technological revolution that occurred in this period. The construction of high-standing Gothic cathedrals called for machines and architectural techniques not employed previously. Admittedly borrowing interculturally from first the Moorish styles that entered Europe no later than the tenth century, but taking these to greater extremes, Chartres, Notre Dame, Cologne all borrowed flying butresses and glass-stone frillery. What might not be noted, however, was a similar shift in imagery in the world of fantasy. The fantasy paintings of the Bruegels remained largely "organic" or "animal-like" fantasies. Devils, dragons, demons, and large monsters clearly were "biomorphic," however fantastical. But by the thirteenth century, machines began to play fantasy roles. Roger Bacon described fantasy machines, such as self-propelled ships, underwater craft, flying machines and other impossible-to-build machines for the times, machines which were later "visualized" in the fifteenth century by da Vinci in his notebooks and which only later (discovered and publicized by the Futurists in the 1920s) came into being in the fifteenth century. I am hinting that a specific mode of technology-imagination or fantasy began to take hold. This probably was a life-world reflection, since many of the radical new machines that began to appear and be developed in Europe had earlier in other forms come from the multicultural trade, journeys, and experiences from the cross-cultural exchanges between Islamic culture, the Mongolian invasions, and the post–Marco Polo adventures to the Far East. Lynn White, Jr., Joseph Needham, and others began to recognize this cross-cultural trade of technologies by the middle of the twentieth century. Spices, gunpowder, the compass, silk, the windmills previously mentioned, all of which migrated to medieval Europe, were adapted and developed. Optics, better known in the east through Al Hazen (1038) than in the West, ended up on a trajectory of lens making which led to the optical inventions of the telescope and microscope which drove the early scientific revolution, instrumental technologies provided the infrastructure of science itself.

All of this today is relatively common tender. But it needs to be seen in the light of the "designer fallacy" I address here. Each new invention that came into Europe, often first a matter of fascination, became adapted into new uses and developments. Although China invented gunpowder, it did not successfully produce a cannon. But by the Thirty Years War, cannons were demolishing French castles at the rate of dozens per week (De Landa, 1987). And it is with this observation that I now begin my move away from the "designer fallacy."

However some material capacity comes to human awareness (discovered by accident, through experiment, found through discovery, or—I suspect rarely—planned out from design), once that capacity is emergent and clear, some possible "trajectory" is suggested. One could say that the explosiveness of gunpowder "suggests" uses. But, those uses will also likely be culture-relative—at least at first. Long before the cannon, feudalism had produced the land-castle system, wherein the lords who were to protect the populace built defensive keeps. A many-centuries-long form of contest centered on strategies of defense with supplies and means of defending against the attackers, a strategy that tended for a time to favor the well-stocked and designed castle. Siege machinery, too, grew in complexity over the centuries, in an evolution from Roman times with trebuchets, catapults, and the like. None of these engines, however, could easily breach walls—which the cannon could do.

In terms of design history, the cannon is in a sense premodern. No one knows who "invented" the cannon, although many attempts to create a workable cannon were made, including the production of early, fire-hardened wooden cannon barrels (not too successful). The cult of the invididual designer had not yet come into being. Visting Meissen in Germany recently, my guide, Professor Bernhardt Irrgang, pointed out that the cathedral there had a room for the architects, and while names of leading architects were sometimes known, the name actually served as something of a "school" of a particular architect—the same was often true for Renaissance artists. The room or office was for the whole entourage that was assigned the task of keeping the cathedral in repair. As Foucault has pointed out, the same frequently applied to authors— individual authors came into being with modernity, thus pointing to an even deeper connection between the "intentional" and the "designer" fallacies.

But let us now return to the designer problem and begin recasting it. I wish to focus upon two interstices in a three-part relation. The first interstice, in the simplest form, is that between the designer-inventor and materiality. What is at play is a set of interactions between the designer and the materials being worked with—it is a two-way relationship within which the "accommodations" and "resistances" Pickering (1995: 22) speaks of, come into play.

The first example I provide is the long fantasized desire of humans for flight. The Icarus story, with its technologies of bird feathers and wax, is clearly fantasy only. Similarly, Roger Bacon's and later Leonardo da Vinci's descriptions of flying machines also remain in the imaginary realm, although da Vinci's recognition of the curved wing-shape of birds was a step in the right direction. Almost everyone has seen the documentaries on early flight-experiments, usually comic with films of flying contraptions—human-powered—and their subsequent falls and crashes. But, note, once again, that the serious experimentation begins with that industrial century, the nineteenth.

From the beginning, it was recognized that wings had to be both light and strong, and the design was at first biomorphic in that bird wings, and sometimes batwings, served as the pattern. Yet, how clumsy the designs seem in retrospect. Gliders began to succeed to some degree, with much experimentation of light materials, wood or bamboo, and glued linen or other light cloth. Interestingly, the reluctance to follow the fantasy trajectory of human-powered flight gave way to the recognition of the need for a light-weight power source, which historically we recognize as the internal-combustion engine plus "screw" or propeller. The Wright brothers' flying machine was a hybrid conglomeration of many technologies. They were experienced light-weight technologists— bicycle makers—who adapted from windmill technologies a propeller for driving through air rather than being driven by the wind. Then, with wing and control designs some modified from others' attempts, they eventually produced the first powered flights (I ignore the historical controversies around who actually first flew, since there were many contenders). What we really have in this history is a competitive "dance of agency" through trials and failures, until finally came the small success that launched the trajectory of human-plus-machine flight. From 1903 to the present century, development also saw flight move away from its biomorphic designs towards more variations of flight that are less and less like flight's origins. The simplest example is that of a fixed wing over a flexible and moveable wing. Flight, originally fantasized as embodied human flight, never really materialized; its closest actualization probably is that of hang-gliding and its kin, restricted to lovers of extreme sports. The one bicycle-technology-based, propeller-driven, light-weight aircraft, flown by a trained cyclist, that successfully flew across the English Channel, could hardly be said to possess anything like birdlike grace in form, even if actually human powered. But with mylar skin, and weighing in at only pounds, it was a culmination of a trajectory towards lightness which was the material need for this approximation of flying. What I am trying to point out is that one does not find anything, like sheer plasticity of the material, over which the designer has a transparency of control. Rather, one finds a process of interrogation of materiality and experimentation with it, which results—sometimes—in fortunate results.

The second interstice would, under the designer-fallacy model, be the "uses" to which the invention, the technology, is put. Maintaining the analogy to literary practices, this would be reader response, or responses. What results from the literary or technological product? In the case of my flight example, the proliferation of uses is historically clear—there is something like an actualization of a possibility tree. In less than a decade, airplanes were beginning to be used militarily; by World War I, there were inter-airplane "dog fights," bomb dropping, reconnaissance. Equally early, commercial developments began, along with recreational uses with the "barnstormers" and stunt fliers; races, distance-breaking flights such as Lindberg's over the Atlantic, and the like. And, in each use, changes in previous practices occurred. By World War II, the *Blitzkreig* employed its own version of "Shock and Awe" with Stuka dive-bombers, to the present, where unmanned Predators and "smart bombs" are employed, displacing what was once trench warfare or disciplined regiments marching at one another. I need not follow each of these trajectories, but it is clear that Orville and Wilbur neither foresaw the speed or the diversity of their invention's results. And, just as the interrelation of designer and materiality contains an indeterminate set of accomodations and resistances, through which may be produced a result never simply planned, so with the results and the indeterminacy of multiple uses.

I have tried to show that the designer-materiality interstice is such that the interrelation of designer-materiality precludes any simple notion of control or transparency over the simply plastic quality or passivity of the material. Instead, the interaction is exploratory, and interactive. In the second, now artifactual-use interstice, the designer has even less control or impact; rather, the user(s) now plays the more important role. The indeterminacy here is multistable in terms of the possible range of uses fantasized or actualized. One particular set of interesting examples comes from the ingenious ways in which technologies may be defeated: defeasability uses. Video surveillance-cameras, for example, may be disabled by laser pointers flashed into the lenses. Hardened-steel steering-wheel anti-theft devices, precisely because hardened steel is vulnerable to fast-freeze brittleness, can easily be broken when sprayed with a freeze spray. Slightly more complex are the "wars" between police determined to trap speeders with radar, now laser speed-detection devices, and the "insurgencies" that develop technologies to detect radar signals or confuse laser-reading devices. And so go the multiple directions from same, different, or differently used technologies.

We are now in a position to draw a few conclusions from this examination of designer fallacies. First, in spite of language concerning designer capacity in textbooks—recognizably there in engineering, architecture, and other design textbooks—I am attempting to show that the design situation is considerably more complex and less transparent than it is usually taken to be. Both the designer-materiality relation, and the artifact-user relations are complex and multistable. While it is clear that a new technology, when put to use, produces changes in practices—all of the examples show that—these practices are not of any simple "deterministic" pattern. The results are indeterminate but definite, but also multiple and diverse. Moreover, *both* intended results and unintended results are unpredictable in any simple way, and yet results are produced. And, finally, what emerges from this examination looks much more like an interrelational interpretation of a human-technology-uses model in which the human, material, and practices all undergo dynamic changes.

I am also implicitly suggesting that the redescriptions that have arisen out of the past several decades of work in the history and philosophy of science, the new sociologies of science, and cultural and science studies, which undertake careful case studies of developments in technologies, give hints of the complexities suggested.

References

De Landa, M. (1991). *War in the Age of Intelligent Machines*. Swerve Editions. New York: Zone Press.

Kittler, F. (1990). "The mechanized philosopher." In Laurence Rickels (ed.), *Looking After Nietzsche*. Albany: SUNY Press.

Latour, B. (1987). *Science in Action*. Cambridge: Harvard University Press.

Nyre, L. (2003). *Fidelity Matters: Sound Media and Realism in the 20th Century*. Doctoral Thesis, Department of Media Studies, University of Bergen, Volda University College: Norway.

Pickering, A. (1995). *The Mangle of Practice: Time, Agency and Science*. Chicago: University of Chicago Press.

Tenner, E. (1996). *Why Things Bite Back: Technology and the Revenge of Unintended Consequences*. New York: Alfred A. Knopf.

Toffler, A. (1970). *Future Shock*. New York: Bantam.

White, Jr., L. (1971). Cultural climates and technological advance in the middle ages. *Viator* 2: 1971: 171.

CHAPTER 9

Human Beings as Technological Artifacts

Joseph C. Pitt

At the risk of oversimplifying, let us assume as a working premise that there are basically two types of people: active and passive. This assumption is introduced in order to open up a way of thinking about the relations between people and the technologies that occupy their world. The basic point is that you can go through life becoming who you will eventually be (a) by simply responding to the various impacts and stimulations you receive, or (b) you can attempt to make yourself into the type of person you think you would like to become. To do the former requires no work on your part. To do the latter requires a lot of work, primarily by way of finding out the limits of your capacities and the nature and range of the options open to you, uncovering the prerequisites for achieving the steps you need to take, allowing for error and the means to correct them, etc. There is an important sense, then, in which the active person attempts to design the person he/she wants to become in much the same way we design an artifact, thereby becoming an artifact himself or herself. To elaborate this idea, I begin by introducing some ideas of John Dewey. I then give a sketch of the design process as we find it in use in engineering. Finally, following Dewey's ideas about the nature of education, and taking the design process as a metaphor, I show how we need to educate our students better for a world of complexity unlike anything we have hitherto experienced. The motivation here is quite straightforward. We live in a technological world that at least appears to be wrapping us up in electronics and other technologies without asking for our consent. The ability to select those technologies I want to be associated with is important to who I am and who I will become. Thus it is important to be able to say, for example, I don't want a cell phone because I treasure my privacy and independence. So far these kinds of decisions have been displayed in the context of resisting technology. But to accept that construal is to accept a picture of human beings as primarily passive beings. The key question is whether we can be active beings in the contemporary environment.

John Dewey and the Aims of Education

In a piece entitled "Education and Growth," Dewey (1916) makes the following claim:

> Education is not infrequently defined as consisting in the acquisition of those habits that effect an adjustment of an individual and his environment. The definition expresses an essential phase of growth. But it is essential that adjustment be understood in its active sense of *control* of means of achieving ends. (494)
>
> The emphasis is on the achieving of certain habits, not beliefs. This stress on habits is a key feature of pragmatism. It comes directly from C.S. Peirce, the founder of pragmatism. Thus Peirce says first, "The essence of belief is the establishment of a habit; and different beliefs are distinguished by the different modes of action to which they give rise. (29)

He completes this thought this way:

> [T]he identity of a habit depends on how it might lead us to act, not merely under such circumstances as are likely to arise, but under such as might possibly occur, no matter how improbable they may be. For what the habit is depends on *when* and *how* it causes us to act. (30)

In his insistence of the developments of habits, Dewey is straightforwardly in the pragmatist tradition. Likewise with respect to the tie of habits to action. Pragmatists are concerned with how we act in the world and why we act the way we do. Thus, according to Dewey:

> The savage is merely habituated; the civilized man has habits which transform the environment. The significance of habit is not exhausted, however, in its executive and motor phase. It means formation of intellectual and emotional disposition as well as an increase in ease, economy, and efficacy of action. Any habit marks an *inclination*—an active preference and choice for the conditions involved in its exercise. (494–495)

Finally he adds, "Above all, the intellectual elements in a habit fixes the relation of habit to varied and elastic use, and hence to continued growth." (495)

So, in the end, Dewey argues for the development of habits that allow for continued growth, which is the heart of education. We aim to inculcate in the young those habits that will give them the capacities to acquire knowledge on their own and then to evaluate it and use it to achieve their goals, adjusting to circumstances and learning from their experiences.

The underexamined component here for Dewey is the selection and evaluation of goals. We do a reasonable job of injecting values into our students, but we rarely give them the means by which to select and evaluate goals or to consider their goals in the light of their values. Often they will choose a goal because everyone else is choosing that goal, for example, to make lots of money. But they usually have not thought through the conflict that arises, for example, between being happy and pursuing a fortune. It may just be, and I put this forth as an unargued-for premise, that, for the long run, the most important thing we can teach our students is how to select and evaluate goals in the light of what they value and what they know. How do we accomplish that goal? Perhaps we can learn something from engineering-design processes.

The Design Process

Design is at the heart of the process of engineering. It consists of a set of steps that lead a team of engineers from the initial postulation of an idea for a product through to its manufacture and marketing. If we break this process up into its major components, design, manufacture, marketing, we find that common to all is the notion of a feedback loop. We begin with some basic assumptions about what is possible, knowledge of some of the constraints under which we will be operating, and a specific goal, that is, you are to build a *whatsit* that will do XYZ. Next comes the process of laying out ideas, examining the assumptions behind those ideas, proposing means by which those ideas can be put into action, and then returning to the original objective to see how far these deliberations have taken us toward that goal.

Walter Vincenti (1988), a Standford University aeronautical engineer, in his *What Engineers Know and How they Know it*—notes that design as a process "typically involves tentative layout (or layouts) of the arrangement and dimensions of the artifice, checking of the candidate device by mathematical analysis or experimental test to see if it does the required job, and modification when (as commonly happens at first) it does not. Such procedure usually requires several iterations before finally dimensioned plans can be released for production" (1988: 7).

The key notion here is that the design process is iterative. Once you have laid out the artifact, determined its components, tested it, and found that it fails, you go back and redo.

Later, Vincenti breaks the process down into finer levels.

Project definition: translation of some usually ill-defined military or commercial requirement into a concrete technical problem for level 2;

Overall design: layout of arrangement and proportions of the airplane to meet project definition;

Major-component design: division of project into wing design, fusalage design, landing-gear design, electrical-system design, etc;

Subdivision of areas of component design from level 3 according to engineering discipline required (e.g., aerodynamic wing design, structural wing design, mechanical wing design);

Further division of categories in level 4 into highly specific problems (e.g., aerodynamic wing design into problems of platforms, airfoil section, and high-lift devices. (1998: 9)

He goes on to note, "Such successive division resolves the airplane problem into smaller manageable subproblems, each of which can be attacked in semi-isolation. *The complete design process then goes on iteratively, up and down, and horizontally through the hierarchy*" (1988: 9, emphasis added). In short, the design process is a process by which goals are given, the means to achieve those goals are broken down into smaller parts, which are then put back together to see how it all shakes down, and the process begins all over again.

Students as Self-Designers

We already know that students in particular are involved in self-design, much to their parents' consternation. Fashion, music, dancing, language are all appropriated by the young in ways they hope will allow them to exhibit their individuality. And if you point out to them the irony of the loss of individuality when they adopt the codes of a group, they have something of a legitimate response when they note that it *their* group. Nevertheless, the *art* of self-design is not foreign to the young. Our objective is to turn the *art* of self-design into the *science* of self-design, if you will. To do that we have to introduce the young to the notion of the consequences of their actions. Thus, "what do you think your body is going to look like in thirty years when that tattoo has faded and is just an ugly black smudge on your arm?" Put that way, of course, the question will only be met with overt hostility. So, the challenge is to find a way to make students fix goals and to think of the consequences of their actions, and to correct for bad choices or unintended consequences.

The key, I believe, is in the distinction introduced at the beginning of this Chapter, active versus passive. We should seek to make our students active participants in their own lives. However, there are problems with the distinction. First, it seems as if some people do not want to, or simply cannot be active players. Further, I am not sure there is a single method for achieving the desired end. Third, the entire idea that everyone should be an active player needs to be examined. Instead of attending to these issues, important as they are, I first try a different approach.

I have argued elsewhere that human being are artifacts (Pitt, 2003: 241–260). That is, by the varied processes of mate-selection, be it deliberate or not, through falling in love, or by arranged marriages, we have made ourselves what we are today. With the possibility of gene therapy on the horizon, we can design our children, fix genetic "defects," etc. No matter that if we start selecting for "beauty" we may be doing our offspring a grave disservice as conceptions of beauty are notoriously fickle. Be that as it may, this is not exactly what I mean when I say, as in the title of this chapter, that human beings are technological artifacts. I mean that we are technological artifacts by way of the enhancements *we* select for ourselves.

We have all had the experience of an electricity blackout. Nothing wakes us up to our almost total dependence on electricity as when it is not there. The interesting part here is that we, for the most part, did not choose to live in an electrified world, we were born into it. Some, for either political or economic motives, are leaving "the grid," choosing a solar-power source or some other. But they are not choosing to give up the technologies that electricity powers, whatever its source. However, others are also beginning to ask questions like "Should I buy that SUV?" given the impact on the environment that increased gasoline consumption produces. But, they are not giving up the idea of a personal means of transportation. Nevertheless in choosing not to pollute the environment as much, they are making some sort of statement. And in making that statement they are saying something about themselves. Just as they are making a statement about themselves by insisting on having a personal means of transportation. Some people I know do not own a television set. They claim they can get all the information they need from newspapers, and they prefer to read. Some people do not own a cell phone, not because they can't afford one, but because they prefer the freedom of being able to walk around and not be summoned by the sound of a phone going off in their pocket, but they have a phone at home and at the office and they answer them when they ring. Part of what we in the United States refer to as a "Soccer Mom" entails owning a mini van or similar vehicle to haul the kids around to soccer games. Everyone has to have a home-entertainment center, fancy or minimal. A house without music is uncivilized, but note, it is increasingly rare that the music is self-generated. We no longer play the piano at home for the purpose of making music; instead we put on the stereo. In short, you are the sum of your choices of technological enhancements, be they books, TVs, stereos, SUVs, or cell phones. The pieces of technology you have selected to be part of your life are as much a part of you as the color of your hair.

Several factors are at play here. First, the idea that you are the sum of your choices is not original—it is certainly a major theme in the work of Jean Paul Sartre. What may be new is the idea that in choosing to employ certain artifacts and technologies in your life they make you what you are. Imagine a teenager without his or her cell phone—he or she would be a totally different person. Think of the changes you undergo when your car is in the shop and not available to you. Sometimes, I am told, the feeling one has when deprived of a favorite piece of technology is like drug or alcohol withdrawal. You are simply not yourself.

If the above claims are correct, it is but a short step to the conclusion that human beings are themselves technological artifacts. If we are the sum of our choices, and if our choices entail making certain artifacts part of who we are, then given our account of design earlier, it follows that we make ourselves what we are in a far more concrete sense than Sartre may have thought. Recall that design is an iterative process proceeding from an idea to a finished product. It involves testing to see if the mini choices we make along the way are going to all fit together to make the thing we are planning work, making adjustments and corrections if they do not is an integral part of the process. The feedback loop is essential to the process: it is what makes the product work at the end; it is what makes it possible for us to change.

Active versus Passive, Redux

Let us, for the time being, put aside the unfortunate fact that there are passive people and that they are perfectly happy being so. Maybe they are not "perfectly happy," but they are at least not willing to try to change.

Instead, let us concentrate on the active person, knowing that there are individuals out there who engage the world and try to make their way in it, overcoming obstacles, seeking their specific vision of the good life. Finally, let us understand that the world they engage in is increasingly populated by a multitude of technological artifacts: the choices of which to adopt will impact who they are, what future choices they have, and who they will become. If those individuals are our students, how do we prepare them to navigate that world?

First, note that we cannot *teach* them how to deal with the technologies that will be available to them. For one thing they are much more adept at manipulating the new information-technologies, in particular, than we are. Second, we cannot begin to imagine what new and transformative technologies the future has in store for them. Third, you cannot anticipate the situations they will encounter, and therefore you cannot teach them how to respond. We can show a student how to use a screwdriver, but we cannot predict the circumstances in which he or she will have to use one nor what type will be needed.

If we can teach our students anything, it is that they will be faced with choices, and that they do have the ability to make choices, and they must evaluate the results of their choices, how to do that, and, finally what to do with the results of that evaluation. How will we know if we have succeeded? Crosby, Stills, Nash, and Young had the answer years ago:

> Teach your children well,
> Their father's hell did slowly go by.
> And feed them on your dreams,
> The one they picks, the one you'll know by

All that said, is there anything more we can say and do? There is; actually there are many things to do. The first is to recognize that many of the technologies that are second skin to our students are also transparent to them. They do not appreciate the extent to which they have incorporated these technologies into their very being. Thus, a major challenge is to find a way to bring that to their attention in a nonjudgmental way. If they are to learn how to and what to choose when we are not around, we must give them those tools. Telling them something is bad for them is not by itself, enough. For one thing, they will not believe us. Giving them the means to find out for themselves that something is bad for them is better. Furthermore, letting them find out that something they thought was going to be good for them was not, *and* also giving them the tools to correct their mistakes so that they learn from them, is even better. What I propose, in effect, is that we teach students how to use something akin to the design process on themselves. This, of course, follows from what I was arguing for when I made the case for human beings as technological artifacts. If we are the sum of our choices and our chosen technological artifacts, then deciding what kind of person we want to become entails learning how to make choices, how to evaluate them, how to evaluate their consequences, and, most importantly, what to do in the light of those evaluations. Our goal should be to make this process a habit, in both Dewey and Peirce's sense.

What I have in mind is an intellectual process that begins by acknowledging that even our youngest students come to us with a given knowledge base, some values, some fears, some hopes, expectations, etc. Given that background, students should be provided with situations in which they must make decisions, that is, they must choose between options. Having made their choice and acted on it, there will be results. The important part comes next. If there is teaching to be done, this is where is takes place. The students must be taught how to evaluate their choices and what to do after that. It is crucial that the outcomes are described in the language of "expected" or "unexpected," *not* in the language of "good" and "bad." For we are not in the business of approving or disapproving of their choices. Rather, we are helping them develop a habit of evaluating the outcomes of their choices in terms directly applicable to their own values and goals. Furthermore, an unexpected result is not necessarily a bad one: although unexpected, it might, nevertheless, lead to alternatives not previously anticipated. If, however, the outcome is not what was expected and, furthermore, not desired, then the students have to be shown how to revisit their previous background assumptions and bases and try to discover what it was that they thought they knew, believed, valued, etc. that needs to be changed, updated in the light of the outcome, or straightout rejected.

Essential to this process is for the student to learn that making mistakes is not such a terrible thing and that there are good things that can come from mistakes: we can learn from them in such a way as to possibly avoid making them in the future. It is in the iterative learning process that we set the stage for the next step: choosing among technologies. Learning how to learn from mistakes and successes is the key to the entire process. And key to that is developing the ability to evaluate your starting point, your assumptions and background knowledge. Further, we absolutely must learn how to avoid the fear-of-failing fallacy.

If you are afraid to fail, you will not choose, but not choosing is itself a choice, the choice to be passive. And to be passive is to put yourself in a position where you cannot learn.

If we now take this iterative learning process and apply it to the problem at hand, we can begin to see some positive results. First, it is important to remind us of the problem with which we are dealing: how do we prepare our students to make intelligent choices about the myriad of technologies they are and will be faced with, insofar as the choices of those technologies create the person they will be?

The wrong thing to do is to approach the problem by announcing that technology is bad or out of control, or some such judgment. They know otherwise. Rather, if you are convinced that a particular technology is undesirable, focus on the consequences of choosing, allowing, adopting that technology on them. The difficult part here is getting them to understand that there are short-term and long-term consequences. Understanding long-term consequences is not easy, even for experienced planners. Putting the issue to them in terms of what kind of a person they will appear to be to the world if this or that consequence does occur will, however, get their attention.

The fact of the matter is that we are our technologies. We would not be designing them if they were not essential to who and what we are. Accepting that as a starting point is not to give up; it is to recognize a fact of our nature. Further, while there are potential negative consequences of any choice, it seems more productive to look at the positive outcomes. In particular, since every choice we make closes down some options and opens up others, we can start our students thinking about their choices of technological enhancements in terms of the options they open up for them. For example, a fancy new computer comes on the market. You can take your hard-earned money and buy it, or rest content with your perfectly good old computer and spend the money on some courses that teach you how to extend your current capabilities. Seeing the opportunities that your choices afford you is the key. Active people can design themselves to be the most flexible and creative people, if they have the habit of iterative reflexive thinking.

References

Crosby, Stills, Nash, and Young (1970). *Teach Your Children* on *De ja vu*.

Dewey, J. (1916) "Democracy and education: the middle years, 1899–1924, Vol 9." In J. Boydston (ed.), *Carbondale and Edwardsville*: Southern Illinois University Press, 1980, pp. 46–58, as reprinted in *Pragmatism and Classical*

American Philosophy, edited by John J. Stuhr, New York, Oxford: Oxford University Press, 2000, 2nd edition.

Pitt, J. (2003). "*Against the Natural/Artificial Distinction.*" In D. Schrader (ed.), *Philosophical Dreams, Oneonta Studies in Philosophy.* SUNY/Oneonta Press.

Vincenti, W. (1988) *What Engineers Know and How they Know it.* Baltimore: Johns Hopkins University Press.

PART III

Considering Aspects of Pedagogy for Developing Technological Literacy

CHAPTER 10

Towards a Philosophy *for* Technology Education

John R. Dakers

The difference between the mathematical mind (*esprit de geometrie*) and the perceptive mind (*ēsprit de finesse*): the reason that mathematicians are not perceptive is that they do not see what is before them, and that, accustomed to the exact and plain principles of mathematics, and not reasoning till they have well inspected and arranged the principles, they are lost in matters of perception where the principles do not allow for such arrangement . . . These principles are so fine and so numerous that a very delicate and very clear sense is needed to perceive them, and to judge rightly and justly when they are perceived, without for the most part being able to demonstrate them in order as in mathematics; because it would be an endless matter to undertake it. We must see the matter at once, at one glance, and not by process of reasoning, at least to a certain degree . . . Mathematicians wish to treat matters of perception mathematically, and make themselves ridiculous . . . the mind . . . does it tacitly, naturally, and without technical rules. (Pascal in Dreyfus, 1660/1979)

Introduction

Pascal highlights an interesting dialectic in the above statement. He sets out two opposing philosophies that can be translated into models for technology education: one that is technical, empirical, and rule driven, versus one that is more hermeneutic and interpretative in nature. This chapter arises out of my wonder, curiosity, and desire to know and understand more about what the objective, aim, or purpose of technology education actually is. I want to examine the two philosophical models alluded to by Pascal, in respect of technology education and its place in culture and society. I will then discuss whether a synthesis of these seemingly opposing stances is possible or even viable. But first, I wish to set the scene, so to speak. I want to explore a genealogy for technology education.

Technology's Influence on Culture and Identity

Human beings have evolved differently from other animals. They have done this by essentially changing the process of "natural selection" with respect to themselves. This was as a direct result of the development of technology. It was *Homo habilis* who, 2.6 million years ago, developed pebble axes that served to completely change the natural order of things (Burke and Ornstein, 1997). It was through the mediation and development of tools that our natural biological evolution was supplanted by new prosthetics that served to exponentially increase our power over the environment "beyond its natural measure" (Arendt, 1998: 140). Tool use thus changed our primordial ancestors' development to such an extent that the trajectory of our evolution, physically, intellectually, and culturally, is a direct result of tool use and technological development. The development of a simple axe heralded the apotheosis of human dominion over the environment.

This synthetic process of "technological," rather than "biological," selection served to separate the flow of human development from that of all other animals. Significantly, it also completely transformed the power relationship among humans themselves. The prehistoric equivalent of Bill Gates et al. became more powerful. By combining a shaped piece of flint with a branch from a tree, the distance between the hunter and his prey was considerably reduced, and hunting, through the mediation of technology, became more "efficient." Whilst many were able to learn to use the spear, and were eager to do so for obvious reasons, it was nevertheless the few who developed technology who reformed and shaped culture. Thus the ongoing development of technology created new ways for humans to live in the world. They moved out of their caves into fabricated artificial lifeworlds, designed by those who were able to develop technologies. The construction of shelters made it possible to locate next to rivers, and proficiency in spear use brought more and varied animal food products to the table, thus enhancing the chance of survival. Paradoxically, proficiency in the use of the same technology could be used to repel unwanted neighbors, thereby forming two new potentialities for the development of the spear: one life sustaining, the other life taking. Technology began to direct the development of possibilities and thus the mind, which in turn led to the innovation of new technologies (Burke and Ornstein, 1997).

The technology–human interface began to change the way in which human beings interacted with their environment and, ultimately, with each other. The evolution of human beings from that of small communities of hunter-gatherers, compelled to follow the food chain, has been dramatically altered over time directly as a result of their interaction with technology. Burke and Ornstein (1997) give an interesting account of this development. They describe the formation of the first ever village economies to emerge over 11,000 years ago. These villages had developed from settlements of hunter-gatherers that had about four families living together, into villages comprising over two hundred houses:

> [T]he new Natufian settlers did not become instant farmers. They were still expert hunters because they had another new tool, a long piece of basalt in which were grounded two deep, parallel grooves. When the stone was heated, wooden shafts could be easily straightened in the grooves. This would greatly improve the accuracy of the arrows and make it more likely that hunting could provide sufficient food for a settled community, even if plant sources failed. (37)

The subsequent mediation of technology, however, not only changed the way these primitive societies survived, but also had a profound impact on the subsequent way in which their lives and identity were formed. The ongoing development of technology facilitated more sophisticated agricultural techniques, whilst the domestication of animals led to the evolution of evermore-sustainable animal husbandry techniques. These two technological developments alone led to an ability to generate a food surplus that could support others within the community, a growing number of whom no longer directly contributed towards the production of food. This allowed for the development of new specializations that became necessary within the new community structures. Craftspeople who could build shelters, or administer health care, or keep records about the community evolved, which in turn, led to the development of "[d]ecision making and social responsibility [becoming] more and more concentrated in the hands of these new specialists." (Burke and Ornstein, 1997: 39)

The social and cultural development of human beings can therefore be seen to have a strong correlation with their technological development. Many different cultures and societies have evolved over time. Some have disappeared or have been overwhelmed by other more-dominant cultures (aboriginal cultures, for example), where the dominant culture has usually been more technologically advanced. The point I am making is that cultural development and technology have always been inextricably bound up with each other albeit in a difficult and complex way. At no time previously, however, has this complexity been more manifest than during the eighteenth-century period of the Enlightenment. This brought in its wake scientific empiricism and the Industrial Revolution, both of which were to have a major impact on society, technology, and technology education.

The Industrial Revolution, the Birth of Public Schooling and Technical Education

The pioneers of the Industrial Revolution were very much guided by Adam Smith who, in his seminal work, *The Wealth of Nations,* presented "a picture of society as an efficient system in which educational institutions play a crucial role, justified in terms of their utility" (Standish, 2003: 224). Smith argued that economic progress in this new "civilized" society was dependent upon the division of labor. The formation of public schooling enabled the retention of class divisions in which those with higher social status attended private schooling whilst those from the lower ranks received a state education. This was not so much intended for the private consumption of the learner, but contributed rather to the "formation of a particular *habitus*. It prepared persons for their position in the social hierarrchy of ranks" (Vanderstraeten, 2004: 196). This social ranking has its roots in Aristotle and Plato who advocated a "hierarchy of theory/practice/production [that] was not only epistemological, but also social in that a person's place in the city state reflected the kind of knowledge that was their daily concern" (Hager and Hyland, 2003: 272). "Early in the [eighteenth] century it began to dawn on the administrators that increasingly sophisticated technology would work unprofitably unless some efforts were made to train more workers in factory skills" (Burke and Ornstein, 1997: 211). Clearly, this utilitarian and vocationally oriented education had less to do with altruism on the part of industry, but was rather more inclined towards increasing productivity and efficiency.

However, this form of educational instrumentality, together with the resulting divisions of labor that emerged, eventually saw the "working classes" express a desire for a more holistic education that went beyond that of industry's immediate needs. This resulted in the establishment of mechanics institutes that offered evening classes.

Following on from this, and largely as a result of it, a strong movement towards the establishment of "working-class" education began to take shape. Funding from the government, and more particularly the trades unions, resulted in the provision of extra-mural evening classes, or continuation classes as they were known. The *raison d'être* for this egalitarian philosophy was very much to enhance "an intellectual understanding, not just technical dexterity" (Cowper, 1970: 115 in Paterson, 2003: 92). Indeed Heriot Watt College (forerunner to Heriot Watt University in Edinburgh), although offering vocational courses, at the same time made it explicit that it sought to attract students who wished to "rise above the position of being mere machines performing certain mechanical and routine operations in order to acquire a fair knowledge of the fundamental laws underlying the science to which they owe their livelihood" (Cowper, 1970: 162 in Paterson, 2003: 92).

But this was a long time coming, and it was not until after the middle of the eighteenth century that a major conference, supported by leading industrialists and, interestingly, John Stuart Mill, agreed that "[t]he time has arrived when it is desirable and necessary in the education of the people that the principles of science (and technology) [*sic*] should form an important element in the tuition of all classes of the community" (Conference, 1868).

A new industrial literacy was deemed essential for the progression of, and participation in, an industrialized society. Technical education began to appear in state-funded schooling, and, in 1890 in the United Kingdom, it was defined as "instruction which aims at communicating to the pupils [students] knowledge and facilities which have a direct bearing upon some special occupation, industrial or commercial" (Cowper, 1970: 47 in Paterson, 2003: 90). This resulted in a two-tier educational system that had, on the one hand, an academic route that saw as its main purpose the development of the individual or citizen, whilst, on the other hand, a vocationally oriented education in the service of industry.

In 1762 Rousseau foreshadowed the argument against the academic/vocational divide by defining the purpose of education as having one of only two choices. For him, the choice lay between making a man or a citizen, for it is not possible to do both at the same time (Rousseau, 1991). Dewey, moreover, echoing Rousseau, later argued strongly that technology education, in particular, should be more orientated towards the formation of informed citizens. For Dewey the segregation of vocational education as favored by industry and commerce struck at the very heart of the democratic process itself:

> Its [vocational education's] right development will do more to make public education truly democratic than any other agency now under consideration. Its wrong treatment will as surely accentuate all undemocratic tendencies in our present situation, by fostering and strengthening class divisions in school and out . . . Those who believe the continued existence of what they are pleased to call the "lower classes" or the "laboring classes" would naturally rejoice to have schools in which these "classes" would be segregated. And some employers of labor would doubtless rejoice to have schools, supported by public taxation, supply them with additional food for their mills . . . [Everyone else] should be united against every proposition, in whatever form advanced, to separate training of employees from training for citizenship, training of intelligence and character from training for narrow, industry efficiency. (Dewey in Apple and Beane, 1999: 50)

Dewey's fears were, however, soon to be realized. In 1917 the United States witnessed the passage of the Smith-Hughes Act. This act promulgated federal support for vocational education, which continues up to the present day (Apple and Beane, 1999). Vocational education in the form of technical education in the United Kingdom and industrialized arts in the United States thus became embedded in a school curriculum.

Technology Education's Renaissance

It became apparent in the 1980s, however, that the industrial arts model of technology education did not reflect the modern technologically mediated world, and a new model was seen to be required. This realization emerged across several democracies at around the same time. It saw technology education as having, as a central tenet, the notion of technological literacy. The process of becoming technologically literate requires participants to become sensitive to the impact of new and emerging technologies upon their technologically mediated world. Moreover, it requires them to engage in a more critical examination of the interplay between technology, the environment, and society.

There is, consequently, a growing movement towards the modern reformation of a technology education curriculum that is more in keeping with the new and emerging technologies of today. The American Standards for Technological Literacy (ITEA, 2000) advocates the study of the nature of technology, including technology and its impact upon society. These include attributes associated with design; abilities required to live an informed and meaningful life in a technologically mediated world;

the study of modern technologies including medical technologies, agricultural and related biotechnologies, energy and power technologies, information and communication technologies, transportation technologies, manufacturing technologies, and construction technologies.

It is clear then, that a genealogy for technology education reveals roots that are firmly embedded within an industrial and vocationally orientated past, originating in the Industrial Revolution. It has also become clear over the last decade, however, that a new rationale for technology education is required. Nevertheless, it is apparent that, in many cases, the older industrial model persists.

The Two Philosophies Paradigm

I want now to explore the two oppositional philosophies for technology education that emerge from the previous discussion. One, the thesis, advocates for a technology education that is technical, empirical, and rule driven and that serves the needs of industry, whilst the other, the antithesis, advocates for a technology education that is hermeneutic, interpretative, and academic. I will then consider whether, out of this dialectic, the synthesis of a new philosophy for technology education can emerge.

Whilst, as was previously mentioned, the antecedents of this dichotomy can be traced back to the ancient Greeks, it is Descartes and the birth of positivism that truly separated the mind from the body, the hand from the head, manual from mental, skills from knowledge, applied from pure, knowing how from knowing that, practice from theory, particular from general, and training from education (Hager and Hyland, 2003).

Technology Education as a Vocational Subject

This paradigm has, as its central tenet, a philosophical framework that considers the subject area as the initial training ground of a future workforce for industry. Learning, or more appropriately, training, becomes instrumental towards that end. Prescribed rules and specific techniques are the subject matter required. These are transmitted from teacher to novice. Technology education, so defined, becomes the acquisition of objectively designed knowledge that serves to train, or more importantly, control, an effective workforce in order to satisfy the perceived needs of a sociocultural industrial economy. Learning in this model conceptualizes knowledge in technology education as the uncritical development of knowledge bases that evolve from an already established hierarchy of "relevant" subject matter. Students conform to the perceived expectations demanded by the system, which in turn serves to inculcate an identity that is hegemonic in nature (Dakers, 2005b). This is "a form of domination so deeply rooted in social life that it seems natural to those it dominates" (Feenberg, 1998: 10). Teachers and learners not only "know their place" in this model, they accept it uncritically. Class divisions occur within a single-state schooling-system in which the formation of the division of labor is based upon the curriculum prescribed, and technology education is clearly the reserve of the technical/vocational classes.

At one end of the technology–vocational curriculum spectrum lies instruction situated in tool and machine use. At the other is, in most cases, design.

Arguments against this epistemological framework centre around the notion that these situated skills are no longer sustainable in today's modern technologically driven world. This has caused policy makers to reposition their thinking away from subject specific skills, in industry terms, towards more generic attributes:

> [A] major interest in generic attributes has become evident at all levels of education in the last decade. The aim has been to identify, teach, and assess generic attributes thought to be common to performance in both education and the workplace. In the United States these generic attributes are known as "workplace competencies" or "foundation skills," in England and Scotland as "core skills," in Australia as "key competencies, and in New Zealand as" essential skills—all reductive expressions and all leading to confusion. (Hager and Hyland, 2003: 274–275)

However, the recent evolution of modern apprenticeships, paradoxically, seems to herald yet another paradigm shift from these generic skills towards a model which sees the formation of the skills required by industry as best acquired within a situated context. In Scotland, for example, students are able to sample modern apprenticeships in the construction industry as part of the curriculum, while partnerships with colleges of education are being formed in order to widen choice. Students are thus able to attend college classes in car mechanics or hairdressing as part of their school curriculum.

There is, furthermore, a growing corpus of modern educational thought that argues for vocationally oriented learning as being best placed within authentic workplace contexts. This is predicated on the basis that skills, generic or otherwise, learned within a school-classroom setting, cannot be transferable from a decontextualized classroom setting into an authentic workplace setting. To design and make a coffee table in school carries with it a completely different set of parameters to that of designing a flat-pack coffee table for a large furniture chain. (see, for example, Hyland, 1999; Dakers, 2005a).

A simple example may help to clarify this notion. A sawer is defined as "one who saws." A sawer, moreover, is usually associated with sawing wood (although not always). These "sawing" skills exist historically and thus, on the sociocultural plane. Skill procurement of "sawing" skills would ultimately be internalised by the learner. If the skill, when acquired, resides outside a specific activity such as sawing down a tree, or sawing which is associated with jewellery making, we must assume that the skill of sawing transcends those activities. The sawer would be skilful, at sawing, in both activities. By the same argument the sawer would also be skilful in the sawing associated with the amputation of a patient's diseased leg. This reduces the concept of sawing to the simple psychomotor actions associated with sawing, and assumes that these skills are decontextualised mental functions contained within the individual, thus rendering these functions as meaningless. Clearly sawing involves action by the sawer upon something external. However, it is the external which gives meaning to the activity. The process involves moving the socially learned cognitive processes associated with sawing "out of the head" so to speak, and locates them in a particular activity in the environment of a particular sociocultural system. In other words, the action of sawing is only meaningful in the context of the sociocultural activity (Dakers, 2005a: 80). Skills and functions are thus embedded in sociocultural activity (Lave, 1988).

Matusov (1998) postulated two models for human development. He considered a model of internalization which emphasizes the transformation of social functions into individual skills. In this model, the transfer of skills from one activity to another suggests that skills exist outside the activity. His model of participation, on the other hand, emphasizes the transformation of individual participation into sociocultural participation. In this model, skills are embedded in social and cultural activities in which meaning is interpreted and renegotiated.

The individual exists in the flow of sociocutural activities and cannot transcend them. Activity is not isomorphic to the unfolding physical time continuum because it is grounded in meaning. Meaning is distributed across time, space, and participants, interpreted and renegotiated. (Matusov, 1998: 330)

The vocational model, therefore, reflects a very restricted view of what technological education should be. As Williams (1996) postulates, it is "more concerned with the development of in-depth manipulative competencies in a narrow range of technology areas than broad based, attitudinal and cognitive competencies" (54).

This definition, moreover, runs counter to social constructivist theories of learning and teaching. Part of the problem may be that the intellectualization of what was traditionally a craft-based, production-oriented subject has led to confusion. "The new broader type of technology education is more complex than that which has sufficed in the past, partly because intellectual processes are not directly observable, in contrast to physical skills" (Williams, 1996: 54).

Social constructivist theories see learning as culturally influenced and set within a socio-historical context. Whilst experiencing the world we inhabit, we develop our understanding and knowledge of it, mediated by antecedent cultural values, artifacts, and skills laid down by our forebears. We construct meaning through direct experience with the natural world, our fabricated world, and our cultural and social environment. Thus, learning is a combination of constructing meaning through interaction with more able humans (such as teachers) and experiencing the world we inhabit. It is not our capacity for picking up rules that directs our perception and understanding; rather, it is flexible styles of behavior (Merleau-Ponty, 1962). As humans, we need to be able to understand the relevance of an artifact in some meaningful context beyond being instructed as to what it is or how it is to be fabricated. For example, for Arendt, "[t]he actual work of fabrication is performed under the guidance of a model in accordance with which the object is constructed. This model can be an image beheld by the eye of the mind or a blueprint in which the image has already found a tentative materialization through work. In either case, what guides the work of fabrication is outside the fabricator and precedes the actual work process." (1998: 140–141). Learning needs to have some rationale that makes sense to the individual. For this to happen the learning situation must be mediated such that abstract, decontextualized rote-learning of prescribed rules is made meaningful by associating it with the spontaneous or tacit knowledge the individual has acquired as a result of being in the world.

Technology Education as an Academic Subject

This paradigm has as its central tenet, a philosophical framework that considers the subject area as theoretical or speculative, without practical purpose or intention. Technology education in this definition is concerned only with scholarship in matters relating to technology and the interrelationship between humans, technology, and the environment. The curriculum would be based upon the history, sociology, and philosophy of technology.

This would, however, require, in most cases, a paradigm shift in terms of pedagogy from that described in the vocational model. The behaviorist transmission paradigm that is dominant in the vocational model, is, by its very nature, a monologue, in which interaction between teacher and student is a one-way process. There is a growing recognition, however, that for children to learn, they have to be actively involved in the learning process. They construct meaning through the process of interaction and inquiry, which involves communicative action.

Bergman (1991) clearly illustrates this point in his criticism of the notion of teaching as a form of the transmission of information.

> If truth is not theoretic but that which a person must verify through his life and the way he lives it, how can one person be another's teacher? A person cannot transmit his philosophy the way an object is given and received. This kind of transmission is impossible in relation to existential truth. The teacher's reality can only open the possibility for the student to live his own truth, to actualize it through his way of life. Therefore, the teacher must not go beyond the limitations of this possibility. We must prevent the birth of a direct relation in which the student passively receives the doctrine of the teacher. (41)

The social nature of this type of learning is also an important factor in current educational thinking:

> We have been moving away from cognitive theories that emphasise individual thinkers and their isolated minds to theories that emphasise the social nature of cognition and meaning. (Resnick, 1987 in Barab and Duffy, 2000: 26)

Learning then does not take place in a vacuum. Children do not learn simply by constructing their own individual realities in isolation from the cultural, historical, and social environment into which they were born. Without those factors there is no conceptual framework to work from (Resnick, 1987 in Barab and Duffy, 2000).

Human development is a process of socialisation. Humans are not born in isolation but into communities, or cultures. These cultures, together with their technologies, have evolved and developed over time.

This pedagogy involves dialogue, not a monologue. Values and issues regarding technology are socially constructed and intersubjective. Learning and teaching is phenomenological. There are no right and wrong answers, only informed or uninformed interpretations. In this model the teacher sees the "end" as the formation of a student's identity in an ever-changing technologically mediated world. The "means" to achieve this "end" requires the teacher to relinquish the "expert" model and devolve responsibility to the creation of a democratic classroom in which a variety of views about technology are discussed.

Towards a Synthesis

Heidegger (1962) and Feenberg, in his critical theory (2003), suggest that a synthesis between these opposing polarities of rules versus interpretation is possible. Both argue that, in association with the instrumental role a technology may have, we must also give consideration to the essence of the technology in terms of its social and cultural implications. Out of this emerges a synthesis that leads to an anamorphosis in technology education. In other words, the technologies that we simply accept as presented are often distortions of the truth, much as the lettering used in road markings appears to be elongated and distorted from the point of view of a pedestrian. However, the same markings when viewed from a driver's point of view, seen head on and from a different perspective, appear, as a result of foreshortening, to be perfectly in proportion. This is deliberate on the part of the designers, but significantly, very few of us, drivers or pedestrians, are actually aware of this. It is only by repositioning ourselves that we may begin to see a different perspective, and this may, in turn, serve to transform our previously distorted values by illuminating and clarifying the controlling logic of the technologically mediated world we inhabit (Dakers, 2005a). A technological literacy in which the dialectics of "calculation versus meditation, objectification versus art, 'world' versus 'earth', identity versus difference" (Kroker, 2004: 38) are explored is therefore a crucial part of a learner's technological development.

Technology education in this synthesis should have a "relationship" with industry, but not a subservient one, not one that is simply in the service of industry. Critical debate about technology and the role that industry has in its development must be encouraged. These debates must engage with global issues relating the sustainable development of technology, methods and patterns of consumption, and their relationship to ecological sustainability. Technology is not neutral, and its proliferation in terms of mass production, if not challenged, threatens the democratic process.

Technology education in the twenty-first century can therefore no longer be programmed instruction with behavioral objectives that set out a "divide and conquer" approach to learning. The vocational and academic polarities in terms of technology education must "dissolve into reciprocity, each constituting the other" (Grumet, 1992: 31). Discourse regarding the very essence of technology, the way technology affects our cultural development and our participation in a global society, must become embedded into technology education. We must learn to interpret the world of technology for ourselves, and we can only do that through the engagement of discourse about technology. In order to do this, we urgently need to develop a new philosophy *for* technology education that has at its center the development of a technological literacy.

References

Apple, M.W. and Bean, J.A. (1999). *Democratic Schools: Lessons From the Chalk Face*. Buckingham: Open University Press.

Arendt, H. (1998) (First published 1958). *The Human Condition*. Chicago: The University of Chicago Press.

Barab, S.A. and Duffy, T.M. (2000). "From practice fields to communities of practice." In David H. Jonassen and Susan M. Land (eds) *Theoretical Foundations of Learning*. New Jersey: Lawrence Erlbaum Associates.

Bergman, S.H. (1991). *Dialogical Philosophy from Kierkegaard to Buber*. Trans. Gerstein, A.A. New York: SUNY Press.

Bruner, J. (1996). *The Culture of Education*. MA: Harvard University Press.

Burke, J. and Ornstein, R. (1997). *The Axemakers Gift: Technology's Capture and Control of Our Minds and Culture*. New York: Tarcher Putnam.

Caputo, J.D. (1987). *Radical Hermeneutics: Repetition, Deconstruction and the Hermeneutic Project*. Bloomington: Indiana University Press.

Conference. (1868).*Conference on Technical Education Held at Edinburgh*, Friday, 20 March, 1868. Neil and Company, Edinburgh. (Publication held in University of Glasgow Special Collection, BG57c. 17).

Dakers, J. (2005a). "Technology education as solo activity or socialy constructed learning." *International Journal of Technology and Design Education*, 15: 73–89.

Dakers, J. (2005b). "The hegemonic behaviouristic cycle." *International Journal of Technology and Design Education*, 15: 111–126.

Feenberg, A. (2003). *Transforming Technology*. Oxford: Oxford University Press.

Grumet, M.R. (1992). Existential and phenominological foundations of autobiographical methods. In W.F. Pinar and W.M. Reynolds (ed.), *Understanding*

Curriculum as Phenomenological and Deconstructed Text. New York: Teachers College Press, pp. 28–43.

Hager, P. and Hyland, T. (2003). "Vocational education and training." In N. Blake, P. Smeyers, R. Smith, and P. Standish (eds), *Philosophy of Education.* (2003) Maden: Blackwell, pp. 271–287.

Heidegger, M. (1962). *Being and Time.* Translated by John Macquarrie and Edward Robinson, San Fransisco: Harper and Row.

Huitt, W. (2001). *Humanism and Open Education.* Educational psychology interactive. Valdosta, GA: Valdosta State University. Retrieved 19 July 2005, from http://chiron.valdosta.edu/whuitt/col/affsys/humed.html

Hyland, T. (1999). *Vocational Studies, Lifelong Learning and Social Values,* London: Ashgate.

ITEA. (2000). *Standards for Technological Literacy. Content for the Study of Technology.* Virginia: International Technology Education Association.

Kroker, A. (2004). *The Will of Technology and the Culture of Nihilism.* Toronto: University of Toronto Press.

Lave, J. (1988). *Cognition in Practice: Mind, Mathematics and Culture in Everyday life.* Cambridge, UK: Cambridge University Press.

Matusov, E. (1998). When solo activity is not privileged: participation and internalisation models of development. *Human Development.* Karger. 41: 326–349.

Merleau-Ponty, M. (1962). *Phenomonology of Perception.* London: Routledge and Kegan Paul.

Pascal, B. (1660). "Pensees." In H.L. Dreyfus (ed.) (1979). *What Computers Can't Do: The Limits of Artificial Intelligence.* New York: Harper & Row.

Paterson, L. (2003). *Scottish Education in the Twentieth Century.* Edinburgh: Edinburgh University Press.

Rousseau, J.J. (1991). *Emile: or on Education* Harmondsworth: Penguin Books.

Standish, P. (2003). "The nature and purpose of education". In Randall Curran (ed.), *A Companion to the Philosophy of Education,* 221–231. Malden: Blackwell.

Williams, J. (1996) "Philosophy of technology education." In J. Williams, and A. Williams (eds) (1996). *Technology Education for Teachers.* Melbourne, Australia: MacMillan Education.

Vanderstraeten, R. (2004). "Education and society: a plea for a historicised approach." *Journal of Philosophy of Education,* 38: 2. Oxford: Blackwell, pp. 195–206.

Vygotsky, L.S. (2000). *Thought and Language.* Ed. Alex Kozulin. MA: MIT University Press.

CHAPTER 11

Innovative Technological Performance

Richard Kimbell

The Rhetoric for Creativity and Innovation

More than half of the "distinctive-contribution" statements in the new national curriculum for England and Wales (DfEE 1999) claim that creativity is part of their core concern. Our political masters—even the prime minister himself—enthuse about the need for a creative Britain.

> "Our aim is that risk-takers are rewarded. Let us believe in ourselves again. Britain's future depends on those with confidence, who take risks, like the creative talents we celebrate here today. They are the people that Britain needs in the next century . . . those who have ambition for our country" (Blair, 1999)

But there is cause to worry that our creative future is at risk. At the launch of National Curriculum 2000, the DfES also created a strategy group to oversee the future development of design and technology. As a first step for that group, we examined the internal coherence of NC2000. Specifically, we examined the aspiration expressed in the "distinctive-contribution" statement, and then analyzed the extent to which that aspiration was evident in the programmes of study (PoS) and the attainment target (AT).

Let us remind ourselves about the aspiration for design and technology.

- Design and technology prepares pupils to participate in tomorrow's rapidly changing technologies.
- They learn to think and intervene creatively to improve the quality of life.

- The subject calls for pupils to become autonomous and creative problem solvers, as individuals and members of a team.
- They must look for needs, wants and opportunities and respond to them by developing a range of ideas and making products and systems.
- They combine practical skills with an understanding of aesthetics, social and environmental issues, function and industrial practices. As they do so, they reflect on and evaluate present and past design and technology, its uses and effects.
- Through design and technology, all pupils can become discriminating and informed users of products, and become innovators (DfEE, 1999).

There is no doubting the thrust of this vision statement. It is explicitly pointing to the need to develop innovative youngsters in exactly the way that Blair and others claim we must.

But What of the Reality?

The DfEE/DfES Strategy Group received and debated an analysis by David Prest—adviser for design and technology in Cornwall—in which he illustrated that both the NC programmes of study, and the attainment target are largely devoid of reference to the need to develop innovative qualities in students' designing. This probably results from the fact that whilst the vision statement was new for NC2000, the programmes of study and the attainment target were modifications of NC 1990 and 1995. No one it seemed had been responsible for making sure of the internal coherence of the whole. Prest concluded that whilst it is possible to *infer* such a connection between the vision statement and the programmes of study, it is explicitly *not possible* to do that with the attainment target. In fact we are—in our assessments—required not to take the least regard of innovative performance.

Taking a lead from this position, the GCSE awarding bodies—making assessments at 16+—do not require students to demonstrate their innovative capabilities. In fact the reverse has become the norm, and for very good reasons.

The percentage of students achieving A–C grades is important to teachers in terms of the league tables of schools that have become ubiquitous in the audit culture of the last ten years (see Shore and Wright, 1999; Tayler and Hallgarten, 2000). Teachers know what is required of their students for them to get A–C grades. Student assessment in design and technology is driven by the *performance assessment* tradition of *design portfolios*. And teachers have developed very well organised systems for guaranteeing that their students' portfpolios contain all that is required for them to get A–C grades. They have checklists of things that have to be in the portfolio to guarantee particular levels.

The result of this checklist approach—both in terms of the portfolio and for the final product outcome is that

- it is (typically) not creative—but formulaic;
- it is (typically) not done in teams—but is individual; and
- it is (typically) not innovative—but safe.

This is not happening because teachers are idle and malign—but because we are systematically rewarding them (i.e., rewarding their students) for producing work that is formulaic, individual, and safe. If we reward those qualities—teachers cannot be blamed for making sure that their students demonstrate them.

The DfEE/DfES Strategy Group concluded that this situation needed urgent attention, and commissioned a research project to develop approaches to assessment in design and technology that would specifically *reward* risk-taking and innovation. Is it possible to develop an approach to assessment that is supportive of the grand vision statement for design and technology? The Technology Education Research Unit (TERU) at Goldsmiths College was awarded the project, which ran from January 2003 to December 2004.

Research Design

Our approach to this research project has moved through three phases: initially exploring performance descriptors of design innovation, then examining classroom practices that encourage it, and finally developing assessment activities that promote the evidence of innovative performance. I provide here the briefest accounts of phases 1 and 2, concentrating attention on phase 3.

Phase 1

At the outset in phase 1 we consulted widely with teachers, advisers and examiners to find work that could be categorised in one of two categories: (a) creative/innovative and (b) competent/adequate. We explored ways of distinguishing between these collections and—at the same time—invited expert groups to use single words to capture the essence of what they saw as creative / innovative. The following list is derived from those processes and is in priority order—the top of the list being mentioned most frequently.

Exciting—unusual—different—novel—risky—bending   the   rules—
brave—determined—marketable—professional—'wow'—confident—
powerful—unique.

Another distinguishing feature that emerged from the critical comparison of the two collections of work was that those projects judged to be creative/innovative were more typically based on *ideas*. This set them apart from the collection of work that was judged to be competent/-adequate, which were more typically based on the conventional steps of project *management* (brief/specification/research/etc). From this process, we derived a preliminary assessment framework that scrutinised the extent to which students were able to:

- *have* ideas
- *grow* their ideas
- *prove* their ideas

The middle one of these—growing ideas (typically through modeling, sketching and discussing)—was seen to be the cornerstone of innovative capability in design and technology

Phase 2

At this point (April 2003) we launched phase 2 of the project—examining the activity "live" in classrooms, studios, and workshops in schools in three LEAs: (Local Educational Authorities) Cornwall, Shropshire and Durham. The purpose here was to get beyond the work itself (the outcome) and examine the *activity* and the *pedagogy* in use with teachers that enabled them to promote creative performance in their students. We asked teachers to run two-day projects (two whole days—typically ten hours) to briefs of their own devising and to feel completely free of the normal constraints of examination assessment criteria. What would they do to encourage design innovators?

Between May and July 2003, schools ran these projects with groups of students in years 2/3 and 5/6 (in primary schools), and with year 9, year 10, and year 12, (in secondary schools) and we observed every minute of each of these two-day projects. Our hope was that we might be able to identify at least some of the qualities (in teachers and students) that might lie at the heart of innovative performance.

The outcome of this round of trials was twofold. First we had masses of interesting work from students—and this work formed the basis of our first assessment trials using the framework derived in phase 1. And second, we had masses of observation data (a) about the kinds of things that teachers did to prompt and support design innovation, and (b) about the ways in which students reacted to those pedagogic prompts.

But overlaying these successes was the undeniable fact that whilst the outcomes were exciting and valuable, the vast majority of the evidence of the *process* that students had undertaken was based on *our* observation data. And this was a real problem, since no examination can realistically be based on a fully employed "observer" recording what students do as they do it. It seemed necessary to find ways of structuring the activity so that, as students undertook it, they would automatically leave behind a *trail of evidence* that would provide some means for interpreting the *evolution* of the outcome and enriching our ability to make judgements about it.

Phase 3

With this at the forefront of our thinking, in September 2003 we launched phase 3 of the project, which involved the construction of assessment activities that would explicitly promote evidence of the *process* of design innovation. We went back to some of our APU thinking from the late 1980s (see Kimbell et al., 1991)—in which we had constructed ninety-minute activities structured into a pupil-response workbook. And we began to explore how the principles embedded in those APU (assessment of performance unit) tasks might be extended into the two-day activities that we had recently been observing.

In November 2003 we launched the first prototype of an assessment activity with a year-twelve group in Saltash School in Cornwall. After the original trial, we modified the structure through a series of trials in ten schools across the United Kingdom between January and September 2004. The format evolved into a 7 hour task: two consecutive mornings of 3.5 hours. In that time, students start with a task and work through from an initial concept to the development of a prototype solution—a "proving" model to show that the ideas will work. The whole 7 hours is run by the teacher—following a script that choreographs the activity through a series of sub-tasks—each of which is designed to promote evidence of students' thinking in relation to their ideas. These "steps" in the process all operate in designated spaces in the booklet.

The finished booklet is a folding A2 sheet that ends up packed with ideas, drawings, notes and photos. It is an immensely rich data source and a vivid record of the students' experience of 7 hours of (often) frenetic activity.

Using various versions of this structured worksheet approach, we have now undertaken trials of ten different tasks ranging from product/packaging design, fashion/textile design, electro-mechanical systems design and food product design. In total we have responses from approx 400 students in 11 schools spread across England and Wales. We have also run one of the activities in a school in Stockholm—using translations of the booklet and teacher script, but otherwise retaining the activity in exactly the same form.

The following comments are from teachers involved in the trials:

- The layout and the way it [the worksheet] folds so that the pupils can see what they have done is great,
- Students *enjoyed* the challenge. Great atmosphere in the room. Students were totally engaged for the majority of the time. Loved the photographs!
- The inspiration table was a really successful way to motivate / excite the students by showing them, and getting them to think about the "wow" factor within a successful product.
- Students were developing products that were more interesting and creative than those that materialise from the brief, specification, research, ideas, development route!
- Through a highly focused activity, students had the opportunity to experiment with a concept that may or may not work. Given permission to take a risk and not to be too worried about a quality outcome
- The pupils think the support team [their group of three] is very helpful in achieving their task and a lot more critical commentary is going on than is recorded.
- One of the remarks that I recall from reading the self assessment sheet was "it shows what I can do in a positive way"—this was written by a pupil who is a school phobic and finds school work difficult.

From the students involved, the message was equally clear. They loved the collaborative element of design development—sharing ideas in their group at the outset and reflecting on them later. And they appreciated the story-line of digital photos that had the effect of showing them their own progress. They also enjoyed working at a fast pace through a concentrated seven-hour activity and having the encouragement to develop really interesting (and somewhat risky) ideas with the confidence that they would not be judged by the craft quality of the final outcome.

When asked to comment on the things they liked/disliked about the activity, the following "likes" were characteristic.

Hull
AB117—The sheet was helpful, as it helped you know what you had to do
AB119—Being able to use my own ideas how I wanted to
AB1111—These have been the best two days in school
AB1117—Its easier to understand when you try it out for yourself
AB1119—The pictures help, cos I could always look back and see how good I'd done

Leicester
AB214—You had more time to get on with it
AB215—Working in groups but having the ability to work independently
AB216—You can make things you didn't expect
AB218—The regular photos
AB219—Working in groups helped for inspiration with ideas
AB2110—Its fun designing
AB2111—Using different materials
AB2116—I could show people my ability

Staffordshire
AB226—Good layout of worksheets
AB228—You got to show your ability
AB2210—Starting from scratch to make you think

Wales
AB314—Using your own ideas; making models instead of drawing—they work better
AB315—It was fun to design something and actually make it
AB319—Seeing your idea develop
AB3111—We got to try out different things, using our ideas
AB323—Being able to make something by myself and what I wanted to make
AB324—I realised that I could do more than I thought I could
AB326—The photos was the best way to show the steps, which I think was good

Berkshire
AB411—I liked getting my imagination go wild
AB4110—It was a very good way of finding how many skills you have
AB4112—I learned how to make a lot more stuff

The teachers have further commented on the extent to which the experience has affected their own classroom practice.

> This trial has had a real effect on my teaching. It has reinforced things I do, reminded me of things that I have done, and prodded me to think of things I have never done. My PGCE student is completely "gob smacked" with the method of working and is implementing many of the principles in the trial in his teaching. His lessons are showing real pace and focus.
>
> We found the project to be a very rewarding experience—we have had time to reflect and it will enrich our learning style considerably.

Factors Underlying the Design of the Activity

There seems little doubt that the activities have been successful in generating excitement in the event and moreover the work-books and the three-dimensional outcomes provide ample evidence through which we can scrutinise a rich variety of student responses. The trials suggest that the following factors seem to be important in creating this effectiveness.

The Script in Association with the Folding Booklet

In line with the original APU principles, the seven hours of activity is structured to alternate between active and reflective sub-tasks. Each sub-task is timed (the shortest is about two minutes and the longest about forty minutes) with specific instructions about what is expected. For example, after the first session of "putting down" their first tentative early ideas, the script then runs as follows:

> We are now going to ask you to help each other take your ideas forward. Can you pass you activity booklet to one of your team-mates.
>
> You now need to forget all about your own ideas and look at what your mate has put in box 1. Imagine you are now taking THEIR ideas forward.
>
> In box 2 put down how you would do this. You have five minutes and remember you are now working in box 2.

The boxes in the booklet are carefully sized to be non-intimidating. They are easy to fill up—and frequently the ideas spill over into the adjoining areas. This all adds to the sense of busy-ness in the booklet, which lends confidence to the students.

In technical terms—for formal assessment purposes—the scripts and the booklet also serve the purpose of standardisation. The activity sits somewhere between what students might see as an *examination* and what they will be familiar with as *coursework*. To overcome the idiosyncrasies of individual teachers and schools, the whole package is supplied centrally and acts to standardise the experience, the process and the focus of students' responses.

But whilst we standardise the *focus* of the response (eg adding ideas to those of your team-mate), we are very careful never to specify the *form* of the response. We use the words 'put down' rather than *write* or *draw*, and at various times we explicitly ask them to use whatever form of response seems most appropriate to them.

> Look at your ideas so far (in box 4)
> Look at your success criteria list (in box 5)
> We would like you to develop your design ideas for your product so that
>   it really works well.
>
> - You can develop your ideas in any way that will be helpful to you
> - you can draw or make notes
> - you can make models,
> - or a combination of both.
>
> Please keep on using box 4 to jot down all your ideas, notes and sketches.
> If you are modeling—use box 4 to make it really clear to us what you are
>   trying to do.

A further feature of the booklet design is its folding. It is based on an A2 sheet but is pre-printed and folded in such a way that whilst you work in box 4, you are immediately presented with what was going on in boxes 2 and 3. This works throughout the whole seven hours—covering both sides of the sheet—but at no time do we cut off the forward moving development process from its own immediately preceding steps. This is *really* important for encouraging students evolving design ideas. There is nothing more depressing than turning over from a full and busy page to a clean and empty one. It is a matter of maintaining the impetus behind the growing ideas—and adding to the confidence of students that they are making progress. They are unaware of the points at which the sheet is turned over—and are typically astonished at the end to look back at the mass of 'stuff' on both sides of the sheet. Hence the teacher comment:

> The layout and the way it (the worksheet) folds so that the pupils can see
> what they have done is great.

At the start of the activity—having been presented with the task—we give each group a "handling collection" of bits and pieces to handle and explore. These have been chosen as "idea-objects," that is objects that are probably nothing to do with the task itself—but contain ideas that might be interesting or helpful. For example, when confronted with a task to redesign light-bulb packages so that the package can be transformed into a lighting feature (or a component thereof), the handling collection is full of bits and pieces that fold, bend & stretch, and generally allow of various transformations. The inspiration table is a kind of collective display for the whole group and comprises bigger things than will fit into the handling boxes—or things that we only had one of. The groups we were testing were typically 21 students, ie with groups of 3, that required 7 handling boxes as well as the central inspiration table.

We believe that the practicality of handling and fiddling with the bits and pieces was important to get the activity going. In the student feedback, the handling collection was judged (on a four point Likert scale of very helpful > very unhelpful) to score an average of 3.27 out of 4.

The Team

There is a mass of literature concerning the importance of team-work both in teaching/learning situations and in designing situations. But for assessment purposes, there is a pathological fear of using the massive support that it provides to students because of the association with "cheating".

We were determined to overcome this problem and arrived at a solution involving the groups of three students—but we used the group explicitly to support and enrich the *individual* work of the team members. It is this individual work that is then assessed. The group is invoked at various points in the activity. Critically it is used to spur and enrich the first ideas—then at the end of the first morning to reflect on the progress of the group members and how they might best move forward in the second morning. And it is used again at the end of the second morning for individuals to reflect on the work of each of the other two individuals in their group. In total the group time is less than 30 mins in the 7 hours, but it is worth it's weight in gold both in getting the creative activity up-and-running, and in sharpening the critical appraisal of the students. Furthermore the working atmosphere in the room is relaxed—with lots of informal chatting within and between groups.

Two of the three highest Likert scores are registered by students for this group activity: 3.63 for group support with generating ideas, and 3.56 for group support in reflecting on/evaluating ideas. And the teachers were very aware of the impact of the groups:

> The pupils think the support team (their group of three) is very helpful in achieving their task and a lot more critical commentary is going on than is recorded.

The Modeling Resources

We are well aware that conventional practice in schools with early design ideas is to constrain it to pencil and paper sketches. We take the view that this ritual is unhelpfully restrictive, particularly for those students (commonplace in design and technology) who are more comfortable with touching and manipulating *things* as a way of developing their *thoughts*.

Accordingly, the activity offers students a range of materials with which to explore their ideas. There is nothing exotic about these materials. They are what might be described as soft-modeling resources. Card, plasticene, string, plastic tube, aluminium foil, paper, lolly sticks, pipe cleaners, etc., along with a wide range of ways for cutting them and fastening them together; staples, eyelets, string, blue-tack, tape, etc. These resources are introduced *after* the "early-ideas" sessions (individual and group) but *before* the main time-block for developing ideas on the first morning. Some students chose to use modelling to develop their ideas from very early on. Others choose to stay with sketching in the booklet and only model later. Neither is right or wrong. The "modeling resources" score 3.38 on the Likert scale, and comments like that below were commonplace, perhaps because modelling it typically not what students are allowed to do when developing their early ideas.

> AB314—Using your own ideas making models instead of drawing—they work better

The Photos

I mentioned earlier the importance of the booklet design for maintaining the impetus behind students' growing ideas—adding to their sense of confidence and the sense that they are making progress. A key part of this is the digital photos that are taken approximately every hour through the activity, growing into a "story line" of six or seven images that are pasted down the spine of the booklet. To take them we used a digital camera, taking photos onto a memory card, and using a small printer that would take the cards direct (i.e., no need for a computer). At a given time we would tell the students that we would be coming round to photograph where they had got to with their work. We took all twenty-one shots, and immediately printed them out as "thumbnails" that were given straight back to the students for pasting in. The whole process takes perhaps ten minutes and one of its strengths is that students lose the fear of cutting up or adapting a preliminary concept model into a developing model. The photos ensure that the original model is not lost.

The "story line of images" that grows in the students booklets scores 3.63 in the Likert scale—joint highest score with team support for generating ideas. And the following student and teacher comment was typical.

> A student: The photos was the best way to show the steps, which I think was good
>
> A teacher: The photos spurred them to work at a pace and also gave a sense of achievement.

The Red Pen and Blue Pen

One of the challenges that exists in conventional design practice in schools is to establish the idea that reflective / evaluative thinking in not something that only happens at the end of the project—but is essential throughout the development process. We developed two strategies for this. In the middle of the first morning we asked students to stop what they were doing, to pick up a red pen, and to make notes and jottings identifying what they saw as the *strengths* and *weaknesses* of the work anywhere in their booklet. The benefit of this is twofold, firstly acting as a *pause-for-thought* in the (often frantic) development process, but also, at the end of the activity, we can see at a glance each student's reflective comment on the work at a moment in time. The same process is then operated on the second morning—but using a blue pen to distinguish it. The difference between red pen and blue pen comments is frequently one of sophistication—the blue pen being comments from deeper into the development process.

The Dice

A completely different approach to encouraging pauses for thought and reflective comment is the dice. This is an octogonal prism about 150 mm long and with a nominal diameter of approx 40 mm. On each of the eight faces is printed a different question, and at intervals the script requires students to stop work—to roll the dice—and to answer the question that comes to the top. It is form of randomised questioning that prompts students to think beyond the current frame of reference of their ideas. Questions such as: How would you idea change if you had to make 100 of them ? What bits of your ideas are risky and which play safe?

The reaction to these dice question is consistent. It is disliked by many students, who see the questions as irrelevant to their immediate concerns and an interruption in the development process. It scored 2.38 on the Likert scale, with almost as many students seeing it as *very unhelpful* as saw it as *very helpful*. But it is liked by teachers, who can see the value of the evidence that is collected as a result. It seems a bit like placing exam-style questions within a piece of personal coursework. The answers are of course personalised to the individual ideas of the students—and reflect where they are in the process—but they still provide interesting comparable data between students.

Deriving Assessment Data

Using these techniques we now have approx 400 pieces of work from approx 200 students (each student undertook two test activities). In addition to the performance data (derived from our marking scheme) we have pupil baseline data both within d&t and in terms of wider school performance (derived from SAT scores, predicted GCSE scores, and other school-based data), and we have teacher data (their areas of experience). Taken together, these provide us with the means for examining the performance of our test activities when set against other measures. And the key question was whether we could identify those students who are really good at design innovation.

There are (at least) two critical aspects to this challenge;

- does the student perform at the same level of innovation across tasks ?
- can two markers agree on the scoring of the work ?

The starting point for the assessment process was the finalisation of the assessment rubric. This required assessors to start with a holistic judgement of the work on a 1–4 scale ("yawn"—"wow")—which was then extended into a 1–12 scale (a *10* is only just a 4, but a *12* is a really good 4). Thereafter in step 2 we ask assessors to tease out the three qualities that were seen to be (from phase 1) central to design innovation;

Table 11.1 Variances between Markers and Research Team

Holistic	having gr/mod	eling gr/	optimizing	proving
1.6	2.3	1.7	2.3	2.0

- having ideas
- growing ideas
   by modeling
   by optimizing
- proving ideas

The descriptors were developed through various assessment trials, looking at a range of work across ten different tasks. Again we ask assessors to assess the work on a 1–4 scale and then refine the judgement to a 1–12 scale.

Table 11.1 illustrates the variance between the markers moderated mark and the research team moderated mark; firstly for holistic and thereafter for the four detailed qualities. All the marks are on a twelve-point scale, and (on average) the markers varied from the team by 1.6 marks for *holistic* (the best fit) and up to 2.3 marks for *having* and *optimizing* ideas (the worst fit). Of the detailed qualities, *modeling* was the best fit with a variance of only 1.7, and this probably reflects the power of the booklet to capture this evidence and give a rich picture of the growth of the idea.

Findings in the Data

There is not space in this brief summary of the research to report all the findings that resulted from our analyses of the data (for the full research report see Kimbell et al., 2004). But three findings in particular are important in the context of this chapter.

Context and Task Effects

Performance assessment in design and technology is typically open to criticism through what the literature terms "context effect." This effect tends to reduce the likelihood that performance on one task is able to predict the likely performance on a different task in a different context. This is clearly a matter of some importance for an assessment that is based on one test activity and is the reason why, in our research design, we had as many schools as possible undertaking two very different activities. Does student performance on these two tasks remain constant? Does performance vary enormously across tasks? In short are our activities measuring students *generalised capability* in design innovation? To answer this question we undertook an analysis of students' holistic performance on their two test activities; with the following results.

On a twelve-point holistic scale, across the whole sample, the mean difference between test 1 and test 2 was $+/-$ 1.6. A student scoring 9 on test 1 would score between 7.4 and 10.6 on test 2. A student scoring 3 on test 1 would score between 1.4 and 4.6 on test 2. This does indicate a level of consistent discrimination in the range of performance of individual students.

Performance against Predicted GCSE Grades

Schools were asked to supply information concerning the predicted performance of students in their up-coming GCSE in design and technology. Across the sample, these predictions ranged from grades A*–D. These scores were then set against the performance scores in our activities to see whether the performances were predicted. Rather than examining the whole sample, we believed that it would be important to examine the extremes. If on our test activities some students had achieved a *very high* score (10, 11, or 12). Would this performance have been expected from the predicted grade? Equally if students were predicted to do very well or very poorly in their design and technology GCSE, how did they perform in our test activities?

In the sample for which we had all the appropriate data, there were four very high scores: three 10s and one 11. Those four students were predicted to achieve the following:

- 10 predicted A
- 10 predicted A
- 11 predicted C
- 10 predicted C

So two of the four most innovative students in our sample were predicted grade C, and none of them was predicted an A*. So how did the students perform who were predicted to get A*?

Seven students were predicted to get A* in their design and technology GCSE and their performance was as follows: 6,7,7,7,7,6,6. In short, they all performed at the middle of the scale, neither particularly innovative nor non-innovative in their designing.

Finally we examined the group of students who were predicted to perform most poorly in their design and technology GCSE. Five students were predicted to get D, and they performed as follows: 4,2,3,2,1. In short their poor performance predicted for GCSE is reflected in equally poor performance in our test activities.

These are of course all small samples, and it would be dangerous to generalise too far. But they do at least indicate that high GCSE predicted scores are not based on (ie do not predict) high levels of design innovation. The most innovative students are not predicted the best marks, and those predicted best marks go instead to those whose performance in design innovation could best be described as "adequate." Predicted poor performance at GCSE is however a better predictor of low level, inadequate, design innovation.

Performance against "General Ability"

The concept of "general ability" is a tortured one in the literature on assessment. Some argue that it does not exist, and others that it is unavoidably present in the sense that the "brightness" of a student (however that is defined) will have an effect across a wide range of capabilities. In order to attempt to investigate this factor, we used KS3 SAT scores for English, Maths, and Science. These were combined into a singe score and used as our "general-ability" measure. This was then divided into three broad "ability" bands; high, mid, low. In each band there were approximately forty-five students and we calculated average holistic scores from our test activities and we noted the range of scores. They are as follows:

> High ability: mean holistic = 6.5 range = 3–12
> Mid ability: mean holistic = 5.3 range = 2–11
> Low ability: mean holistic = 4.5 range = 1–10

Another way of looking at the range data is to see how many students in the sub-groups achieve the lowest scores (1,2,3) and the highest scores (10,11,12).

> High ability: 4 lowest and 7 highest
> Mid ability: 5 lowest and 2 highest
> Low ability: 9 lowest and 1 highest

Two things are evident in these data. First, "general ability" is *not* a determinant of design innovation—since the lowest ability band has a student performing at the highest level, and the highest ability band has several student performing at the lowest level. Second, there is however a general trend such that performance follows the "general-ability" spectrum. On average performance is higher in the high ability band and lower in the low ability band.

Issues for the Future of Design and Technology

This project was launched from a concern that conventional approaches to assessment in design and technology were not identifying innovative performance in students. Furthermore the question was posed as to whether it is possible to create an assessment scheme that will enable such assessments to be made—or whether it is self-defeating to seek to assess the quality of design innovation.

I believe that we have shown that it is possible to identify this quality in students' work. Moreover we have shown that—for an individual student—it is *a consistent quality* that transfers across tasks; that it is currently *not registered* in teachers' predictions of GCSE performance; and that it is *not predicted* by measures of general ability. It is a *different* quality and—if we believe the vision statement for design and technology—it is an *important* quality.

In making recommendations for teachers' classroom practice or for GCSE Awarding Bodies developments of assessment policy, we would draw attention in particular, to the following key issues.

First, there is a real counter-intuitive conundrum in this project. Students are effectively frog-marched (by the teacher script) through a series of steps that are tightly timed and within which they have to put their thoughts in delineated sections of a pre-printed worksheet. At first glance it might be thought to be a bit like painting-by-numbers. And yet the comments of both teachers and students all talk of the *freedom* they feel in developing their own ideas. Why is it that such a tightly structured and choreographed experience can feel like freedom?

We looked at parallel creative disciplines to explore this question—and music provides an interesting example. It is like jazz. There is a rigid twelve-bar rhythm with a clear beat and a predictable series of phases to the music. And within that tight structure, the most outlandish improvisation can be liberated. So too with our design worksheet and the teacher script. By taking away from students the need to think about how they will organise and present their work, they are empowered to concentrate on the ideas that drive their designing. Our constraint of students was entirely procedural. *We did not constrain (at all) their ideas or how they chose to develop them.*

This distinction between procedural constraint and idea constraint is one that teachers and awarding bodies would do well to note.

Second, the power of modeling. Many (probably a majority) of the students in our sample chose to do most of their development work through progressively more sophisticated models—supported by (not led by) sketching. This is NOT the normal approach in schools, but it chimes very closely with practice in the commercial world of design innovation. Myerson J (2001) talks to IDEO designers about the centrality of modeling.

> [W]e build lots and lots of imperfect prototypes not because we think we've got the right answer, but to get responses from buyers and users. Then we can fix their complaints. We're into multiple realisations of what the future can be. "Faking the future" describes the rough and ready IDEO formula of building lots of crude prototypes . . . Kelley describes this as "fast fearless prototyping." (Myerson 2001)

I am delighted that our activities have had the effect of liberating students to create "*multiple realisations of what the future can be*" through "*fast, furious, prototyping*". The current fixation of examinations in design and technology is to reward the absolute opposite of this; ie slow, painful, beautifully rendered, nonsense (with pretty borders).

Third, comes the issue of pace, for it has to be said that at the end of our seven hours of activity, the students leave in a state of near exhaustion. Through a combination of the continuous mornings, the relentless script, the structured booklet, the photos and the team support and appraisal, the overall effect is to drive the activity forward with a furious pace. Teachers frequently comment that students have achieved more in seven hours than in their more normal twenty-hour coursework projects.

Fourth, in the APU project (Kimbell et al., 1991) we became very aware of what the literature refers to as the "school effect"; that is, all the students in school A outperforming all those in school B. We showed that the school effect was far greater than in other subjects and attributed it to the relative youth of design and technology. At first glance we appear to be picking up a similar trend in our current data—though here it can more properly be termed a "teacher" effect. Even with a script to read, it can be read in many ways, and the workshop/studio setting has a culture that pre-exists the test and is, principally, the product of the teacher. There are real and powerful messages here for teachers' professional development.

Fifth, is the power of ideas. This is the centre-ground of the whole project and it is already abundantly clear, in the 400 or so pieces of work, that they are full of interesting, novel, unusual, risky ideas that students are struggling to grow into new products and systems. Back in 2002, in my keynote lecture to the DATA conference that pre-figured this research project, I analysed five student qualities that I thought might shape the future of performance assessment in design and technology. And from those five, I pointed to the central importance of two of them.

I have two nominations for you—the terrible two—the intractable two—the tantalising two—without which design can be *effective but lifeless*; can be *adequate but unexciting*. I suggest to you that the central qualities that we should be assessing if we value design innovation are the ability to be *playful in restructuring the world* and the ability to *spark ideas*. Where do you find these qualities in the current assessment regime? Nowhere. So at the least we can look carefully at these qualities and tease out criteria that reward them in students' designing (Kimbell, 2002).

I believe we may have gone further than that. It is one thing to recognise these qualities when they arise but quite another to deliberately promote them. And I believe we have developed a structure for assessment activities that does deliberately promote these vital qualities and make them accessible for assessment.

References

Blair, T. (1999). *Speech at the Millennium Products Awards—Millennium Dome.* London. December 14, 1999. (see www.design-council.org.uk)

Department for Education and Employment (DfEE). (1999). "The National Curriculum for England: design and technology." *Qualifications and Curriculum Authority* (QCA) London.

Kimbell, R., Stables, K., Wheeler, T., Wozniak, A., and Kelly, V. (1991). *The Assessment of Performance in Design and Technology: The final report of the Design and Technology APU project.* Evaluation and Monitoring Unit; Schools Examination and Assessment Council (SEAC) for the Central Office of Information and HMSO D/010/B/91 London.

Kimbell, R. (2002). *"Assessing design innovation: the famous five and the terrible two."* The 1st John Eggleston Memorial Lecture at the DATA International Research Conference. 2–5th July 2002, Proceedings (ed.) Norman E. 19–28., DATA Wellesbourne.

Kimbell, R., Miller, S., Bain, J., Wright, R., Wheeler, T., and Stables, K. (2004). *Assessing Design Innovation: A Research and Development Project for the*

Department for Education and Skills (DfES) and the Qualifications and Curriculum Authority (QCA) December 2004. London: Goldsmiths College.

Myerson, J. (2001). *IDEO: Masters of Innovation.* London: Laurence King.

Shore. C., Wright. S. (1999). "Audit culture and anthropology: Neo Liberalism in British Higher Education." *Journal of the Royal Anthropological Institute*, 5: 4 (December): 557–575.

Tayler, M. and Hallgarten, J. (2000). "Freedom to modernise." In *Education Futures,* published in London by a collaboration between the Design Council and The Royal Society of Arts.

CHAPTER 12

Pedagogy to Promote Reflection and Understanding in School Technology-Courses

David Barlex

Introduction

In England, the school subject "technology" is known as design and technology. This naming is not accidental. The working party set up to articulate the unique contribution of technology education to the curriculum produced an interim report that clarified and justified the term design and technology.

> Our understanding is that whereas most, but not all, design activities will generally include technology and most technology activities will include design, there is not always total correspondence. Our use of design & technology as a unitary concept, spoken in one breadth as it were, does not therefore embody redundancy. It is intended to emphasize the intimate connection between the two activities as well as to imply a concept which is broader than either design or technology individually and the whole of which we believe is educationally important. (Accordingly, we use design & technology as a compound noun taking the singular form of verbs in what follows.) (Department for Education and Science and Welsh Office, 1988: 2)

This indicates that design and technology is a construct designed specifically to meet the educational goal of teaching the "capability to operate effectively and creatively in the made world." This is its greatest strength and also a weakness in that it ensures that is not a subject with venerable roots in the academic tradition, which values particularly the acquisition of knowledge for its own sake. Here again the interim report was clear in its thinking about the place of knowledge in design-and-technological activities.

> We have argued above that because knowledge is a resource to be used, as a means to an end, it should not be the prime characteristic of attainment targets for design & technology. This is not to devalue knowledge, but rather to locate it in our scheme according to its function. What is crucial here is that knowledge is not possessed only in propositional form ("knowing that"), but that it becomes active by being integrated into the imagining, decision-making, modeling, making, evaluating and other processes which constitute design & technological activity. (Department for Education and Science and Welsh Office, 1988: 29 and 30)

The pedagogy described here was developed during the period 1990–2005 in England as a response to the introduction of design and technology in 1990 as a new subject in the National Curriculum for England. During this time, the orders for design and technology went through several changes and currently their intention is best summarized by the unique contribution statement that occurs at the beginning of the 2004 Orders (Qualifications and Curriculum Authority, 2004a):

The Importance of Design and Technology

Design and technology prepares pupils to participate in tomorrow's rapidly changing technologies. They learn to think and intervene creatively to improve quality of life. The subject calls for pupils to become autonomous and creative problem-solvers, as individuals and members of a team. They must look for needs, wants, and opportunities and respond to them by developing a range of ideas and making products and systems. They combine practical skills with an understanding of aesthetics, social and environmental issues, function, and industrial practices. As they do so, they reflect on and evaluate present and past design and technology, its uses and effects. Through design and technology, all pupils can become discriminating and informed users of products, and become innovators (15).

> Design and technology is compulsory in England for all pupils aged from 5–14 years, with schools statutorily obliged to make significant provision for pupils aged from 14–16 years who wish to study the subject although it is not compulsory for pupils in this age range (Qualifications and Curriculum Authority, 2004a).

The pedagogy described here was developed as a result of the activities of three curriculum projects: Nuffield Design and Technology (Barlex, 1998; Givens and Barlex, 2001 and see also www.secondary-dandt.org), Young Foresight (Barlex, 2001, 2003, and see also www.youngforesight.org), and Electronics in Schools (Barlex, 2004 and see also www.electronicsinschools.com). Each of these curriculum projects involved a dynamic relationship between curriculum development and research. The Nuffield Project called on the work of the Assessment of Performance Unit in Design and Technology (Barlex and Welch, 2001). Two independent evaluation exercises informed the final form of the Young Foresight project (Murphy et al., 2000, 2001). The independent evaluation of Electronics in Schools (EIS) has validated the approach to design-and-technology professional development initially elaborated through international research from four different countries—England, Canada, Finland, and New Zealand (Banks et al., 2004).

In the period 1990–1995, the Nuffield Design and Technology project developed three types of learning activity: Capability Tasks, Resource Tasks, and Case Studies. A Capability Task requires pupils to design and make products that work and in so doing learn to become capable and at the same time reveal their capability. This will involve the pupil in generating design ideas, developing these, and combining them into a clear visualization of the product, so clear that they can communicate this through sketches, drawings, and three-dimensional models that they can use as a guide when they make the product. This product will embody their design ideas and reveal both their designing and making abilities. This is an engaging but highly demanding activity. Pupils are unlikely to be successful if they cannot build on prior learning. This prior learning is provided by Resource Tasks and Case Studies. A Resource Task is a short activity, often practical, that requires pupils to think and helps them to learn the knowledge and skills they need to design and make really well, that is, be successful in a Capability Task. Through Resource Tasks, pupils learn design strategies, communication techniques, making/manufacturing skills, technical knowledge and understanding, and commercial matters. A Case Study is a true story about design and technology from the world outside school. Through Case Studies, pupils learn about the way firms and business design and manufacture goods and how goods are marketed and sold. Pupils also learn about the impact that products have on the people who use them and the places where they are made and used. These impacts can be economic, social, or environmental and may be unanticipated by both producer and user. In both Resource Tasks and Capability Tasks, the emphasis was on individual learning and performance. However, in Case Studies there were sometimes instructions requiring pupils to work collaboratively and discuss the contents of the study with a partner.

The Young Foresight project, which began in 1997, adapted the Nuffield Capability Tasks and Resource Tasks in four important ways. First, it removed the requirement to make from the Capability Task so that pupils could concentrate on designing without being limited by their personal making skills and the facilities available in their school. Second, it required pupils to work collaboratively in this design activity. Third, it reconceptualized the supporting Resource Tasks into a tool-kit of tasks to support designing rather than designing and making. Fourth, it required pupils to discuss their work with one another when tackling tool-kit tasks. The emphasis on collaboration and communication is in considerable contrast to the mainly individualistic way in which pupils were expected to work within the Nuffield approach to design and technology.

The emphasis on design *and* making in the Nuffield Design and Technology project was maintained in the Electronics in Schools project, which began in 2001, but the design decisions made by the pupils were made more explicit by considering them as belonging to one of five sets: conceptual, technical, aesthetic, constructional, and marketing. These sets of design decisions are mutually interdependent. A change of decision in one set will almost certainly lead to changes in the other sets. By making the possible design decisions more explicit, the Electronics in Schools project was able to provide teachers with an audit tool by which they can scrutinize the range of designing required in Capability Tasks and ensure that pupils are properly prepared to make and justify these decisions.

Understanding Needs and Wants and How These May Be Met by Technological Products and Services

If pupils are to move away from an egocentric approach to designing it is important that they design for others rather than themselves. To do this they will need to have some understanding of people's needs and how these might be met by products and services. The Nuffield Design and Technology project developed the PIES approach to identifying human needs. PIES is an acronym standing for physical, intellectual, emotional, and social and provides a simple conceptual framework for classifying needs. People need food, water, and air to breathe. We need to keep warm and be protected from the weather, and to take regular exercise.

These are physical needs. We need to be mentally active, learn new things, and to be stimulated. These are intellectual needs. We need to feel safe and secure. We need to feel that others care about us and to have ways of expressing our feelings. These are emotional needs. Most people like to spend time with their friends, talking and sharing joint activities. These are social needs. The Resource Task that introduces this approach asks pupils to identify the needs of people in three different situations: in a hospital ward, in a hotel room, and on a train journey. It then requires the pupils to identify products that meet these needs. In this way, the pupils can learn about the relationship between needs and products. It provides pupils with a conceptual tool that they can use to interrogate both situations and product. They can ask of situations they observe, "What are the needs of people in this situation?" and "What products do they use to meet these needs?" They can ask of existing products, "What needs will be met by this product?" and "In what situations are people likely to have these needs and hence use these products?" They can put their own product-design ideas into a variety of situations and scrutinize them for their potential usefulness. Teachers can encourage pupils to use this approach throughout a design and technology course of study in ways that become more sophisticated as the pupils become more adept at using it and hence develop pupils' understanding through reflection.

The Young Foresight tool-kit introduces the PIES approach through considering the needs of people who are waiting at a bus stop, a railway station, and an airport and identifying the needs meet by a mobile phone, laptop computer, and newspaper. This is then extended by means of a second activity in which pupils explore the differences between needs and wants. This is done by means of two short vignettes that describe how the needs of people in very different situations are met. This leads pupils to appreciate that what we want and can hope to acquire to meet our needs are determined largely by the nature of the society in which we live.

Several of the Case Studies in the Nuffield Design and Technology Study Guide (Barlex, D., 1995a) reinforce the relationship between people's needs and the products and technologies they use. "Printing—from wood-blocks to computers" illustrates how technological advances in printing have been used to meet changing needs. "Designing houses to suit people's needs" describes housing projects in Peru that illustrate how important it is to involve local people in making design decisions. "Designing maths instruments for different users" describes how a compass was redesigned to suit the needs of young children. By regularly requiring pupils to read and discuss such Case Studies, teachers can reinforce understanding of the important relationship between needs, wants, and the nature of available products.

Understanding How the Outcomes of Technology can Have Impact beyond the Intended Benefits

The brief history of the motorcar, invented a little over one hundred years ago, shows that some technologies have far-reaching effects, beyond their intended benefits. The development of the internal-combustion engine gave rise to a transport system that completely revolutionized our way of life. To accommodate the needs of the motorist (and to provide for movement of goods by lorries and tankers), a large network of roads and motorways have developed. The use of motor vehicles on this transport network contributes significantly to pollution of the atmosphere and global warming. Learning to drive and acquiring a motorcar have become a rite of passage for most young adults, male and female, in many countries. The opportunity to move from your place of birth to new and different places, to gain employment, to meet new people, to form friendships and relationships is facilitated by the motorcar. This physical and social mobility can have a deleterious effect on small, localized communities. In the United States, in 2002, there were an estimated 63,16,000 car accidents, resulting in approximately 2.9 million injuries and 43,000 people killed. Since the first road-crash fatality in 1896, motor vehicles have claimed an estimated 30 million lives globally. On average, someone dies in a motor-vehicle crash each minute in the world. When the motorcar was invented and the automobile industry was born, no one envisaged that subsequent design iterations would be responsible for environmental damage, social upheaval, and a colossal death-toll. What would the Victorian designers and engineers responsible for developing the motorcar have done if it had been suggested to them that their work would harm the planet, erode family values, and kill millions of people? They would probably have been incredulous. They might have argued that society would step in and stop all those dreadful consequences by managing the way this new technology would be used. But they would have been wrong. We know this because these events have come to pass. And of course, those Victorian engineers and designers were not of malign intent. They saw what they were doing as providing considerable benefit to many people. And, in that respect, they were correct. The motorcar has been highly beneficial to many individuals, communities, and societies but at a cost: the cost of impact beyond intended benefit.

The Nuffield Design and Technology project developed a simple yet effect device to enable pupils aged from 11–14 years to consider impact beyond intended benefit. It involves identifying all those likely to be affected by a product or technology and deciding whether this affect will cause them to be winners or losers. Pupils use a target chart composed of three concentric circles to identify those affected by the product or technology and highlight winners in one color and losers in another. They can use the color balance to decide whether they think the product or technology is good or bad in terms of a winner/loser balance. The work can be extended by two further activities. First, pupils who think the product/technology is a good idea write down how they would persuade the losers to agree with them. Second, pupils who think the product/technology is a bad idea write down how they would persuade the winners to agree with them. Teachers can use the winners-and-losers approach to consider the impact of a product or technology as a starting point for developing a critique of products and technology, which can be extended to include essay writing by older pupils in which the history of a technology can be discussed in terms of impact beyond the intended benefits.

One of the Case Studies in the Nuffield Design and Technology Study Guide is particularly useful for considering impact beyond intended benefit. "Winners and losers—fish processing in Lake Victoria" describes how the introduction of the Nile perch into Lake Victoria led to a large export-crop of Nile perch but a decline to almost extinction of the indigenous Enkejje fish, which kept the algae growing in the lake under control and was used by local people as a vital food-source for young children.

Conceiving Products and Services that Use New and Emerging Technologies and Justifying Their Worth

Insisting that pupils should always make what they have designed can undermine their autonomy especially if they have limited making skills. The Young Foresight project deliberately avoids this difficulty by requiring pupils to work collaboratively in designing but NOT making products and services for the future. The Young Foresight approach identifies four factors that teachers should encourage their pupils to take into account:

1. The technology that is available for use. This should be a new and/or emerging technology and be concerned primarily with how the new product or service will work. Pupils should not concern themselves with manufacture.
2. The society in which the technology will be used. This will be concerned with the prevailing values of the society, what is thought to be important and worthwhile. This will govern whether a particular application of technology will be welcomed and supported.
3. The needs and wants of the people who might use the product or service. If the product does not meet the needs and wants of a sufficiently large number of people then it will not be successful.
4. The market they might exist or could be created for the products or services. Ideally, the market should one with the potential to grow, one that will last, and one that adapts to engage with developments in technology and changes in society.

Clearly, these factors interact with one another and influence the sorts of products and services that can be developed and will be successful. Using this way of thinking, unencumbered by the necessity of making the proposed designs, enables pupils to be creative and develop highly original, conceptual design-proposals.

An important decision for the teacher is the order in which to ask pupils to tackle the task. One way is to start with a particular new technology and ask a sequence of questions like this:

What sorts of thing can we use this technology for?
What needs would the technology meet?
Would meeting these needs be seen as important and worthwhile in society in the future?
Would people want products or services to meet these needs?
What sort of market is there likely to be for these products and services?

If this approach is adopted it will be important to be wide ranging in answering the first question. For example, in asking this question about the possible application of quantum tunnelling composite (QTC), a new material that can be used to make pressure-sensitive conductors, a group of pupils identified the following areas in which this could have applications: sport and leisure, transport, medicine, environmental monitoring, and aids for the handicapped. Eventually they focused on producing a range of sport-and-leisure goods and developed two ideas from this range: a device that could be used to help people recover from hand injuries and overcome arthritis, and a textile product that could be used for step exercises and would keep an accurate record of exercises performed. They were able to justify both of these product ideas in their answers to the other questions. And they were able to explain how the technology they had started with would be utilized in their designs.

Another way is to start by asking pupils to construct a scenario of what a future society will be like and what life will be like for particular groups of people in that society. Pupils can then explore a sequence of questions as suggested below:

What needs would there be in that society?
What products and service would people want to meet these needs?
What sort of market is there likely to be for these products and services?
What technology do I need to make the product or service work?

This is a much more demanding approach but offers more scope for considering the nature of a future society and the impact of technology on that society. It is an approach that is more likely to stall, as the starting point is much less concrete than a particular technology. However, it does have the potential for developing some really big ideas. For example, a group of pupils constructed a scenario in which only the rich had access to anti-ageing technology through private medical care. And the government refused to make it available on the National Health Service because this would lead to an increase in demand for health and other social services that would be unsustainable. In this scenario there was considerable social unrest, and action groups used the Internet to mobilize opposition to the government. The pupils created another scenario in which this technology was available to all and explored ways in which the active elderly could make a financial contribution to society by means of limited home-working using the Internet. The limited home-working involved a wide range of activities using the Internet, as follows:

Providing companionship for the lonely.
Providing tutorial support for those studying at school using e-learning.
Supporting a forum for the discussion of local issues to develop participation in local government.
Providing examples of oral history from their memories of times past.
Guidance to those involved in work similar to that which they did when in full-time employment.

The design that the pupils produced was a guide to anti-ageing services provided by new technology. A comparison of the two scenarios revealed that the way a society makes such technology available to its people has consequences, and shows how the same technology, in this case use of the Internet, could be used for very different purposes.

Developing Products Using Existing Technologies by Making and Justifying a Wide Range of Design Decisions Needed to Bring the Product into Existence as a Prototype

The Electronics in Schools project is a professional development-initiative and during the on-going evaluation that took place during its first year of operation it was realized that the majority of the in-service training taking place was concerned with technical subject knowledge about electronics. This is not surprising, but dealing with these technical issues while important was not sufficient to ensure that there was an impact on pupil learning in design and technology lessons. It was important to focus on the totality of electronic product design and consider the wide range of design decisions, including the technical, that pupils would need to make if they were to be successful in electronic product design. Subsequently this holistic approach to electronic product design was found to generate tasks that were authentic in that they were personally meaningful and set in culturally authentic contexts (Murphy and Hennessy, 2001). The view of the EIS project was that pupils should be given the opportunity to learn to make five types of design decisions:

1. Conceptual (e.g., what is the overall purpose of the design? What sort of product will it be?)
2. Technical (e.g., How will the design work?)
3. Aesthetic (e.g., What will the design look like?)
4. Constructional (e.g., How will the design be put together?)
5. Marketing (e.g., Who is the design for? Where will it be used? Where will it be sold?)

This can be represented visually, with each type of decision at a corner of a pentagon, with each corner connected to every other corner. This interconnectedness is an important feature of design decisions. A change of decision within one area will affect some if not all of the design decisions that are made within the others. For example, if the way a design is to work is changed this will almost certainly affect what the design looks like and how it is constructed. It may also have far-reaching effects in changing some of the purposes that the design can meet and who might be able to use it. Usually the teacher identifies the sort of product the students will be designing and making. This makes it very difficult for students to engage in conceptual design. Even if the type of product is identified for the pupils, there are still many opportunities for making design decisions in the other areas. Consider the designing and making of a puppet theatre and puppets. The pupils can make decisions about who will use the puppets and what for (marketing decisions), what sort of puppets would be appropriate, the sort of theatre such puppets would need, the nature of props and scenery, plus any special effects that might accompany the performance. These decisions will encompass a host of technical, aesthetic, and constructional design decisions.

It is through a combination of the learning from appropriate Resource Tasks and previous experience within Capability Tasks that students will be empowered to make these design decisions. Teachers are able to use the idea of design decisions to scrutinize their design and technology curriculum. The first step is to audit the range of design decisions that are likely to be made by pupils tackling a particular designing and making assignment. The second step is to carry out this audit across all the designing and making assignments tackled by pupils across a key stage. This gives an overview of the designing that is taking place. If an area of design decision making is missing, under-represented, or over-represented the nature of the assignment can be adjusted accordingly. Teachers can adapt their curriculum to include Resource Tasks that are relevant to the required design decisions. In this way the demands for reflection within designing can be orchestrated by the teacher so that pupils are required to make and justify their design decisions in ways that are challenging without being daunting and without being overwhelmed with design tasks that are too complex.

The role of Case Studies in supporting designing and making is less direct than that of Resource Tasks but no less important. The particular content of a any one Case Study is unlikely to be relevant but it is the intention that the broad learning acquired across several Case Studies, that is, becoming informed about a design-based approach and appreciating the pitfalls of making assumptions about user's needs and wants, will enable students to take a more mature and considered attitude towards their own design decisions.

Discussion

As a science teacher, before I became a design and technology teacher, I had been considerably impressed by the work of Rosalind Driver and her ideas of alternative frameworks (Brook and Driver, 1984).

> Before students experience any formal teaching in science, they are likely to have formulated their own intuitive ideas, which enable them to explain and predict familiar phenomena to their own satisfaction. When students are presented with ideas in science lessons, they have to modify and re-structure their own ideas in order to accommodate new ideas. This requires a willingness and effort on the part of the learner. (109)

I believed that the alternative frameworks pupils possessed regarding simple electrical and mechanical systems might be challenged through a design situation in which misconceptions led to technical failure of a proposed design solution. The failure of the design proposal would provoke both willingness and effort on the part of the pupil to modify and restructure their understanding.

The Nuffield Design and Technology Resource Tasks, developed to teach the technical understanding required for pupils to be able to design simple products containing mechanical, electrical, and electronic systems, were formulated to provide concrete experience through investigation of sub-system assemblies of components and through structured questioning require the pupils to consider the functional characteristics of the sub-systems and to reflect on how they might be used to solve technical problems in simple design-tasks. See, for example, the set of Resource Tasks concerned with mechanical control: MRT1—changing types of movement; MRT2—changing axis and direction of rotation; MRT3—changing force, speed, and distance; MRT12—introducing mechanism design (Barlex, 1995b).

At this stage of development of the Nuffield Design and Technology project, in the early 1990s, this simple constructivist view did not acknowledge explicitly the social nature of knowledge construction, and the Resource Tasks were written to be tackled on an individual, almost private, basis. Inevitably, the effective teacher would disrupt this introspection by interacting with the pupils through discussion and questioning on an individual, small-group and whole-class basis. A similar approach was taken in developing the strategy Resource Tasks such as the PIES approach to considering people's needs. The situations used to engage pupils in reflecting on needs in both the Nuffield Project and Young Foresight (hospital ward, hotel room, rail journey, bus stop, railway station, and airport) were chosen because all pupils were likely to have experienced most if not all of these situations. This can be seen in terms of a Vygotskian framework. The pupils would have significant and highly relevant "everyday" knowledge that would be needed to make sense of the "scientific" concepts that would be taught by the teacher—a classification of needs and the relationship between a product and the needs it might meet. The dynamic interaction between the spontaneous and scientific concepts is in keeping with Vygotsky's view concerning their interdependence.

> We believe that the two processes—the development of spontaneous and non-spontaneous concepts—are related and constantly influence each other. They are parts of a single process: the development of concept formation which is affected by varying external and internal conditions but is essentially a unitary process, not a conflict of antagonistic, mutually exclusive forms of thinking. (Vygotsky, 1986: 157)

The use of Case Study reading can be put into Vygotskian perspective. The reading can be shared among the pupils in a class. The contents of the study can be discussed. The teacher can ask questions that encourage pupils to ask further questions. Through these socially shared activities of the classroom, the individual pupil is able to develop his or her own personal understanding, that is, to internalize the co-constructed knowledge. To help explain the way that this social and participatory learning took place, Vygotsky (1978) developed the concept of the zone of proximal development (ZPD), which he defined as "the distance between the actual developmental level as determined through independent problem solving and the level of potential development as determined through problem solving under adult guidance or in collaboration with more capable peers" (86). Rogoff (1994) views the ZDP as the means by which learners participate in a community of practice.

The winners and losers approach to developing an understanding of impact beyond intended benefit engages pupils in discussion and argument, which, if carefully orchestrated by the teacher, can lead to considerable learning. The project has anecdotal evidence of this approach being used with pupils at a school located in a mining community that had suffered considerably during the miners' dispute with the government and subsequent pit-closures. Using winners and losers to discuss the impact of nuclear-power stations gave fourteen-year-old pupils a voice with which to articulate powerfully held views. This is a stark example of the importance of a sociocultural perspective for school technology. In this case, the experience and knowledge of some of the pupils were greater than that of the teacher; they were indeed more capable peers.

In the Young Foresight project, deliberate steps are taken to enhance both the role of peer collaboration and adult guidance. Pupils are expected to work collaboratively in developing design concepts for products and services needed by a future society and are supported in this collaboration not only by the teacher but also by a mentor from industry who can bring a commercial perspective to bear on the pupils' suggestions. The evaluation of the Young Foresight (YF) project (Murphy et al., 2001) indicates the importance of this adult guidance:

> "The YF teacher-mentor partnership is very effective. It represents an important development for ensuring curriculum innovation and reform" (3). Pupils valued the mentor input as this description from one pupil indicates: "[The mentors were] pointing us in directions to go and head that way . . . They said you could try this just giving ideas. I think everyone really liked that they were coming over to talk to us" (85).

The social situatedness of concept formation has been studied by Moll (1992) who uses Vygotsky's analysis to gain insight into providing effective education for linguistically and culturally diverse students. The evaluation of the Young Foresight project (Murphy et al., 2000) reported a particularly striking example. The schools in phase 1 of the pilot scheme had pupils from very diverse cultural backgrounds. It is difficult to include and give value to pupils' cultural knowledge in a prescribed curriculum. The Young Foresight approach appears to be enabling this, as one teacher noted.

> One of the pupils was seeing the future very much on a political level. She came from Africa, a recent arrival and was talking about the need to get policies right. Things like policies towards aid to the third world, policies on afforestation and stuff like this which was really operating above the level I expected. That [her homework] was read out [to the class] and I thought that there was a lot of students they're thinking "yes, this is what it's all about" (7).

The evaluation of the Young Foresight (Murphy et al., 2000) approach indicated clearly that pupils valued the collaborative approach to designing and saw benefits in comparison with working as an isolated individual.

> You get a better product as a group. You don't get "Ah, you're doing this wrong";

They help you out and say you could have done this . . . help you evaluate your product sort of.

You're not like "do this, do that", you've got more ideas to do it. More opportunity.

Not just using your own ideas, you get other people's and you can work off them.

It works better when we're in groups, more ideas than if you work as an individual. You can see things from different perspectives.

It's really shown me what I can achieve, and as a group as well. (3; 4)

A key question for those who argue that learning involves the co-construction of knowledge is to what extent this is possible for a pupil acting as a "solitary" designer/maker? Sim and Duffy (2004) provide an intriguing picture of designing as a learning/activity. They argue that the designer is learning about the design that he/she is conceiving through successive iterations that give increasing clarity to the design proposal and its worth. The designer is learning about what he/she is creating as he/she creates it. From a pedagogic viewpoint this is fascinating—it is the pupil who has the knowledge and expertise in this situation, only he/she knows about his/her design. The teacher's role is one of enabling that learning to progress according to the pupils' design intentions. This is very different from the traditional role of the teacher which is to help the pupil' learn about that which the teacher, already knows. Clearly, the role of the teacher is that of an adult guide here and this is stated quite explicitly in the Teacher's Guide (Barlex, 1995c).

A Capability Task must make appropriate demands on a student's resources, and this requires careful matching. At the level of the whole class, this will take into account the position in the key stage and hence the previous experience plus any overall strengths and weaknesses of the class. While all students in the class are tackling a common task, you can use negotiation and intervention to help students adjust their response to the task so that the challenges it provides are appropriate for that student (66).

The role of other pupils as more capable peers is also reinforced in the Nuffield approach in the Study Guide (Barlex, 1995a), which describes clearly by means of a comic-style illustration the role of fellow pupils in helping a pupil review the progress of his/her designing. This is also made explicit in a later edition of the Teacher Guide (Barlex, 2000) in which the role of peer-to-peer evaluation of design ideas is described in a section on teaching a Capability Task.

The design ideas are now more fully developed but it is still important that they are scrutinized. This process can be more dynamic if pupils carry out peer review while working in pairs, taking alternate roles of client and designer. The client has the specification and the designer the prototype product (in whatever form this has been developed). The client has to question the designer about the prototype. You can provide questions or expect the pupils to make them up. It is important that this feedback informs the final design (19).

This places a particular pedagogic burden on the teacher and fellow pupils; a burden that requires them to make constructive criticisms of both the decisions made and the results of those decisions, to be supportive of the pupil as he or she responds to these criticisms.

Conclusion

Some might argue that it would be unwise to use the ideas of Vygotsky to inform education in today's schools. Developing a classroom in which collaboration, as opposed to competition, underpins the educational endeavor is extremely difficult in the current assessment-driven environment. Acknowledging, valuing, and utilizing the cultural diversity in a classroom is a demanding task. Supporting individual pupils in their designing and making through teacher and peer mentoring as opposed to instruction moves teachers and pupils into unfamiliar territory. However, I believe that I have shown that the pedagogy associated with three significant curriculum-development initiatives can be understood by considering them in the light of the sociocultural approaches to learning and development advocated by Vygotsky. Furthermore, I believe that the effectiveness of this pedagogy is directly linked to this strong theoretical foundation and that the subject of school technology, design and technology as it is called in England, is particularly suited to a Vygotsky-based pedagogy. It will, however, require a combination of initial teacher-education and substantial continuing professional development in which this pedagogy can be explored and internalized for it to become prevailing good practice.

References

Banks, F., Barlex, D., Jarvinen, E., O'Sullivan, G., Owen-Jackson, G., and Rutland, M. (2004). "DEPTH—Developing Professional Thinking for Technology Teachers: An International Study." *International Journal of Technology and Design Education*, 14: 2, 141–157.

Barlex, D. (1995a). *Nuffield Design and Technology Study Guide*. England: Longman.

Barlex, D. (1995b). *Nuffield Design and Technology Resource Task File*. England: Longman.

Barlex, D. (1995c). *Nuffield Design and Technology Teacher Guide*. England: Longman.

Barlex, D. (1998). "Design and technology: The Nuffield perspective in England and Wales." *International Journal of Technology and Design Education*, 8, 139–150.

Barlex, D. (2000). *Nuffield Design and Technology Teacher Guide*. England: Longman.

Barlex, D. (2001). *Young Foresight*. New Media in Technology Education, PATT11 (Pupils Attitudes Towards Technology) Conference Proceedings, 2001, 31–33.

Barlex, D. (2003). *Considering the Impact of Design and Technology on Society— the Experience of the Young Foresight Project*. The Place of Design and Technology in the Curriculum, PATT13 (Pupils Attitudes Towards Technology) Conference Proceedings 2003, 140–144.

Barlex, D. (2004). *Creativity in School Technology Education: A Chorus of Voices*. Learning for Innovation in Technology Education, 3rd Biennial International Conference on Technology Education Research Proceedings, 2004, 24–37.

Barlex, D. and Welch, M. (2001). "Educational research and curriculum development: The case for synergy." *Journal of Design and Technology Education*, 6: 1, 29–39.

Brook, A. and Driver, R. (1984). *Aspects of Secondary Students' Understanding of Energy: Full Report*, Children's Learning in Science Project. Leeds: England.

Department for Education and Science and Welsh Office (1988). *National Curriculum Design and Technology Working Group INTERIM REPORT*, London, UK: DES and Welsh Office.

Givens, N. and Barlex, D. (2001). The role of published materials in curriculum development and implementation for secondary school design and technology in England and Wales. *The International Journal of Technology and Design Education*, 11: 2 (137–161).

Moll, L. (1992). "Literary research in community and classrooms: A sociocultural approach." In R. Beach, J. Green, M. Kamil, and T. Shannon (eds). *Multidisciplinary Perspectives on Literacy Research*. Urbana, IL: National Council of Teachers of English, 211–244.

Murphy, P., Lunn, S., Davidson, M., and Issitt, J. (2000). *Young Foresight Phase 1 Evaluation Report*, Bucks, England: Open University.

Murphy, P., Lunn, S., Davidson, M., and Issitt, J. (2001). *Young Foresight Summary Evaluation Report*. Bucks, England: Open University.

Murphy, P. and Hennessy, S. (2001). "Realizing the potential—and lost opportunities—for peer collaboration in a D&T setting." *International Journal of Technology and Design Education*, 11, 203–237.

Qualifications and curriculum authority (2004a). *Design and Technology. The National Curriculum for England.* Crown Copyright.

Qualifications and Curriculum Authority (2004b). *Changes to the Key Stage 4 Curriculum: Guidance for Implementation from September 2004* Available at http://www.qca.org.uk/4146.html Downloaded 03.01.05.

Rogoff, B. (1994). Developing understanding of the idea of communities of learners. *Mind, Culture and Activity* 4: 209–229.

Sim, S. K. and Duffy, A. H. B. (2004). Evolving a model of learning in design. *Research in Engineering Design*, 15, 40–61.

Vygotsky, L. (1978). "Mind in society: the development of higher psychological processes." Edited by: M. Cole, V. John-Steiner, S. Scribner, and E. Souberman. Cambridge, MA: Harvard University Press.

Vygotsky, L. (1986). "Thought and language." Edited by: A. Kozulin Cambridge, MA: MIT Press.

CHAPTER 13

"Technology, Design, and Society" (TDS) versus "Science, Technology, and Society" (STS): Learning Some Lessons

Frank Banks

Introduction

A few years ago, I was talking about an examination entry by a sixteen-year-old pupil with his teacher. The pupil had designed and made a "panic alarm" in case he was attacked late at night. In a technical sense it was very well done indeed with proper consideration of the alarm's weight, power supply, loudness, ease of action, and so on. If anyone had attacked that boy, everyone would have heard about it. I asked his teacher whether the pupil had considered the issue of *why* such an alarm was needed in his neighborhood. The teacher looked puzzled by the question as he obviously thought it irrelevant; why such a panic alarm was needed (in terms of the wider values exhibited by those in the pupil's locality) was not part of the examination-marking scheme. However, I wondered if this alarm was the best solution to the problem he faced. Here was the dilemma. His school technology-examination regime did not give any credit for considering the values that impacted on the problem. However, by not considering *why* he was afraid at night due to few late-night buses or limited and poor street-lighting, his solution was, in some senses restricted. Maybe the sixteen-year-old could not do much himself about the wider context of supplying maybe free buses or better street-lighting. However, the well-crafted and technically sound panic alarm provided only a partial solution to the youth's problem, as it certainly did not reduce his fear. In some ways, the merely "technical" solution increased it.

Both science and technology are often held up as school subjects, that are particularly concerned to develop two types of knowledge, "conceptual" and "procedural" (See McComick, chapter 3). Procedural knowledge is "know-how-to-do-it" knowledge, and conceptual knowledge is concerned with relationships among aspects of what a learner knows, and being able to make and identify the links one says that they have by "conceptual understanding." Hodson (1998) has similarly characterized these in the science domain as "doing science" and "Learning science." Over the last twenty years, there has been much debate in both subjects as to the relative weight that should be given to these types of knowledge. Technology should be more than just acquiring procedural skills and science should be more than the memorizing of facts and the manipulation of abstract concepts. Few would disagree. In addition, both science and technology makes claims to link school-based work to the "real world" outside the classroom and indeed the relevance of these subjects to every-day life has been part of the rationale for making the subjects a part of the compulsory curriculum in many countries.

In this chapter, however, I will explore other types of knowledge and understanding that should also feature as part of these subjects: what, in science, Hodson calls "Leaning about science—developing an understanding of the nature and methods of science, an appreciation of its history and development, and an awareness of the complex interactions among science, technology, society and environment" (Hodson, 1998: 5). Science, technology and society (STS) has been a movement in science education which has tried to humanize the curriculum and to make it relevant to the majority of pupils (Aikenhead, 2003). Similarly, for many years in a range of countries there have been concerns to address the values implicit in the design and making activities in technology classrooms (DfEE, 1995; MoE, 1995; ITEA, 2000).

What lessons do the success or otherwise of the "values agenda" in curriculum developments around the world in both science and technology have for us as we consider how we should take technology and design forward? In this chapter I look at the two subject areas in turn, draw conclusions, and suggest a few possible teaching strategies.

Science, Technology, and Society (STS): What is STS?

STS education is dedicated to the proposition that it is well worth learning about the knowledge and perspectives of the different groups involved in the technological issues of our times, for only with such understandings can decisions about the issues be made. (Solomon, 1993; cited Banks, 1994: 153).

STS, therefore, is a move to widen science education to consider the interrelationships between science, scientists, and their place in society, and the way that one impacts on the other and on the "products" of science. Building on the discipline of science studies in higher education, STS was advocated for schools as a way of providing "science for citizenship" or "Scientific Literacy" to enable those who, although they will not become practicing scientists themselves, will better understand what scientists do, their contribution and responsibilities to society, and which questions are and are not amenable to a scientific response. This STS movement has had, to varying degrees over the years, implications not only for the traditional science-curriculum but also on the question of how schools and teachers position a subject (for better or worse) in the eyes of pupils and their parents.

Writing as long ago as 1971 in "Science Education," Jim Gallagher noted:

> For future citizens in a democratic society, understanding the interrelationships of science, technology and society may be as important as understanding the concepts and processes of science. (Gallagher, 1971: 337)

In 2000, the sociologist Harry Collins wrote:

> [W]e teach science for the benefit of potential scientists rather than to enable the vast majority of those who will not become scientists to gain an understanding of the world we live in. This degree of specialization means Britain gets its scientists to their PhDs by the age of 24 or so, much earlier than other Western countries, and produces some of the most creative specialists in the world, but only at enormous cost to the non-specialists and, hence, to the economy and the society as a whole. (Collins, 2000: 169)

And in 2005, the resources guide to a set of school textbooks called *Twenty-First Century Science* comments:

> Educating the next generation of scientific practitioners is crucial, yet only a minority of pupils go on to become career scientists . . . Everyone, as a citizen, needs to be able to cope with the science that shapes modern life. Parents, patients, householders, and voters have to understand and interpret scientific ideas and technical information to make good decisions. With this in mind, a new framework for the . . . science curriculum

will be introduced in 2006, and the 21st Century Science initiative is expected to play a major role. (Nuffield, 2004: 1)

These quotations indicate a number of themes that need to be explored in order to learn lessons from the long history of STS initiatives around the world. First, STS has been on the curriculum agenda for some time; thirty-five years separate the first and last quotations, and many other changes to schools and the curriculum have vied for priority in that time. Second, that it has such a long history indicates that the nature of the science curriculum for all pupils has been hotly contested and there are strong interest-groups involved both within and outside the STS "movement" which have firm views about what STS means. Third, even if the principle of a curriculum wider that the traditional concepts and processes of school science is accepted, the *nature* of that wider science-curriculum is not clear. In what sense is the technology, "T" in STS, stressed and how much does the "S" for society help pupils "interpret scientific ideas and technical information to make good decisions"?

The Coming of STS?

The launch of Sputnik in 1957 is credited with shocking much of the Western world into a re-evaluation of the number and quality of scientists it was producing. In many countries, the 1960s saw a move away from rote-learning of science facts to an attempt to understand concepts by engaging with experimental work directly. Heavily influenced by the ideas of Jean Piaget, pupils became a "scientist for a day." By encouraging an emphasis on the processes of science through hands-on practical work, it was assumed that understanding of the concepts would follow. The science taught, however, was largely abstract (especially that taught to "academic" pupils) and not clearly linked to every-day life. This lack of links between science in educational contexts and the application in the "real world" led to a number of curriculum initiatives around the world at a number of levels. For example, in higher-education programs such as *Science in a Social Context* in the United Kingdom and Deakin University's *Knowledge and Power* in Australia were developed. At the school level in the 1970s the United Kingdom's Schools Council Integrated Science Project produced *Patterns* (Hall, 1973), the PLON (Project Curriculum Development Physics) was developed in the Netherlands (Raat, 1979; Eijkelhof and Korland, 1982), and in Canada *Science: A Way of Knowing* (Aikenhead and Fleming, 1975). A decade later came *Science in Society* in the United Kingdom (Lewis, 1982).

It is clear that these initiatives were running alongside other political pressures on the curriculum. The most important of these was the move to make science a compulsory subject for all pupils, including its introduction into primary schools in both developed and developing countries.

In many countries, such as France, Germany, Sweden, and Japan, science is now a compulsory subject in secondary education, with a major expansion of primary science teaching in most countries over the last fifteen years or so. The political thrust to make science compulsory has, to some extent, cut across the school initiatives to widen what pupils consider as part of science lessons. Any curriculum-development initiative must be considered in the day-to-day context in which it exists. Teachers' confidence is dependent on subject knowledge and teaching expertise which, along with adequate resources and appropriate accommodation, all play a part in the acceptance of curriculum reform.

Primary science has grown in importance in many countries in recent years and all programs have faced similar implementation problems of improving the science knowledge of primary teachers, lack of equipment, and, just as significantly, lack of agreement about what *sort* of science should be taught to young pupils.

Taking a pragmatic line as to what could be achieved in a "science curriculum for all," governments were rather conservative in scope, wishing to emphasize the need to move away from rote-learning rather than stressing the impact of science in the wider world. For example, the United Kingdom government policy document *Science 5–16* (DES,1985) did not merely define what should be taught in terms of *content* such as "electricity" or "plants," but instead rather emphasized the importance of a *process* approach. Indeed, science curriculum innovation in the middle to late 1980s in England saw a large number of new courses such as *Warwick Process Science* and *Science in Process* for secondary schools. These focused not on science concepts but rather on processes such as observation, interpretation and classification—aspects critical to "the scientific method." Another strand of development was the illustration of how science phenomena are used or impact on every day contemporary life. Textbooks and teacher-support materials such as *SATIS* (Science and Technology in Society; ASE, 1988) encouraged teaching strategies such as the use of newspapers to promote debates and broaden the learning aims of lessons. In developing counties such as Botswana, resources such as *Science 6–14* and *Science Alive* emphasize processes and relate science to the environment and everyday life (Stannard and Williamson, 2002).

This mood for an emphasis on science "processes" has been picked up in the primary science-curricula around the world. Although not totally accepted by some (for example, Jenkins, 1987), the teaching profession generally welcomed a move away from what was often considered as merely the memorizing of poorly understood facts. In contrast, there emerged a curriculum that might be more accessible to *all* pupils and which emphasized skills applicable to other areas of life both inside and outside school. The attention to "doing" science—raising questions that could be answered by an investigation—became the corner-stone of primary science.

The content–process debate became rather heated, and still arouses strong passions. However, as the debate focused closely on that area, concern was also expressed about whether a science curriculum (as Gallagher had said in 1971) built around just the concepts and processes of science (whether "watered down" or not) was indeed appropriate for all pupils or even the majority of them. By the turn of the century, there was considerable criticism in England, for example, about what should be included as part of the science curriculum for all pupils in order to fully engage them with the subject. As evidence of the state of science, in 2002, the Westminster Parliament Science and Technology Committee reported on "Science education from 14 to 19" and said the following as part of the document summary:

> Current . . . courses are overloaded with factual content, contain little contemporary science and have stultifying assessment arrangements. Coursework is boring and pointless. Teachers and students are frustrated by the lack of flexibility. Students lose any enthusiasm that they once had for science. Those that choose to continue with science post-16 often do so in spite of their experiences . . . rather than because of them. (House of Commons, 2002: 5)

This more severe criticism led to a new consideration of science for citizenship and funding for new curriculum-initiatives such as *Twenty-First-Century Science* (Nuffield, 2004) that attempt to address the lack of enthusiasm for science and to provide an appropriate education for those who will be citizens and voters, and, in addition, a grounding for those who will use science professionally in the future.

Interest Groups

Any consideration of the lessons to be learned from the long gestation of the movement (or lack of movement) of STS ideas from the fringes to more mainstream thinking has to consider the influence of different groups. I have indicated above that any attempts at curriculum change have to take account of the wider school context and other educational debates prevalent at the time. Issues such as teacher expertise and resources are vitally important to success. Equally important, however, is the influence of the various interest-groups involved.

Any curriculum innovation has to be supported by an appropriate assessment regime. This is especially true in those countries that operate examination systems largely independent of teacher assessment. The science schemes of the 1960–1970s, for example, that emphasized conceptual understanding over rote-learning had to have an examination scheme to match. There is a world of difference between a closed question such as "Calculate the pressure of a gas initially at 20 Pa of volume 1000 mm^3 when the volume is reduced to 750 mm^3," and the rather more open "Calculate the pressure on a tent during a thunderstorm." However, a prescribed curriculum needs to fully embrace the STS agenda if it is to thrive and—even if curriculum elements are there—in practice, only what is assessed will be taught.

There were other critics of the move to introduce STS. Some suggested that using the argument that not enough pupils were being motivated by science so, therefore, one should change what is taught is "throwing the baby out with the bath water." More recently, for example, STS ideas were advocated in a report called *Beyond 2000* (Millar and Osborn, 1998). They suggested looking at the "big ideas" of science rather than building up from the learning the historical "laws": looking as it were at the building of science rather than scrutinizing its individual bricks. Joe Vinen, an eminent physics professor from the University of Birmingham, may express views that are representative of the constituency of professional scientists who are concerned that any course which focuses on consideration of the impact of science on society rather than on the processes and concepts may result in a course in which "the approach is so superficial as to be inconsistent with the stated aim of giving young people a real understanding of science and its methods," (Vinen, 2000: 175). He wonders if we can dismiss the knowledge base so easily and also questions the premise that not all pupils need the same sort of scientific preparation

The [Beyond 2000] Report notes that only a small minority of students who study science up to 16 will become professional scientists, and that this group must not be allowed to have undue influence on the curriculum. This argument has some validity, but it ought to be treated with caution, for three reasons. First, school science can be the first stage in the training of not only the "science specialist" but also the professional engineer. Secondly, there is a shortage of students, especially good students, wishing to be professional scientists or engineers; surely the schools must accept some responsibility for this situation. Thirdly, so many areas of employment now call for a significant knowledge and understanding of science that the distinction between professional scientists and others may, especially in the future, become less and less clear. (Vinen, 2000: 175)

Throughout the last thirty-five years hand in hand with the desire of some to widen the science curriculum have been the views of others to press for caution and, to some extent, maintaining the status quo.

STS—"T" or "S"?

The emphasis that I give here to the "T" for technology or the "S" for society is a crude short-hand way of pointing to two traditions within STS. As might be expected when one considers the range of different curriculum-projects that have been advanced under the banner of STS, there are a number of different aims for the proposals for change. The technology emphasis is to stress the applications route for science and this naturally gives an applied-science bias. The motivation for this is that pupils will find science relevant and interesting if it is clear how the phenomena illustrated with "mahogany-and-brass" school laboratory apparatus is useful in everyday life. A number of published curriculum-materials developed in the 1980s and 1990s such as *Salter's Science* (Burton et al., 1994) and the Australian *Science World* used in New South Wales and Queensland take this view (Stannard and Williams, 2001). A problem with this approach is the very limited conceptualization of technology that is used and the "add-on" nature of technology examples. In such a view, technology is seen to follow scientific discovery and, for better or worse, seen as a consequence of science. Technology is configured as "artifacts" as the teaching of technology is often not seen as a goal but rather a spin-off from science.

An alternative approach sees the introduction of STS principally as having an ethics dimension. Here the focus would be on consideration of the impact of scientific endeavor on the environment and on the way society conducts itself. Consideration of the morality of genetic engineering and cloning, stem-cell research, animal experimentation, and assessing the balance of risk in the use of nuclear power or mobile phones would exemplify this approach. Here the need to open up the issues to debate is clear and teaching strategies encouraging pupils to explore each-other's views are common.

It can be seen that those in the STS "movement" who were challenging the traditional approach to science education were a loose federation of groups with different fundamental motivations.

Lessons to Be Learnt

Throughout the past fifty years, science educators have unsuccessfully wrestled with the same dilemma: how do we prepare students to be informed and active citizens, and at the same time, how do we prepare future scientists, engineers, and medical practitioners? (Aikenhead, 2003)

If that is the principle aim of STS, a science education for all citizens and embracing their different needs, what lessons are there for those who have argued for both a science and a technology curriculum for all? I would suggest the following:

- Traditional views of subject are very strong within schools and if curriculum change is required it needs to be a "root-and-branch" reform including locking the intended reform into associated assessment materials.
- Making a subject compulsory for all pupils at all ages, may re-enforce traditional views of the subject as teacher training and resources often lag behind rather than lead the reform.
- External constituencies have views as to what should be taught and these need to be accommodated. This is particularly so in science and technology where higher education and professional bodies have particular expectations of schooling.
- Pressure groups, such as those clustering under the title STS, need to agree on priorities for curriculum change if they are to effectively challenge the status quo.

Technology, Design, and Society (TDS): What Is TDS?

The first thing to note is that there is no movement under the banner "TDS" as there has been for STS, however there is most certainly a similar desire to include in the technology curriculum in many parts of the world a consideration of the values implicit in technological activity. Although technology as a general subject for all pupils has a much shorter curriculum-history than science, there are clear parallels with the development of STS and other lessons to learn for how the developing technology-curriculum moves forward. There is also the commonly recognized difference in the *goal* of science and technology. Sparkes (1993: 36) has suggested that there are some key differences between science and technology. Most fundamentally, he suggests that the goal of science is the pursuit of knowledge and understanding for its own sake whereas that of technology is the creation of successful artifacts and systems to meet people's wants and needs. Inevitably, what people value impacts on what they want and need. Although the traditional science curriculum has endeavored to make value-free statements, technological activities are by their very nature value laden. The question in teaching technology, therefore, is not whether values should be considered, but (even more so than in STS) *whose* values should they be?

The Coming of "TDS"—Considering Values

The 1990s saw a trend around the world to move the technology curriculum away from its craft or industrial arts roots to one that embraces design and a fuller consideration of the user of the outcomes of technology within their environmental context. In New Zealand for example, the technology curriculum states that pupils should follow a strand called Technology and Society which includes understanding the ways the beliefs, values, and ethics of individuals and groups:

- promote or constrain technological development
- influence attitudes towards technological development

and understanding the impacts of technology on society and the environment:

- in the past, present, or possible future
- in local, national, and international settings (MoE, 1995)

Another example would be the United States where, although a "National" curriculum would not be possible, many states have considered the adoption of the Technology Content Standards which similarly include a strand on technology and society:

- Students will develop an understanding of the cultural, social, economic, and political effects of technology.
- Students will develop an understanding of the effects of technology on the environment.

- Students will develop an understanding of the role of society in the development and use of technology.
- Students will develop an understanding of the influence of technology on history. (ITEA, 2000: 4)

The curriculum statement for England indicates the sort of outcomes of pupils who have studied design and technology suggesting (among other attributes) that:

They must looks for needs, wants and opportunities and respond to them by developing a range of ideas and making products and systems. They combine practical skills with an understanding of aesthetics, social and environmental issues, function and industrial practices. As they do so, they reflect on and evaluate present and past design and technology, its uses and effects. ((DfES/QCA, 1999)

Consideration of values and the interaction of technology with the specific context of the design and make task and its environment more generally are, therefore, an integral part of the specified or suggested curricula in many parts of the world. But does the rhetoric match the reality?

The traditional approach to the teaching of manual subjects before the mid-1970s with roots in Swedish Sloyd was largely restricted to the development of excellence in practical skills. These outcomes were achieved by adopting pedagogy not so very different to the "master–apprentice" model of a medieval guild. The pupil would be given "a job"—perhaps to produce a pipe rack, (now occasionally seen as a CD rack!), coat-hook, pencil box, pin-cushion, or sponge cake—and shown all the skills and techniques necessary to produce a (more or less) satisfactory outcome. Such approaches are still very regularly used in many parts of the world, and no doubt, you mentally added your own common "design and make" artifacts to my list. But given the wider conceptualization of what should now be embraced by the subject of technology in schools, it is clear that a traditional "show-and-copy" apprentice model of teaching is inadequate. However, the long-established aim to enable a pupil to produce an artifact which he or she is proud to own and take home is very strong. Enacting this wider view of technology education puts severe constraints on time and resources and the nature of the pedagogy that teachers adopt in the technology workroom. As with the developments in science education since the 1970s, so too with technology: curriculum development has not taken place in a vacuum. Practical constraints on the extent of teacher preparation and adequacy of resources have impacted on the desire to fully engage with the wider issues of "Technology and Society." This was particularly acute in England in which the technology curriculum introduced in 1990 underwent many rapid and fundamental changes but was also true, for example, in New Zealand and Australia.

Interest Groups

As the recent histories of the emergent technology curricula around the world indicate, a number of interest groups have been active in influencing the emphasis of school technology. Following the broad classification suggested by Leyton (1993: 18) the first would be those who see technology as a precursor to vocational education and serving an economic function. In the power-play that accompanied calls to remove the compulsion to study design and technology in England this argument was used with politicians by advocates of technology for all and led to a new high-tech influence particularly with regard to the adoption of widespread computer aided design and it was a strong argument for the introduction of the subject into Western Australia where it is called "Technology and Enterprise." A second group would be the professional technologists. Taking a stand similar to that suggested by Vinen above, the Engineering Council produced a damning report on the first iteration of the technology curriculum in England which declared that "Technology in the National Curriculum is a mess" and that the process-based format of the curriculum was not sufficient (Smithers and Robinson, 1992: 1). The report advocated the critical evaluation of existing products as an element of study and, in that regard, opened up the curriculum to a better consideration of an artifact's purpose and its social and environmental impact. In the United States too, NASA, for example, was heavily involved in the production of the technology standards. Both of these constituencies were keen to stress the skills and processes of technology.

These interest groups, however, were, and are, still balanced by those who see technology as a key player in educating for a sustainable future. For example, the Intermediate Technology Group within the United Kingdom works as a consulting body with national and local education-authorities, advising on how to deliver education for sustainable development, particularly within the design-and-technology curriculum. Their focus is on appropriate technologies for the developing world and provides a basis for discussion of how technology is not "neutral." Similarly, in Canada, both Petrina and Elshof have criticized the lack of proper consideration of sustainable issues they consider should be part of the technology curriculum of the differed states, Elshof being particularly critical of Ontario and British Columbia (Elshof, 2000; Petrina, 2000; Elshof, 2005). As Layton has pointed out, "an artifact can reshape people's values and call new ones into play. It makes possible new kinds of action between which people have to choose . . . [T]he chainsaw opened the way to rapid deforestation . . . at the expense of ecological balance and the loss of rainforests. Because it created new possibilities for action, can we call the chainsaw 'neutral'?" (Layton, 1993: 31)

As in STS, assessment in technology tends to drive what is taught—particularly when that assessment is high stakes and external to the schools. The anecdote about the "Panic alarm" mentioned in the introduction is a case in point. An analysis of suggested assessment tasks in New Zealand and of examination specifications in England suggest that social aspects are to be assessed, but a search of corresponding examination papers is rather disappointing.

TDS—"D" or "S"?

As was the case for STS, the different groups advocating a proper consideration of values in school technology would give different weight to the "D" for design and "S" for society. Such as distinction is very crude, and would not apply to all advocates for change, but it does highlight two sub-cultures prevalent in those advocating a fuller consideration of values in technology lessons. The following table 13.1 adapted from Leyton, (1992: 36) illustrates the division.

A full consideration of values would look at all aspects. The values on the "D," *left*-hand side of the table, are usually considered in the design "process" although perhaps those nearer the top of the table often take priority over those nearer the bottom. Less common are consideration of the values on the "S," *right*-hand side promoted by those individuals and schools which have a strong commitment to "equipping pupils to become active collaborators in the creation of a more peaceful, just and sustainable society" (Pitt, 1991: 34). These schools would wish to promote technology tasks that favor particular users such as the disabled or the poor.

Table 13.1 Categorizing value judgments

Technical	Moral
Pupils consider questions of "quality"; who is the product for? How should it be used and with what quality of finish? This is balanced against the extra time required for improvement.	There may be a market for the product but given the responses to the social and environmental considerations—should it be made? Are people's lives enhanced or diminished and how is that judged?
Economic	**Spiritual/ religious**
Pupils should consider the idea of value for money or a thrifty use of resources.	Is there a consideration of the technological Process and consideration of artefacts as to *who* should primarily benefit from the development?
Asethetic	**Social**
Pupils should consider the quality of the images that are used in similar products and what that suggests about the user, the product, and its longevgity in the market.	Is the product appealing to all or restrictive to just one sex or to the able-bodied? What impact does the product have on the way people behave? who wins—who loses?
Enviromental	
Is it justifiable to use materials for the product? "Where do the materials come from?" and "Where do they go?"	

Lessons to Be Learnt

Ruth Conway, writing in the early 1990s, illustrates the need, particularly acute then, to develop ideas on *how* pupils could consider values as part of the work done in technology lessons:

> Faced with the same problem or situation, a person with a techno centric perspective may see a technological outcome that is different from that of a person with a humanistic perspective. When addressing the problem of bicycle theft, for example, a techno centric perspective might suggest stronger locks or an alarm mechanism. Consideration of the social aspects of the problem might suggest public use of a fleet of community bikes, active senior citizens staffing bike parks, or perhaps better sports facilities for young people to "keep them out of mischief." The most effective action would probably include elements from both perspectives. (Conway and Riggs, 1994: 227)

Over a decade on, what lessons have been learned? I would suggest the following:

- In most countries in the world, technology is a subject derived from an earlier tradition, usually craft or industrial arts. If a broad consideration of values is important it needs to include change in the weight given to it in assessment materials.
- Unlike science, pedagogy in technology is commonly directed to the support of the individual in a lone task. Opportunities for full discussion, so as to share experiences for example, need to be built in to lesson planning.
- External constituencies to schools and government agencies also have a view as to what should be taught. In technology, to establish or maintain credibility, this has manifested itself in gaining approval of professional bodies and political groups who may have a limited view of the purpose of a technology curriculum for all.
- Pressure groups, such as those which have promoted a consideration of values in technology education, have been largely successful in winning official support. They may be more disappointed in the extent to which they have impacted on schools.

TDS versus STS: Putting Some Lessons into Practice

Every year I teach and observe both science and technology lessons across the nation-states of the United Kingdom and often abroad too. There are many similarities. Both subjects make much of "hands-on" learning; both promote problem solving and other "processes"; both try to explicitly link school tasks to useful learning for every day life and the needs of the work place. There are differences too. In addition to the different subject goals mentioned above, there is often a noticeable difference in the classroom culture.

Science classrooms engage in practical work usually in groups. This is partly driven by the need to share apparatus but is also due to a tradition of discussing ideas and concepts as part of social learning. Since the 1980s, a "constructivist" view of learning has had a large impact on science-classroom practice and associated published resources. Technology lessons, in contrast, are more solitary. Although pupils are often given common briefs and engage in similar preparatory activities, most of the time work is done by each pupil on his or her own, and the later making stage is almost always done individually. However, to explore the values, perspectives and opinions of others, discussion is essential.

For the remainder of this chapter I suggest some classroom organization strategies that can encourage fruitful collaborative activity, and some resources that might be used to raise the awareness of the values implicit in technology lessons. The position taken is that, to make the often *implicit* value position *explicit*, it is necessary for pupils to more actively interact with the teacher and other pupils than is often the case in technology lessons.

Group Work

Care has to be exercised if a group activity is part of teacher assessment of practical outcomes in giving credit for different aspects of the project to the appropriate pupils. However, in setting up group discussion to be meaningful, I have found I have to consider the makeup of the groups carefully. Questions that arise include: Is friendship grouping the most appropriate? If not, what criteria should be used to form more effective groups? Is the grouping a temporary measure or a more permanent arrangement which needs monitoring? I have to ensure each group has short-term strategies to achieve long-term goals. This is best achieved by visiting each group quickly once they have started, still keeping every group in view. The different groups must know that their progress is being monitored even though I am principally occupied in a different area of the room so that I can make sure all groups are kept busy and on task. If a group appears too rowdy or too many pupils appear to be moving around on short excursions, I check that it is to do with the organization of their task, rather than just an excuse to have a social conversation with friends.

Later, as pupils become more experienced, a more flexible approach may be possible. The techniques in which pupils note ideas individually, then share them with a partner, then in a group of four and finally reporting to the whole group can work well; however, the agenda for discussion needs to be tight and the time kept short, especially if pupils are not used to this way of working.

There are many benefits that this "snowball" technique of small-group discussion can bring to technology lessons. For example, it enables pupils to contribute their own ideas to less-threatening scrutiny before exposing them to a wider audience as they pool ideas and half-formed opinions, which can develop, especially if the values of different experiences and cultural groups can be considered. I have used this technique with preparatory-school teachers in Egypt and, although very different from their usual teaching strategy, they engaged with it enthusiastically and saw how they could embrace it in their classroom.

A stumbling block, however, was the school principal who would have to be convinced of the learning that was taking place in such "noisy" classrooms.

Teachers engaging in structured group-work have found it valuable for pupils to sort out their own rules for discussion. The following suggestions for the organization of discussion work are adapted from the STS-inspired science and technology in society (SATIS) teachers' guide:

- Seating is important. The usual classroom arrangement, with the teacher at the front facing the students, encourages a flow of discussion from teacher to students and back again, but discourages communication between students. Wherever possible, discussion groups should be arranged so everyone can see everyone else in the group. [In the final reporting-back arrangement, a circle of seats is best although the conventional technology workshop or studio may make this difficult.]
- Discussion rarely goes well without an initial stimulus. SATIS units include many discussion questions and stimuli, but there are plenty of other sources such as newspaper cuttings, pictures from magazines, a recent TV program, a provocative statement from the teacher and so on.
- The teacher's role is very important. He or she needs to avoid dominating the discussion: remember that the teacher's views will carry disproportionate weight. Try to give support and encouragement, and to draw out the quieter pupils.
- It is important to get the right atmosphere at the start. The teacher needs to be enthusiastic, lively and well organized (ASE, 1986: 27–29).

Circle time is a discussion technique used with young pupils. Often a ball or soft toy can be used to establish that the one who holds the toy is the one who speaks while the others listen.

Product Evaluation and Values

Evaluating an existing product can do more than merely suggest ideas for design and make assignments. Questions can be asked of the product that can be used to generate discussion and reveal values judgments when considering an actual product. Working in pairs or groups of three to encourage interaction, the pupils can rotate round the room to different stations where there is an example artifact or a picture of the product. On a work-sheet, they can cover issues such as:

1. Responses to the product
   a. Who might the owner be?
   b. Why might they buy it?
   c. Would I want to own or use it?
   d. What would this reveal about me?
   e. Is it really needed?

2. Exploring design, production, promotion, use and disposal
   a. Whose needs and wants were considered during each stage from design to disposal? Who might have been consulted?
   b. What materials were used and why?
   c. Where do the resources come from?
   d. Are they likely to run out?
   e. How is the product promoted and packaged?
   f. What assumptions appear to have been made about the potential buyers/users?
   g. What effect will its use have on people's lives and relationships?
   h. How long will it last? What happens to it after use?
   i. What factors limit/lengthen its life span?

3. Values embedded in the product

Pupils can group their answers to the questions to around the values set out in table 13.1 above (adapted from DfEE, 1995: 4).

A Few Exemplar Resources

There are a number of simple resources that focus consideration of values such as "who wins, who loses" but space is limited here. Nuffield design and technology and materials from the *Sustainable Technology Education Project* (STEP) suggest using a diagram like an archery target as a means of generating discussion concerning the affects and impact of technological products. Working in groups, pupils write in the "bulls-eye" the product or process under discussion. Then in the ring closest to the centre, they write down all the groups of people who are directly affected by the product for good or ill. In the outer ring segments, they write down all the groups of people who are indirectly affected by the product. As a group they discuss who benefits and color in that segment, the groups they think will lose out are shaded a different color. The groups' colorful results are shared with other groups. As is usually the case with such activities it is the engagement with the issues that is important, not the results as such, and pupils need to be put at ease that there are no real right or wrong answers.

Alternatively small groups can use pictures cut from old magazines to create contrasting "image boards"; collage composites around value-laden themes such as "Green or Greedy" and "Hero or Zero." Consideration of what the images convey can compliment the product evaluation questions.

Learning Lessons

In their consideration of the relationship between science and design and technology in the secondary school curriculum in England, Barlex and Pitt advocate greater collaboration between science and technology teachers in schools to the benefit of pupils.

> The result of this collaboration should be that pupils will be able to articulate their ideas in both subjects much more easily so that the focus of discussions with teachers and other pupils becomes the nature of the idea and its viability or significance. (Barlex and Pitt, 2000: 42)

As indicated above, technology teachers can learn much from the approach to STS developed in science over so many years. To share experience and develop joint practice is essential. Few in a democracy would disagree with the proposition that all future citizens need to engage with and debate the values they and others hold. A consideration of values made explicit through learning about technology, design and society are key to that process. If education is the conversation we have across the generations, how we use and value subject disciplines is crucial to the society we create. Neither science nor technology are value-free. It is the mutual consideration and debate of the values that we and our society hold that lies at the heart of schooling.

References

Aikenhead, G. (2003). "STS education: A rose by any other name." In R. Cross (ed.), *A Vision for Science Education: Responding to the Work of Peter J. Fensham*. London: Routledge.

Aikenhead, G. and Fleming, R. (1975). *Science: A Way of Knowing*. Saskatoon, Canada; Curriculum Studies, University of Saskatchewan.

ASE (1986). *Science and Technology in Society: General Guide for Teachers*. Hatfield, Association for Science Education.

Barlex and Pitt (2000). *Interaction: The Relationship between Science and Design and Technology in the Secondary School Curriculum.* London: Engineering Council.

Burton, G. Holman, J., Pilling, G., and Waddington, D. (1994). *Salter's Advanced Chemistry.* Oxford: Heinemann.

Collins, H. (2000). "On Beyond 2000." *Studies in Science Education*, 35 169–173.

Conway, R. and Riggs, A. (1994). "Valuing in technology." In F. Banks (ed.), *Teaching Technology.* London: Routledge.

DfEE (1995). *Looking at Values Through Products and Applications.* London: Department for Education and Employment.

DfES/QCA. (1999). *The National Curriculum.* London: HMSO.

Eijkelhof, H. and Kortland, K. (1982, July). *The Context of Physics Education.* A paper presented to the 2 IOSTE Symposium, Nottingham, UK.

Elshof, L. (2000). "Technological education for critical citizenship or consumerism?" *Orbit' Science, Math & Technology Learning for All* 31: 3 25–29.

Elshof, L. (2005). "Technological Education and Environmental Sustainability, a Critical Examination of Twenty years of Canadian Practices and Policies." *Poc of PATT-15*, Haalem, Netherlands. http://www.iteawww.org/PATT15/PATT15.html.

Gallagher, J. (1971). "A broader base for science education." *Science Education*, 55, 329–338.

Hall, W. (1973). *Patterns: Teachers' Handbook.* London: Longman/Penguin Press.

House of Commons. (2002). *The House of Commons Report: Science Education for 14 to 19. Volume 1: Report and Proceedings of the Science and Technology Committee*, London: HMSO.

ITEA (2000). *Standards for Technological Literacy.* Reston, Virginia: International Technology Education Association.

Jenkins, E. (1987)."Philosophical flaws." *Times Educational Supplement*, 2 January.

Layton, D. (1993). *Technology's Challenge to Science Education.* Buckingham: Open University Press.

Millar, R., and Osborne, J. (eds). (1998) *Beyond 2000: Science Education for the Future.* London: King's College London.

MoE (1995). *Technology in the New Zealand Curriculum.* New Zealand: Wellington, Learning Media Ltd for Ministry of Education.

Nuffield (2004). *Pilot Resources Guide, 21st Century Science.* Oxford: Oxford University Press.

Petrina, S. (2000). "The politics of technological literacy." *International Journal of Technology and Design Education*, 10: 2 (181–206).

Raat, J. (1979). "The education of physics teachers in the Netherlands." *Physics Education*, 14. London: Institute of Physics.

Smithers, A. and Robinson, P. (1992). *Technology in the National Curriculum: Getting it Right.* London: The Engineering Council.

Solomon, J. (1994). "Teaching STS." In F. Banks (ed.), *Teaching Technology.* London: Routledge.

Sparkes, J. (1993). "Some differences between science and technology." In R. McCormick, C. Newey, and J. Sparkes (eds), *Technology for Technology Education*. Addison-Wesley Publishing Company.

Stannard, P. and Williamson, K. (2001). *Science World*. Australia: Macmillan.

Stannard, P. and Williamson, K. (2002). *Science Alive*. Botswana: Macmillan.

Vinen, W. (2000). "Science, or science appreciation?" *Studies in Science Education*, 35, 174–180.

CHAPTER 14

Gender and Technology: Gender Mediation in School Knowledge Construction

Patricia Murphy

Introduction

Historically, technology education was perceived as an instrument of social reform and control designed to maintain and reinforce the social spheres of males and females. Current representations of technology, which cohere around notions of technological capability, are considered to be "free" of symbolic gendering. This assumption fails to take account of the deeply gendered nature of technology. As Layton (1993: 35) observed technology is understood as a "masculine" preserve, not a place for women, who are relegated to the roles of users and consumers. This phenomenon can be traced to the historical exclusion of women from skilled work, which was appropriated by men, who restricted "women's work" to the unskilled and routinized and set up a pattern regarding women's involvement with technology (Wajcman, 1991). Consequently, "technical competence" came to be understood as an integral part of hegemonic masculinities and positioned women in opposition to this as the "outsiders" or the technically incompetent (Wajcman, 1991). Thus in the discourses that circulate about technologies, women's and girls' technical competence is denied and beliefs about their "lack" and men's and boys' "expertise" become part of our "common-sense" knowledge about the way people are. Women's involvement in technology continues to be problematic with product design, decision-making, and development dominated by men (Southwell, 1997). This coupled with beliefs about girls' and boys' technological competence has major implications for the social construction of technology and for the ways in which teachers represent, and students experience, technology education.

The chapter examines some of the evidence derived from an English curriculum context about gender–technology interactions that have international relevance. It examines first the roots of the subject and how these position teachers and students in relation to it. Next, students' course choices and performance are discussed as outcomes of the way gender mediates knowledge construction. To gain insights into the meanings that students construct in their technology education, findings about gendered views of salience are discussed. Researchers have challenged the emphasis on the individual in the study of gender, arguing for a shift in attention towards the social relations in which gender is used, that is, the situated meanings of gender (Stepulevage, 2001). In the final section, evidence from an ethnographic study in a coeducational school that adopted a single-sex grouping strategy to enhance access and learning is discussed to consider how girls and boys feel positioned in technology.

Reforming Technology Education

Lewis (1999) in his argument for a more authentic curriculum challenged the devaluing of the "practical arts" which included technology education and attributed this to the Platonic conception of knowledge that dominated Western cultures. The current curriculum in England was seen as narrow with its emphasis on academic knowledge excluding many human practices including those concerned with the solution of existential problems connected to everyday life. The bringing together of subjects in the reconceptualisation of technology education was intended to bring it into the mainstream of all students' educational experience, increasing its breadth, quality, and status. In that sense it was conceptualised as a "new" subject that would enable young people to "learn to think creatively to improve the quality of life . . . become autonomous and creative problem solvers . . . look for wants, needs and opportunities and respond to them . . . with an understanding of . . . social and environmental issues, function and industrial practices" (DfEE, 1999). Such a subject would therefore benefit all students whatever their career aspirations. Currently all students in England have a legal entitlement to study technology education from five to fourteen years of age. Before 2004 this statutory entitlement extended to students aged from fifteen to sixteen but since 2004 the requirements became nonstatutory. Schools, nevertheless, are required to make available at least one technology course to all students aged from fourteen to sixteen.

Like the domain itself school subjects are social constructions that have a social history and making a subject compulsory and changing its specification and purpose cannot eradicate the influence of these historical roots. The technology curriculum specification for England drew together subjects which had "deeply gendered histories" (Paechter and Head, 1996: 23). Two of the main contributing subjects were craft, design, and technology education (CDT) and home economics (HE) which traditionally were taught to boys and girls as separate groups with the expressed aim in HE of training working-class girls into the domestic roles that they were destined for. CDT, which was a subject taught to boys, drew on the workshop skills traditionally associated with male working-class occupations and crafts, skills that have been associated with forms of hegemonic masculinity. Both subjects were aimed at nonacademic students and were viewed as lower status than academic subjects like science and maths. These subject roots can be traced to the development of technical education in England based on an apprenticeship model which left technology education rooted in workshop practices, hostile to academic theoretical knowledge and "perennially low in status" (Green, 1999: 60).

Teachers' Professional Identities

The significance of this gendered history relates to the way that subject identities are generated and made available through dominant subject discourses. The discourses in a subject are constantly reproduced and reconstructed in the classroom setting and teachers are pivotal in regulating and legitimising ways of knowing, acting, and being. James (1999) citing Gleeson's work described the culture of crafts and trades teachers as an "exclusive masculinity club" and that prevailing views within the culture included the belief that teaching girls was acceptable but girls taking up careers and "men's jobs" was not. She argued that technology studies teachers' construction of masculinity could be traced in part to the discourses shaping their histories and current lives, and a socio–historical relation to the physical world and labour bound up with hegemonic masculinities (398). It is to be expected that in technology education, with its very different subject roots there will be competing and conflicting discourses circulating about what should be taught; who should be educated in this way; and by what means.

Paechter and Head's (1996) characterisation of the subject cultures of technology education teachers in England in the early 90s has significant overlaps with that of James' technology-studies teachers. They referred to the significance that teachers gave to close relationships with students, particularly disaffected and working-class boys, in their construction of their professional identities. They related teachers' beliefs, particularly those of CDT teachers, in the importance of students creating individual products with the need for boys to present to their parents the results of their physical labours and argued that it reflected the importance of physical work to working-class masculinity. Female technology teachers in the study were described as a minority of pioneers whose views of the subject were losing out to dominant perceptions of curriculum based on segregation. Paechter (2003) found that the reasons for taking up teaching careers mediated teachers' professional identities. CDT teachers valued craft skills as a source of professional satisfaction and regretted the increased emphasis on design in the reformed curriculum. This, Paechter argued, led some to attempt to reinterpret the curriculum to reflect "more closely the areas in which they felt powerful and comfortable" (137).

Students' Agency

Although the teacher is identified as a key agent in maintaining or contesting the gender order of the classroom (Dixon, 1998) this is not to deny students' agency. The view of gender increasingly advocated in the field is that gender is constructed in social interaction and is not a fixed attribute of an individual. Different contexts and the discourses within them offer a range of ways of being male and female but some are privileged and these become hegemonic reinforcing certain practices in a setting and subordinating others. Gender from this perspective is understood as a hegemonic social representation that circulates as a set of norms, ideas, and conventions and provides some of the resources from which individuals construct social identities (Lloyd and Duveen, 1992; Ivinson and Murphy, 2003). Some of the symbolic resources that students draw upon to manage a social identity in a subject are from representations of gender that provide them with clues about what are socially legitimate ways for them to act. In this way gender mediates knowledge construction as part of a more general process in which identity formations structure and frame educational choices and performance (Murphy and Ivinson, 2004).

Course Choices

Brooks (2003) commented on gendered option-choices in technology at age fourteen that "there are still many areas of life where boys will be boys and girls will be girls" (4). The author is far from alone in representing students' choices as a passive response to socialisation processes. Murphy and Whitelegg (2005) however noted that studies about girls' participation in physics showed that students' self–concept, that is their sense of current and future possible selves in relation to physics, interacted with their experience of the subject to mediate their course choices. Roger and Duffield (2000) in their review of the factors underlying girls' persistent opting out of science and technology courses in the context of Scottish schools similarly identified students' self-concept, and career awareness as influential. They described the relationship between self-concept and career awareness as the "interaction between the way pupils see themselves and the opportunities they perceive are open to them. If they way they see themselves excludes technical or scientific competence, then the opportunities perceived as realisable will also exclude science, engineering and technology" (374).

Since the introduction of a national curriculum in the late 80s, the study of technology education in England is a statutory requirement but post-fourteen it is optional in terms of the particular aspect of the subject studied. The General Certificate of Secondary Education (GCSE) examination taken by the majority of students at age sixteen offers a range of technology courses. All courses share a common structure based on design-and-making skills and content is considered in terms of materials and components, design and marketing influences, and processes and manufacture. The courses differ in their subject content in terms of the types of materials and systems studied and the skills and processes associated with their use. The entry figures for males and females for 2002–2004 showed continuing major differences in course entry patterns. For example electronics has a male entry of around 17,000–18,000 compared with between 1,000–2,000 for females. Textile technology has a female entry of around 50,000 compared with less than 2,000 for males. About three times as many girls as boys enter for food technology and the converse is the case for resistant-materials technology. Graphics is the one subject in which entry is more equivalent. Entry for systems-and-control technology remains male dominated. Study post-sixteen at advanced level reveals the same pattern of entry for males and females but the gaps are more dramatic.

The entry figures represent student choices but choices that are reinforced by teacher and institutional discourses. There are small sub-groups of males and females crossing gender boundaries but no evidence that this phenomenon is on the increase. The figures suggest that many girls and boys studying technology education post-fourteen continue to feel a sense of belonging in the subjects that were traditionally constructed for them. Their course choices being mediated by the discourses about what it is to be a successful person in the various realms of technology and what they, in turn, understand to be appropriate "masculine" and "feminine" behaviors. Students' decisions also reflect their views of what it is worthwhile to study, that is, what makes sense, has personal relevance and engages them, which may reflect career aspirations for some students but not for others.

The GCSE examination results for 2004 show that across all the technology courses, girls achieved significantly more passes than boys as a group. It would be assumed that where there is a major imbalance between girls' and boys' entry that the smaller group is the more highly selected and a performance advantage for that restricted group would be anticipated. There is some evidence that this may be the case with girls taking electronics, and systems and controls, and this is also the case in the advanced-level examinations but it does not hold for those girls choosing to study resistant materials or for those boys choosing to study textiles and food Technology. In the advanced-level examinations taken at age eighteen girls continue to achieve more of the higher grades, A–B, in food technology even though they significantly outnumber the boys. These results may suggest something about the sub-populations but might also indicate that for some of these boys and girls once their choices are made the gender-boundary crossing is experienced as difficult and hazardous and this in turn constrains their access to and engagement with their chosen subjects.

"Boys Will Be Boys and Girls Will Be Girls"

Teachers' common-sense beliefs about the way boys and girls are can lead them to accept that students' choices reflect the "natural" order and their role in regulating and reproducing gender orders is often not recognised. The Electronics in Schools (EIS) project funded by the Department for Trade and Industry (DTI) in England was a national project to increase students' access to electronics in both primary and secondary schools through a combined process of teacher training, and funding of resources (Murphy et al., 2004). The evaluation of the project surveyed hundreds of teachers and undertook case studies in twelve schools. The study found that most schools had very low numbers of girls studying electronics post-fourteen. Teachers generally had definite views of the type of student that studied electronics. The characteristics of a successful male student were associated with high intellectual achievements, logic and rationality and a successful female student with neatness, attention to detail and artistic responses:

> The lads who are really good scientists, mathematicians, they tend to go for the electronics side of it.

One teacher commented, "Electronics in the end isn't a girls' thing" even though he described girls who opted for his electronics groups as doing 'fantastically well'. He characterised girls' approach to the subject:

> [T]hey're neat about what they do. Their attention to detail is often better than the boys, so the chances of their products working are great.

Another teacher who had successfully motivated girls to study systems and controls having almost equal numbers of girls and boys in his groups described his perception of boys and girls:

> [G]irls are better at a lot of the programming work and their graphical work is usually better. You have your high technological boy . . . and he is able to work at very high level, logical, technical, mathematics etc. The girls are more artistic in their approach. They're far more quality-conscious than the boys.

While this teacher was successful in motivating girls it is interesting to note that "technological" is associated with boys and "artistic" with girls in his discourse about success. The extent to which students, particularly girls, associate themselves with teachers' representations of success will affect their self-concept and their course choices. Clegg et al. (1999) described how students in higher education discussing choices about design and IT were "making statements about their perceptions of the dominant disciplinary discourse" (54). Unsurprisingly the EIS project found that about a third to a half of the boys in the case-study schools thought they would continue with their study of electronics post-sixteen. No girls reported that they would continue to study the subject either because it was too difficult or because they had plans to study other subjects.

Students' Responses to Technology Tasks

Social constructivist views of learning based on Vygotskian theorising recognise that knowledge emerges first between people and it is this shared understanding that is appropriated by individuals. Students' ability to appropriate shared knowledge depends on their prior experience, understanding and commitments. Human understanding of the world develops through a process of simple associations between characteristics of objects, people and experience. These associations lead to objects and people gradually acquiring "ever more eccentric and intense degrees of significance" (Greenfield, 2000). In this way people and events acquire differential degrees of importance. This individualised way of knowing begins to determine our interpretations of, and responses to, new situations. Social representations of gender divide social life into masculine- and feminine-marked activities, objects, and attributes. Thus human experience is shaped in part by what is represented as legitimate ways of behaving for boys and girls, and in this way gender mediates what we come to pay attention to and consider salient.

Views of Salience

Studies, which make problematic what students' bring to technology activities, have identified differences in views of salience between girls and boys as groups. A common finding is that girls more than boys are concerned with the social context, and this is reflected in the details they include in their initial designs. Murphy (1991) found that all students identified essential and nonessential details but showed clear differences in their initial interpretation of needs and wants in their designs for boats to go round the world. Girls' concern with the social consequences of their designs directed their attention to peoples' needs. In contrast boys tended to design without reference to social and environmental consequences and included detail about mechanisms and structures. To exemplify this further Murphy reported on a study where secondary students were given the opportunity to design a moving vehicle. A group of girls focused their design on improving the stability and efficiency of a pram for transporting a baby and redesigned the wheels and the pram shape. A group of boys also chose a pram design. They wanted to amend the design to computerise the pram so that a baby could be taken for walks without an accompanying adult.

In a study of secondary students technological problem-solving given the opportunity to generate authentic designs it tended to be girls who situated their response in the context of the person's needs and the circumstances of use (Murphy 1999). Thus water sensors were used to create a bath-alarm for a grandmother housed in a "water-drop"-shaped casing. A rain alarm for a mother's wash-line involved a sock-shaped housing. Brunner, Bennett, and Honey (2000) reported similar findings in their study of middle-school students' fantasy designs. They described girls' vehicles as household helpers or improvements to technologies that solved real-life problems. Boys' vehicles were characterised as having the capacity to take them wherever they wanted to go instantly.

Girls' attention to aesthetic details and boys' to mechanisms and structures has been widely noted but needs to be understood in relation to the purposes that students perceive for their designs which mean that different details become more or less significant. This impacts on students' opportunities to learn. For example, in a study that evaluated the Nuffield primary technology resources for teachers one activity had children designing a bus. In response to this most boys began their making task with the moving parts whereas girls generally focused on the interior features for the passengers and the exterior appearance. When the topic ended many girls' buses looked like buses but lacked wheels or else had rather inefficient wheels whereas many boys' buses looked like moving cardboard boxes (Murphy and Davidson, 1997). Rennie (2003) working with elementary pupils making pirate boats also noted this effect referring to the different levels of construction skills as well as differences in how the boats were designed and furnished. Only boys made boats from wood and girls made all the boats that were less well constructed. This reflected the different value the students gave to the design features of the boat, as the girls were more likely to have furnished their boats and to have made model pirates.

The Electronics in Schools (EIS) project found that in the settings in which girls were motivated to study electronics, tasks were set in contexts where their social significance was obvious. The choice of task alone is not sufficient to engage girls, the social circumstances have to be integral to the solution. One task observed involved programming a pelican crossing, that is, a road crossing controlled by traffic lights. The following excerpt is from a discussion with a student about how to think about the three waiting times for the traffic lights to change from red–amber; amber–green and green–red. The design decisions involved giving thought to the context of use and to the users.

> *Teacher*: Well, one of the three ones [wait times] will be determined, say, by road conditions or by the amount of traffic. You've pressed the button; this automatic would link; amber appears; so, wait there.
> *Girl*: Where?

Teacher: There's a timed wait. You put it in between the commands. So, you just put a little arrow there and say: here we'll wait. We don't know how long the wait is at the moment—we don't really mind—but there is a specific wait time band between you pressing the button and the system operating, and there are two more. It might be a wide road.

Girl: Longer for an old person.

Teacher: Yes, for granny pushing a trolley, easy to hit.

Girl: We put that in there?

Teacher: OK, when the people are crossing. It goes, yes, there.

Girl: Wait's put in it or . . . ?

Teacher: Yes, put a wait there. OK, we're stopping the traffic here . . . so the traffic's stopped here. What are the people doing? They're going. The wait light is on, so you actually have to tell them to wait all the time.

The excerpt shows how the teacher maintained the authenticity as a reference point for students' decision making and how this in turn enabled the student to engage with the users' problems.

Situated Meanings of Gender

Markwick (2001) argues that to explore how girls and boys are positioned in technology there is a need for discourses that legitimate crossing gender boundaries. Insights from a study of a coeducational school, which had chosen to organise students into parallel single-sex groupings for teaching shed some light on the discourses that legitimate boundary crossings. The strategy was based on two assumptions, one educational—that girls and boys learn in different ways and have different needs and the other political—that single-sex organisation is associated with high-achieving schools in England. The study observed classrooms across the curriculum and only some findings from the technology classes are reported here.

The Study

In the research a sociocultural view of learning was adopted which allowed a focus on the embedded nature of classrooms in which teachers' practice are understood as forms of mediation that regulate the boundary between classroom settings and the other social contexts that students negotiate (Lave, 1988). During the pilot, two technology teachers were observed. The intention was to identify a teacher who used the strategy to attempt to develop a discourse that enabled gender boundary crossings. The selected teacher was observed over several weeks as he taught the same task to two single-sex classes of students age thirteen to fourteen. Data was collected by observation (video, audio recording, and field notes) and interviews (the teacher and eight students).

Some Findings

The teacher spoke of teaching the "whole student," that is, preparing them for their future life and for flexible work careers by providing them with generic transferable skills, in particular "problem-solving." The teacher recognised the low status of the subject seeing it as "much maligned." However, he took pride in being seen by students as "not like other teachers." The dynamic nature of the subject was evident in the teacher's account of the "old" versus the "new" technology teacher.

> My background is electrical engineering control systems etc. although I've worked in engineering environments so I'm familiar with all the processes and everything else. People like myself, who've been in architectural product design etc and who hadn't been anywhere near a machine or a tool in their life we're the second breed [of teachers] . . . Sometimes it's quite difficult for some of the older lot to have to change and accept that change.

The images the teacher portrayed of the future that he anticipated for the students were overwhelmingly of the domestic realm. In so doing he gave value to the domestic while allowing for both "masculine" and "feminine" behaviors within it.

> [D]ecorating your house, doing little jobs around the house themselves, the ability to cut a bit of wood, the ability to join a bit of wood, help my mum, put a shelf up, hang wallpaper, arrange tiles, carpet fitting, buying a microwave, get the dimensions [for the space of the microwave].

He referred to the decline in the manufacturing base in the United Kingdom and made no reference to technology education as a preparation for future jobs.

In his social representation of gender, he drew on the "feminine" behavior of "learned helplessness." This was in conflict with the teacher's aims for the subject, which were to promote learner autonomy and willingness to take risks, in the teacher's words, "to be adventurous and/or dangerous." Although he made no reference to "masculine" behaviors, risk taking and acceptance of danger are part of a hegemonic social representation of masculinity. He compared himself as a teacher with his role as the "workshop supervisor" when he was an electrical engineer. He was anxious to stress the way he saw the setting as a social space where "nonacademic" conversation was legitimised. He described his view of children as social beings which he saw as in opposition to how they were positioned in academic subjects where isolation was the norm in his view. The community he was trying to reconstruct related back to the workshop. Both of these aspects of his characterisation of the setting reflect the historical subject roots and suggest that boys more than girls might feel a sense of belonging in the setting.

Girls and boys from their interviews understood that designing and making artefacts was the overarching aim of technology education. All students highlighted the dangerous nature of the subject and how important safety and learning how to use tools appropriately was. Only one student, a girl, described the subject aims in terms of her own autonomy to function competently within and beyond school. This was interesting given the extent to which the teacher emphasised capability in life beyond school in his representation of the subject.

The activity the teacher identified was to design and make a vehicle with four wheels that could carry a 2 lb weight and travel 16 feet. For the teacher the skills acquired through the design and making of artefacts such as a model-car had an obvious relevance to life. Thus, measurement in relation to where to drill the holes for the model-car axles was linked to the context of putting up a shelf and buying a microwave to fit a given space. Creating joints was another feature of the activity and for the teacher this knowledge would enable students to "do those little jobs around the house." However, for the students their actions and their learning were associated with the task, as they understood it and this was determined by what they valued and considered important.

All the boys identified meeting the design brief as the main aim of the activity, that is, the task represented by the teacher. The activity had value in its own right. Its purpose was experienced as unproblematic on the whole. One pair of boys turned it into a competition to make the fastest vehicle, which was not a criterion in the brief. The boys worked first on the structure to ensure that it met the design criteria of stability, strength and movement. Two boys emphasised the significance of the movement in terms of structures for example that the wheels should not rub the chassis and the axle should turn smoothly. Only one boy mentioned appearance and talked of making his car "eye catching" but in elaborating this he talked of detailed structural features such as the bonnet. Two boys were explicit that appearance was a secondary consideration. As one put it "it's the capability [not the appearance] of the designs that's key."

The girls tended to put design as the primary concern and meeting the brief as a secondary criterion. Three of the girls gave priority in their design to presentation and the appearance of the finished product. These were considered as important as structures. For one the main concern was appearance, she wanted her car "to be like neat and nice on the top and to be different." This had led her to work with plastic and vacuum formation. The students related these views of salience to the teacher's concerns and his representation of the subject. Yet they suggest a gender–technology interaction that is shaped by students' values that conflict, for some girls, with what is considered legitimate ways of doing technology. For boys there is congruency between their values and those legitimised by the teacher.

Girls were aware of conflicts. One girl explained that the teacher valued meeting the design brief but her personal commitment was to the design. Another student was conscious that the value she placed on design might prevent her from achieving the aim of the activity as she observed, "I don't think mine will make it." This girl sought validation for her product outside of school. In her interview she emphasised the importance of her parents and brother in validating her subject identity in technology to the extent that she was prepared to take a risk. "I'm just hoping that the design mark is really good and it will make the five metres [the 16 feet distance specified]." The study found that for several girls their identity as technologically competent came from the home and allowed them to resist aspects of the teacher's representation of success. Donna's father's active encouragement was important in determining her self-concept in technology.

> My Dad's a builder and he's got them sort of things [tools] at home. I always go out to the garage and play with them and build things . . . Little aeroplanes and things but I'm making a doll's house at the moment.

> When I was little I used to watch him making things and when he did things around the house I used to always do that and want to help make it with him.

Donna was aware too of the gender valence of the technology practices describing them as things "girls don't normally do." She went on to explain:

> When they grow up they're just beauticians or working on computers and all things like that and when something goes wrong, like, my Mum, she can never do [fix] it . . . When I get older I just want to be able to do it all myself instead of relying on everyone else.

Donna understood technology to be about learning how things work "even if you don't get it right." This emphasis on learning through your mistakes was part of the way the teacher addressed girls' perceived technological incompetence. For some girls this was empowering within the setting but it is questionable whether such a view would translate into a positive career aspiration. Donna talked of wanting her artefact "to be different" and how she liked "doing it my own way." The teacher had stressed in his interview that he valued individuality, and Donna saw this as legitimising her reformulation of the teacher's task. Donna was expressing a social identity as a competent female. She was able to take up this identity and manage it because of the teacher's valuing of the domestic realm where Donna already experienced herself as technologically competent. Although the teacher was unaware of this, his representation of the subject provided the possibility for Donna to cross gender boundaries. It also enabled girls to create meaning in the subject as they identified family members as the clients for their products, which enabled the home-school boundary crossing. The home-school boundary crossing was more complex for boys.

The strategy of single-sex organisation was predicated on the need to address girls' deficits within a safe learning environment. Boys were not considered problematic in the context of technology and so common sense beliefs about the way boys are were not challenged. The boys assumed that technology was a "masculine" subject. They did not have to create meaning in the subject but rather assumed it. The teacher's discourse about the relationship between technology and the domestic realm disrupted the assumption that boys' identities were bound up with their relationship to the physical world and labour and therefore valued the opportunity to take home the product of their physical labours. Consequently the role of individual products in enabling the home-school boundary crossing was only supportive for boys with an identity as technologically competent, an identity the teacher assumed. One boy said it was important to him to show his parents what he had achieved. This boy considered himself to be "very competent . . . I always get high marks." Another boy described how he policed what he took home as he anticipated negative feedback particularly from his mother. He saw himself as not very good at technology an identity he was not comfortable with, and an individual product made visible his inadequacies. The assumption of boys' technological competence positioned some boys as "outsiders." Two boys commented on their dislike of the subject and would not continue with it. They considered themselves to be insufficiently skilled to participate successfully. One of these boys related his feelings about the subject to his fear of the machines. "I'm just afraid of hurting myself." The positioning of boys as competent risk takers in technology education does not allow the possibility of the "frightened" boy and seeking help would risk revealing this. The practices of technology education including the emphasis on products made the boundary crossing hazardous for these boys and not worth it. Three of the girls referred to the machines as "scary," "dangerous," and "worrying." However their experience of the single sex setting had been empowering in relation to their access to the machinery. They talked of "knowing how to work it [the machine]" and that "it is nice to be trusted to use the machine." The gender valence of the machines and tools was disrupted in the girls' setting but reinforced in the boys' setting.

Discussion

Large numbers of boys and girls continue to take up traditional subjects in technology post-fourteen. Furthermore achievement patterns suggest that for those who risk crossing gender boundaries the success of these depend on changes in the practices and discourses within technology subjects to transform dominant gender orders and these have yet to be achieved. It is argued that women's marginalisation in technology is a problem for technology itself. Similarly continuing to practice technology in schools without attention to gender mediation is to undermine the purposes and values of the subject, and students' experience of it. Constructivist approaches to science education emphasise the significance of students' prior knowledge in the learning process, although rarely its social and cultural situatedness. However, it is rare for teachers to elicit what students bring to their technology projects and to use these insights to inform their approach. Technology activities typically start with a brainstorm of needs and wants. The needs and wants that students identify reflect their values and commitments. The needs and wants that emerge in turn define the problem space in which students work. While it is essential to allow for and recognise diversity between students it is also important for teachers and students to be aware of the different learning opportunities that may result from students' diverse commitments. Understanding what students consider salient and how that might direct their attention to certain solutions is important for three reasons. First, it impacts on learning; second, it helps to understand how students' may feel positioned in technology education when they struggle to make sense of the value and purpose of tasks; and third, it provides the insights for both teachers and students to challenge gender constructions.

Technology by its very nature is diverse and wide ranging and this provides the possibility for students to engage with it according to their commitments. Students would need however, to understand how their commitments might limit both their solutions and their learning about the subject. To do this the discourse in classrooms has to develop to allow students a voice and a critical stance to what they are asked to study and how they study it. Differences between students in their consideration of the social circumstances of tasks point to the gap between the rhetoric and practice of a subject that has at its core an understanding of social and environmental issues. If the subject were achieving its purposes and giving value to social considerations then teachers' representations of successful students would begin to shift, and "technological" would not be associated with boys' achievements alone. Furthermore boys' tendency to ignore social and environmental circumstances would be seen as a matter for teaching rather than something to be accepted. That these differences remain invisible to most teachers suggests that the gap between rhetoric and practice is not a small one. Teachers' choice of tasks and their understanding of how to consider social issues in a culturally as well as personally authentic way are crucial. Yet evaluation studies suggest that in both respects teachers need support to change their practice.

Evidence from the single-sex classes revealed that the teacher's discourse allowed girls to create meanings in their technology experience that was empowering. He also ensured that their relationship with the tools and machinery was transformed creating a sense of belonging in the workshop. However he did not challenge some of his assumptions about gender–technology interactions and remained unaware that girls' identities relied heavily on validation outside of school in order to resist the view of them as technologically helpless. While some girls' identity in the domestic realm was transformed through the experience, it was not clear that this would in any way impact on their understanding of themselves in relation to the workplace. The research also provided insights into the commitments of girls and the conflict that they experienced between their values and those of the teacher's. From the students' perspective a wider range of learning tasks including an emphasis on design in its own right would enhance their motivation to study at the same time as giving them a more authentic understanding of technology as it is practised in the world. Importantly, practice that represents a broader, holistic vision of the subject would allow students to understand the important relationships between design and production and manufacture. Boys' relationship to technology continues to be viewed as unproblematic. Yet the evidence from the "all-boys" class revealed how a hegemonic representation of masculinity constrained boys' learning. The assumption of boys' expertise denies access to some boys in the same way that an assumption of girls' incompetence denies access to them, positioning them both as outsiders.

Gender–technology interactions are complex and are mediated by students' self-concept in relation to technology and their perceptions of future possible selves, as one girl from the EIS project noted, "although I enjoy electronics and am fascinated by it, I am not thinking of doing it more seriously, I don't see the point." Paying attention to gender and the language of discourse requires a revolution in pedagogy and technology education has long way to go if gender is to become less significant in students' construction of identities in relation to it. The direction in which to move though is increasingly clear and the reward at a minimum might be students who understand themselves to be technologically competent and increasingly see the point of their engagement with it.

References

Brooks, Y. (2003). "Breaking with tradition." *Modus* 3: 4–5.

Brunner, C., Bennett, D.T. and Honey, M. (2000). "Girl games and technological desire." *The Jossey-Bass Reader on Technology and Learning*. R. Pea (ed.), San Francisco: Jossey-Bass Inc., 168–183.

Clegg, S. and W. Mayfield (1999). "Gendered by design: how women's place in design is still defined by gender." *Design Issues* 15(3): 3–16.

DfEE (1999). *The National Curriculum, Handbook for Secondary Teachers in England*, key stages 3 and 4, jointly published by DfEE and QCA.

Dixon, C. (1998). *Action, Embodiment and Gender in the Design and Technology classroom. Gender in the Secondary Curriculum*. A. Clark and E. Millard (eds). London: Routledge, 145–162.

Green, A. (1999). *Technical Education and State Formation in Nineteenth-Century England and France. Perspectives on the Context of Curriculum*. Moon, B. and Murphy, P. (eds). London: Paul Chapman Publishing Ltd, 44–62.

Greenfield, S. (2000). *The Private Life of the Brain*. London: Penguin Books Ltd.

Ivinson, G. and Murphy, P. (2003). "Boys don't write romance: the construction of knowledge and social gender identities in English classrooms." *Pedagogy, Culture and Society* 11(1): 89–111.

James, P. (1999). "Masculinities under reconstruction: classroom pedagogy and cultural change." *Gender and Education* 11(4): 395–412.

Lave, J. (1988). *Cognition in Practice.* Cambridge: Cambridge University Press.

Layton, D. (1993). *Technology's Challenge to Science Education: Cathedral, Quarry, or Company Store?* Buckingham/Philadelphia: Open University Press.

Lewis, T. (1999). *Valid Knowledge and the Problem of Practical Arts Curricula. Perspectives on the Context of Curriculum.* B. Moon and P. Murphy (eds.). London: Paul Chapman Publishing Ltd, 130–147.

Lloyd, B. and Duveen, G. (1992). *Gender Identities and Education: The Impact of Starting School.* Hemel Hempstead: Harvester Wheatsheaf.

Markwick, K. (2001). *Deconstructing Discursive Borders: Conflicting Discourses of Femininity and Techno-Scientific Nationality in the Context of Educational Computing.* AARE 2001 Annual Conference, 2–6 December 2001, Fremantle, WA: Australian Association for Research in Education.

Murphy, P. (1991). *Gender Differences in Pupils' Reactions to Practical Work. Practical Science.* B. Woolnough (ed.). Milton Keynes/Philadelphia: Open University Press, 112–122.

Murphy, P. (1999). *Supporting Collaborative Learning: A Gender Dimension. Learners, Learning and Assessment.* P. Murphy (ed.). London: Paul Chapman Publishing Ltd, 258–276.

Murphy, P. and Davidson, M. (1997). *Evaluation: First phase, Nuffield Design and Technology in the Primary Curriculum.* London: Nuffield Foundation and The Open University.

Murphy, P. and Ivinson, G. (2004). *Gender Differences in Educational Achievement: a Socio-Cultural Analysis. Culture and Learning.* M. Olssen (ed.). Connecticut: Information Age Publishing, 365–386.

Murphy, P., McCormick, B., Lunn, S., Davidson, M., and Jones, H. (2004). *Evaluation of the Promotion of Electronics in Schools Regional Pilot: Final Report of the Evaluation.* London: The Department of Trade and Industry and The Open University, 204.

Murphy, P. and Whitelegg, E. (2006). *Research Review for the Institute of Physics on the Participation of Girls in Physics.* London: The Institute of Physics.

Paechter, C. (2003). "Power/knowledge, gender and curriculum change." *Journal of Educational Change* 4: 129–148.

Paechter, C. and Head, J.C. (1996). "Gender, identity, status and the body: life in a marginal subject." *Gender and Education* 8(1): 21–29.

Rennie, L.J. (2003). " 'Pirates can be male or female': investigating gender-inclusivity in a years 2/3 classroom." *Research in Science Education* 33: 515–528.

Roger, A. and Duffield, J. (2000). "Factors underlying persistent gendered option choices in school science and technology in Scotland." *Gender and Education* 12(3): 367–383.

Southwell, M. (1997). "Black stockings and pot pourri: gender issues in design and technology." *International Journal of Art and Design Education* 16(2): 181–189.

Stepulevage, L. (2001). "Gender/technology relations: complicating the gender binary." *Gender and Education* 13(3): 332.

Wajcman, J. (1991). *Feminism Confronts Technology.* Pennsylvania: The Pennsylvania State University Press.

CHAPTER 15

Implicit Theories: Their Impact on Technology Education

Wendy Dow

There is a growing recognition among educationalists and policy makers at an international level that in order to promote an active interest in technology education, significant changes are necessary. These include the promotion of pedagogies that provide for authentic and relevant learning experiences, opportunities to develop creativity, and the development of autonomous and motivated learners able to engage with the profound social and cultural changes brought about by the impact of technological advancement upon society. Central to this notion is the development of a technological literacy for all. In a number of countries across the Western world, policy has consequently been adapted in an attempt to accommodate this new view of technology education. There has been a subsequent move away from the view of technology education as a prescriptive skills-based, vocationally oriented subject most suitable for less academic pupils, towards a view that technology education must equip all pupils with the skills necessary for active and critical engagement with an increasingly technologically mediated world.

Despite these shifts in thinking, however, there is increasing evidence at an international level that these policy changes are too frequently failing to have any significant impact on practice in the technology classroom. Despite the development of new curricula and the promotion of the most recent theories of effective learning and teaching in courses for both pre-service and experienced teachers, the gap between policy and practice, between rhetoric and reality, remains an important area of concern (Dakers, 2005; Volk, 2005).

A wide variety of factors can clearly account for this. In many countries, for example, an increasingly aging teaching population is perceived to be a significant barrier to change. Assessment methods that drive the curriculum and encourage the regurgitation of earlier-learned facts is another factor, as is a lack of resources and materials to accommodate new ways of teaching in the technology classroom (Dakers and Dow, 2004).

This tension between theory and practice, and between policy and practice, however, is by no means new, and there would appear to be two main areas of concern in relation to this. The first is the resistance to change of teachers already in place, with Yerrick, Parke, and Nugent (1997), for example, demonstrating that resistance can persist even in the face of intensive courses designed to encourage change.

The second is the difficulty of persuading student teachers to adopt current theories and policies in the face of opposition in schools (Zeichner and Tabachnick, 1981). Student teachers traditionally complain about the "ivory tower" attitudes of policy makers and academics, claiming that what works in theory seldom works in the real world of busy classrooms. More recent research, moreover, has highlighted the almost insurmountable difficulties experienced by those new teachers who *do* attempt to introduce innovative methods into a system in which attempts at innovation are too often met with lukewarm support or outright resistance. (Long, 2004).

> Because they are weary of the constant battle to find a place to learn and grow, too many teachers join the status quo or leave teaching altogether. They lose hope, confidence, and, most frighteningly, a sense of themselves as knowledgeable professionals. (Long, 2004: 142)

Indeed, there appears to exist at all levels of the profession, a resistance to change that may not be easily overcome, but the source of which must be identified and addressed if the changes envisaged by academics and policy makers are to become a reality in the technology classrooms of tomorrow.

It is the contention of this chapter that an important source of this resistance is the implicit theories that both teachers and student teachers of technology hold, about not only such issues as the nature of their subject and its place in the curriculum, but the nature of effective teaching and learning itself.

The idea that implicit belief systems inform and shape our social worlds has been a recurring theme throughout the history of psychological research. Heider's (1958) notion of the social perceiver as "naïve scientist" and Kelly's (1955) theory of personal constructs, for example, have helped to lay the foundation for the investigation of the types of lay theories or folk psychologies that influence our every-day thoughts and actions. These beliefs are not necessarily easily articulated, nor are they even always available for conscious scrutiny. Acquired gradually through experience, these implicit systems (variously defined as theories, beliefs, attitudes, values, or knowledge) have origins, which are shrouded in the mists of the past, but can nevertheless exert a powerful influence both upon our interpretation of new information and upon how we act in any given situation.

Consider, for example, a group of student teachers embarking upon a course designed to produce teachers of technology education for deployment in secondary schools. Each will have had a minimum of ten or eleven years' intensive personal experience as pupils within the existing education system. This experience will have started at an early and impressionable age, and each will consequently have developed important underlying assumptions (or implicit theories) about what education in general and technology education in particular is all about. Unlike novices entering other professions, these particular novices will have extensive, deep-rooted knowledge and firmly formed conceptions of the world they are about to enter. Whereas most students approach their chosen academic disciplines as strangers entering unknown environments, pre-service teachers are in fact insiders entering familiar territory. They have no need to define their surroundings, accommodate new information, or assimilate new ideas or beliefs. Prepared, as Lortie (1975) suggests by an apprenticeship of many years' observation, commitment to prior implicit theories and beliefs may be particularly strong.

There is, then, an important distinction to be made between the "expert" theories developed by academic researchers through the systematic collection and investigation of data, and these spontaneous implicit or tacit theories, attitudes or beliefs that are developed through our personal perception of, and every day interaction with, the world. Indeed, many writers highlight this distinction between academic (or espoused) theories, which are used to *explain* action, and implicit theories, which are often evident only *in* action (see Schon, 1983). This distinction has particularly important implications for the development of teachers of technology education.

It has perhaps been too easy to assume that, when confronted with academic theories, these earlier theories will be altered or replaced. What is perhaps more likely is that these previously formed theories will be overlaid but will remain, albeit perhaps at a less accessible level. They may nevertheless be activated when circumstances permit and can thus exert a profound but subtle influence on classroom practice.

Once formed, moreover, these implicit attitudes or theories form frameworks within which new information is interpreted and stored. Thus information and material that validates the implicit theory held are more readily selected and accepted while material that contradicts or threatens is rejected or ignored (Kennedy, 1997). Thus, aspects of theory taught in initial-teacher-education courses may be distorted or rejected, making little overall impact on the underlying theories held.

Context, however, is also an important factor, and a complex relationship will exist between implicit and explicit theories and the context within which action occurs. The context of any technology classroom will result from a subtle and intricate interaction of, for example, school ethos, central policies governing curricula and assessment, the demands of head teachers and department heads, and pupil expectations. The extent to which implicit theories will govern action will depend on the extent to which the context is supportive of the particular implicit theories held.

Consider, for example, the experience of a student who has been educated at school within a behaviorist tradition of technology education and whose implicit theories are therefore firmly embedded within this model. These implicitly held theories will influence ideas relating to the nature of knowledge within the subject, how that knowledge is to be presented, the degree of teacher control over learning considered necessary or desirable, and beliefs about how pupils are motivated to both learn and behave. The initial teacher-education-course attended may include many sessions promoting theories of teaching and learning intended to challenge and change these views. These newly encountered theories will have been espoused in written assignments, discussion groups, and examination answers. But whether or not they will translate into practice will depend on a complexity of factors. Where there is a mismatch between the implicit theory and the espoused, such aspects as the degree of motivation to override the implicit theory versus the extent to which the implicit theory finds validation in the context of the school or department will ultimately determine which will exert the greater influence.

While it is possible to have implicit theories about any aspect of our social world, there are clearly some aspects that will have particular importance in the field of technology education.

Dweck Chui and Hong's (1995) model of implicit theories provides one conceptual framework for analyzing ways of responding to our social world that has important implications for technology classrooms. According to this model, two fundamentally different worldviews exist, which in turn influence how we process and respond to a range of social information. A core assumption of these views relates to the stable, versus malleable nature of human attributes. Thus, constructs such as intelligence and personality can be implicitly regarded on the one hand as global, stable, and innate or, on the other hand as flexible, fluid, and context dependent.

One construct that fits into this category and that has particular importance for technology teachers is that of creativity. The most recent "expert" sociocultural theories of creativity stress the importance of the environment in engendering interest, motivation, and commitment (Amabile, 1983), thus suggesting an incremental view of creativity, and this has found reflection in modern policy-documents (see Scottish 5–14 National Guidelines, for example). Like intelligence, however, creativity can also be regarded as a fixed and global personality trait. Teachers who hold an implicit-entity theory of creativity are less likely to create the kind of motivational climate suggested by current policy and research.

The characteristics associated with the creative personality in Western cultures moreover, are not those that are generally valued within the traditional Western behaviorist tradition of education. Although the majority of teachers traditionally *espouse* support for the fostering of creativity in the classroom (Feldhusen and Treffinger, 1975), studies have demonstrated that this explicit view has not always translated into classroom practice, with recent studies suggesting that children rated as highly creative tend to be regarded as belligerent, defiant, or more disruptive than the "less creative" pupils (Scott, 1999). Teachers who hold implicit-entity theories of creativity are therefore more likely to use teaching methods designed to control behaviors considered undesirable, thus in fact stifling creativity. Teachers who hold incremental views on the other hand are less likely to associate creativity with particular personality traits and will therefore take contextual and other factors into account. In this case, creativity will be regarded as a quality that all pupils possess, not just a privileged but difficult-to-deal-with few. These teachers are more likely to create the kind of environments in which tasks offered are open ended to allow for individual choice, in which autonomous learning is encouraged, and time is given for the genuine development of ideas.

Dweck's conceptual model also has important implications for motivation, identifying "the contemporaneous, dynamic psychological factors that influence such phenomena as the choice, initiation, direction, magnitude, persistence, resumption and quality of goal directed (including cognitive) activity"(1983: 645).

Pupils will clearly select motivational goals for themselves, based both upon their own implicit conceptions of ability and on the type of structures created within the classroom. However, the role of the teacher in fostering these views is a crucial one.

For example, the extent to which a technology teacher implicitly believes that motivation comes from within as opposed to without, or is fostered by competition rather than cooperation, and the extent to which these views are supported or challenged by the school and classroom context will have important implications for the ways in which tasks are structured and how children are encouraged to engage.

In the technology classroom in which motivation is implicitly seen as arising from competition and external rewards, prescriptive tasks are more likely to be evident. Control will be in the hands of the teacher as each small step in the process of manufacture of an artifact is demonstrated and copied by the pupils in unison. Each stage of the work will be assessed by the teacher, with praise or admonishment delivered according to the degree of satisfaction with the outcome. Comparison with the work of others will be encouraged and an individualistic competitive environment fostered. The focus will be on performance, rather than on learning, with marks awarded for the quality of completed artifacts, rather than what has been learned.

In the technology classroom in which motivation is implicitly seen as arising from cooperative working, interest in, and intrinsic enjoyment gained through, active engagement with the process, however, a very different picture will emerge. Within this environment, tasks will be structured to ensure what Johnson and Johnson (1999) define as "positive interdependence"—a situation in which a successful group-outcome is entirely dependent upon the success of each individual member of that group. Assessment within this structure will be formative, with a focus on the development of peer and self- assessment. Emphasis will be placed on individual and group improvement over time, rather than a comparison of one person or group with another. Thus, any competitive ethos will be reduced or eliminated. Collaboration will be further encouraged through the fostering of group discussion and debate, problem solving and decision-making. Within this structure, the role implicitly adopted by the teacher will be one in which the focus is on challenge and facilitation rather than control.

The structuring of technology classrooms arising from these differing implicit-theoretical stances will, moreover, have important implications for achievement. Whereas environments that have been structured to foster collaboration have been found to result in increases in academic success (Slavin, 1995), the fostering of a competitive ethos has been found to have the detrimental effects of reducing both intrinsic motivation and creativity (Ryan and Deci, 2000) and adversely affecting both interpersonal relationships and attitudes towards school (Nichols, 1989).

The very nature of technology education and its role within the school curriculum are other areas in which the powerful impact of implicit theories can be found. The extent to which technology education is implicitly regarded as a haven for the less-academic pupil or an entitlement for all, the extent to which importance is attached to the production of future skilled-members of the workforce or to the development of technologically informed and literate global citizens will have a profound effect on all aspects of content and delivery and will in turn influence the perceptions of pupils and teachers alike.

Where technology education is implicitly regarded as a vocational subject for less-academic pupils, for example, the emphasis is more likely to be on the acquisition of psychomotor skills and the production of artifacts of varying degrees of meaningfulness and authenticity. Where it is implicitly regarded as an entitlement for all, and an important part of the development of the individual, however, both content and delivery will be markedly different. Within this framework, there will be a recognition that all young people exist in a technologically mediated world and that the nature of their experience within this world will to a large extent be dependent upon the degree to which they are prepared to enter an informed debate regarding the impact of technologies upon their lives. The emphasis within this theoretical framework will be less on the development of skills and the production of artifacts, and more upon debate and discussion, upon the development of a technological literacy—an awareness of the impact of technology, both desirable and undesirable, upon humans at the level of both the individual and society.

Closely connected to this is the variety of ways in which the concept of technological literacy can be perceived and consequently delivered within the school curriculum. This again may be an important function of the implicit theories that technology teachers hold. The term "technological literacy" can for example be defined in a number of different ways and at a number of different levels, each of which will impact upon both content and delivery within the curriculum. At the most basic level, technological literacy can be perceived as the acquisition of the skills necessary to make effective use of the various forms of technology encountered in the modern world. At this level a demonstration of competence in the use of, for example, the computer, the mobile tele-phone, or the fax machine will be regarded as sufficient evidence of technological literacy. The adoption of this type of implicit theory of technological literacy in turn lends itself to an expert, transmission, skills-based model of teaching in which the focus is on the passing on of previously existing knowledge.

At the next level of definition, there may be an emphasis, not simply on the acquisition of skills, but also upon the development of under-standing. Where this level is adopted, however, it is likely that this will simply involve an understanding of the various functions of the tech-nologies, rather than a consideration of their impact upon either the individual or society. Where technological literacy is interpreted at its deepest level, however, there will be an implicit recognition of its role in the processes of empowerment and democratization. This in turn will result in the adoption of a very different type of pedagogy involving dialectic argumentation and debate (Dakers, 2002).

If, as has been suggested, implicit theories can impact so powerfully, this raises the question of what can be done to affect the type of change to the system of teaching considered necessary in order to develop a truly technologically literate population. Two main problems appear to exist. One concerns the covert nature of implicit theories, the other the extent to which they may be resistant to change.

If, as Schon (1983) has suggested, implicit theories that influence action are evident only in action, the question of how technology teach-ers can be made aware of the implicit theories that they hold is one that must be addressed.

The very range and variety of methodologies employed in attempts to expose implicit theories to scrutiny and challenge, however, in itself bears testimony to the problems involved in making the implicit explicit. These include standardized questionnaires specifically devised to explore entity or incremental theories of intelligence and personality, the use of concept-generation exercises such as the Kelly (1955) Repertory Grid, narrative studies, exploration of the metaphors that people use to describe education and teaching, in-depth stimulated recall interviews, observation to explore theory in action, and case stud-ies involving multiple methods of investigation. There is evidence to suggest, moreover, that even when these are made explicit, this in itself may not be sufficient to affect changes in practice.

Although it has been demonstrated, for example, that changes in implicit theories can be manipulated under laboratory conditions (e.g., Hong et al., 1999), studies carried out under more natural conditions have proven more problematic with Entwistle, Skinner, and Entwistle (2000), for example, concluding that implicit theories may, in the final analysis, be resistant to change. "The course did not seem to change firmly held views about teaching, rather it showed how those beliefs could be justified from evidence, and "operationalized" within teaching practice" (1).

The fact that implicit theories may be difficult to elicit and are resistant to change does not, however, mean that change cannot be affected.

One important factor may be the degree of opportunity provided for the new teacher to engage in *action* that directly challenges the implicit theory held. Research into attitude change may be useful in this respect. Where there is a match between classroom structures and policy, and academic theories, but where these are at odds with the implicit theories held, there will be pressure on teachers to act in ways in keeping with the context, rather than with the implicit theories held. Acting in a way that runs counter to implicit theories held will, according to Festinger's (1957) theory of cognitive dissonance, result in one of three possibilities. One is that the behavior will change to bring it into line with the implicit theory, thus reducing cognitive dissonance. This is, however, unlikely since the new teacher will generally be anxious both to fit into the system and to succeed. The more likely possibility therefore is either that the implicit theory will be overridden or suppressed in order to reduce dissonance or that new reasons to justify the actions that are in conflict with the implicit theory held will be sought. Either way, the more frequent the opportunities for putting espoused academic theory into practice and the greater the feelings of success encountered by so doing, the greater the likelihood of espoused theories becoming an automatic part of action.

Where implicit theories are supported by school structures and policies that do *not* reflect current policy-measures and academic theories on the other hand, the result will be an absence of cognitive dissonance. In this case, implicit theories will be supported by context and evident in action. The chances of practice endorsing changes in policy will be remote.

This has particularly important implications for the careful choice of school placement for student teachers of technology education. Where the academic theory taught on university or college courses promotes a collaborative, creative, critically analytic approach to technology education, and the implicit theories held by student teachers tend towards a reductionist, behaviorist skills-acquisition approach, if the school context supports the former, there is a greater likelihood of change than if the school context supports the implicit theories held. Thus a careful matching of school placement and student teacher in accordance with the implicit theories held will be necessary in any attempt to bring about change.

In-depth opportunities to explore, make explicit, and challenge the implicit theories held by both student teachers and experienced teachers should become an integral part of technology education courses. A critical analysis of the practice both encountered in schools and of student teachers in relation to both academic and implicit theories and recent policies could be used to identify crucial matches, mismatches, and potential pitfalls.

Change, of course, is not only imperative at the level of initial teacher-education. The resistance of teachers already in place is also an issue in challenging the status quo. Here again, it has perhaps been too easy to assume that the provision of in-service courses promoting recent policy and academic theories of teaching and learning are sufficient to impact upon the implicit theories that teachers already hold. This is where carefully developed policy-measures have an important part to play. Where policies can bring about changes in actual *behavior*, there may be a greater chance of change. Policy measures that firmly place the focus of assessment on the processes of learning, rather than on performance, for example, may go a long way to change the way that teachers of technology not only act on, but ultimately believe, at an implicit level about content, delivery, and the type of classroom structures best designed to promote effective learning.

In addition, there may well be a need for lecturers of technology education courses in universities and colleges to explore, through a careful analysis of their own practice, the implicit theories that they themselves may hold. Whereas such courses may well *espouse* the importance of developing creativity, authenticity, agency, and technological literacy within a social constructivist pedagogy, the manner in which such courses are delivered may well in fact reflect and thus reinforce a reductionist transmission, behaviorist approach to the teaching of technology education. As long as this is the case, the potential for any significant change in the subject may continue to be problematic.

References

Amabile, T.(1983). *The Social Psychology of Creativity*. New York: Springer-Verlag.

Dakers, J. (2005). "Technology Education in Scotland. An investigation of the past twenty years." In: Marc J de Vries (ed.) (2005). *PATT-15 Pupils Attitudes*

Towards Technology. International conference on design and technology educational research proceedings. available on line at: http://www.iteawww.org/D4c.html

Dakers, J. (2002). Dialectic methodology: The impact of incorporating a Neo-Vygotskian approach to design and technology. In E.W.L. Norman (ed.), *DATA International Research and UK Education Conference Book*: 45–50. http://www.iteaconnect.org/PATT15/PATT15.html

Dakers, J. and Dow, W. (2004). *Implementation of "Education and Training 2010"* Work programme. Working group D; "Increasing participation in math, science and technology." Mapping of policies supporting the implementation of the 2003 Recommendations agreed upon by working group D: Annex to the progress report. Published by the European commission. Available at: http://europa.eu.int/comm/education/policies/2010/otherdoc_en.html

Dweck, C., Chiu, C., and Hong, Y. (1995). "Implicit theories and their role in judgements and reactions: a world from two perspectives." *Psychological Inquiry*. 6: 4, 267–285.

Dweck, C. and Elliott, E. (1983). "Achievement motivation." In P. Mussen (ed.), *Handbook of Child Psychology (4th Ed.) 1V: Socialisation, Personality and Social Development*. New York: John Wiley and Sons.

Entwistle, N., Skinner, D., and Entwistle, D. (2000). "The nature and possible origins of 'good teaching' among student teachers." Paper presented at the *European Conference on Educational Research*, Edinburgh, 20–23 September. Available at http: www.leeds.ac.uk/educol/documents/00001604.html

Feldhusen, J. and Treffinger, D. (1975). "Teachers' attitudes and practices in teaching creativity and problem solving to economically disadvantaged and minority children." *Psychological Reports*, 37, 1161–62.

Festinger, L. (1957). *A Theory of Cognitive Dissonance*. Stanford, CA: Stanford University Press.

Heider, F. (1958). *The Psychology of Interpersonal Relations*. New York: John Wiley and Sons.

Hong, Y., Chui, C., Dweck, C., Derrick, M., and Wan, W. (1999). "Implicit Theories, attributions, and coping: a meaning system approach." *Journal of Personality and Social Psychology*, 77: 3 588–599.

Johnson, D. and Johnson, R. (1999). *Learning Together d Alone: Cooperative, Competitive, and Individualistic Learning* (5th Edition). London: Allyn and Bacon.

Kelly, G. (1955). *The Psychology of Personal Constructs* (Vols 1–2). New York: Norton.

Kennedy, M. (1997). *Defining an Ideal Teacher Education Program* (mimeo). Washington DC: National Council for the Association of Teacher Education

Long, S. (2004). "Separating rhetoric from reality: supporting teachers in negotiating beyond the status quo." *Journal of Teacher Education*, 55: 2, 141–153.

Lortie, D. (1975). *School Teacher*. Chicago: University of Chicago Press.

Nichols, J. (1989). *The Competitive Ethos and Democratic Education*. Cambridge, MA: Harvard University Press.

Ryan, R. and Deci, E. (2000). "When rewards compete with nature: the undermining of intrinsic motivation and self regulation." In C. Sansone and J. Harackiewicz (eds), *Intrinsic and Extrinsic Motivation: The Search for Optimal Motivation and Performance*. New York: Academic Press.

Slavin, R. (1995). *Cooperative Learning* (2nd Edition). Boston, MA: Allyn and Bacon

Schon, D. (1983). *The Reflective Practitioner: How Professionals Think in Action*. London: Ashgate.

Scott, C. (1999). "Teachers' biases towards creative children." *Creativity Research Journal*, 12, 321–328.

Volk, K. (2005). "The rhetoric and reality of technology education in Hong Kong." Paper delivered at the 15th PATT (Pupils' Attitudes Towards Technology) Conference. Haarlem, Netherlands.

Yerrick, R., Parke, H., and Nugent, J. (1997). "Struggling to promote deeply rooted change: the 'filtering effect' of teachers' beliefs on understanding transformational views of teaching science." *Science Education*, 81, 137–159.

Zeichner, K. and Tabachnick, B. (1981). "Are the effects of university teacher education 'washed out' by school experience?" *Journal of Teacher Education*, 32: 3, 7–11.

PART IV

Considering Globalization, Computers, the World-Wide Web, and their Impact in Developing Technological Literacy

CHAPTER 16

Reconstructing Technoliteracy: A Multiple Literacies Approach

Richard Kahn and Douglas Kellner

The application of electric agencies to means of communication, transportation, lighting of cities and houses, and more economical production of goods . . . are social ends, moreover, and if they are too closely associated with notions of private profit, it is not because of anything in them, but because they have been deflected to private uses: a fact which puts upon the school the responsibility of restoring their connection in the mind of the coming generation, with public scientific and social interests.

(Dewey, 1916)

The ongoing debate about the nature and benefits of technoliteracy is without a doubt one of the most hotly contested topics in education today. Alongside their related analyses and recommendations, the last two decades have seen a variety of state and corporate stake holders, academic disciplinary factions, cultural interests, and social organizations ranging from the local to the global weigh in with competing definitions of "technological literacy." Whereas utopian notions such as Marshall McLuhan's "global village" (1964) and H.G. Wells's "world brain" (1938) imagined a technological world of growing unity in diversity, ours is perhaps better characterized as the highly complex and socio–politically stratified global culture of media spectacle and the ever-developing mega-technics of a worldwide information (Castells 1996), cum technocapitalist infotainment society (Kellner, 2003a: 11–15). As such, there is presently little reason to expect general agreement as regards what types of knowledge are entailed by technoliteracy, what sorts of practices might most greatly inform it, or even as to what institutional formations technoliteracy can best serve and be served by in kind. Further, despite the many divergent and conflicting views about technoliteracy that presently exist, it is only relatively recently that existing debates have begun to be challenged and informed by oppositional movements based on race, class, gender, anti-imperialism, and the ecological well-being of all. As these varying movements begin to ask their own questions about the ever-dovetailing realms of technology and the construction of a globalized culture, political realm, and economy, we may well yet see technoliteracy become more multiple in one sense, even as it becomes more and more singularly important in another.

Much has been written that describes the history of the concept of "technological literacy" (Petrina, 2000; Selfe, 1999; Jenkins, 1997; Waetjen, 1993; Lewis and Gagel, 1992; Dyrenfurth, 1991; Todd, 1991; Hayden, 1989) and, as noted, a literature attempting to chart emancipatory technoliteracies has begun to emerge over the last decade (Kellner, 2004, 2003c, 1998; Lankshear and Snyder, 2000; Petrina, 2000; Luke, 1997; Bromley and Apple, 1998; O'Tuathail and McCormack, 1999; Burbules and Callister, 1996; McLaren, Hammer, Sholle and Reilly, 1995). We do not seek to reinvent the wheel here or reproduce yet another account of the same. However, considering that tremendous variance exists in the published definitions of technoliteracy, it will prove fruitful to begin with a brief examination of the meanings that "technology" and "literacy" have received towards achieving insight into what sort of knowledge and skills "technoliteracy" hails.

From this, we will seek to summarize the broad trajectories of development in hegemonic programs of contemporary technoliteracy from their arguable origins as "computer literacy" in the United States' *A Nation at Risk* report of 1983, through the Clinton years and the economic boom of information-communication technologies (ICTs) in the 1990s, up to the present call for integration of technology across the curriculum and the standards-based approach of the *No Child Left Behind Act of 2001* and 2004s U.S. *National Educational Technology Plan*. Agreeing with Petrina (2000), that such U.S. government policies are largely the construction of a neutralized version of technoliteracy which bolsters a conservative politics of ideological "competitive supremacy," we will show how this has been tacitly challenged at the global institutional level through the United Nations' Project 2000+.

We aim at showing how these contestations link up with the oppositional democratic project for the re-visioning of education though multiple literacies. Finally, in closing, we think about what it will mean to reconstruct "technoliteracies" with pedagogies and social movements that can actively transform mainstream understandings, policies, and practices of technoliteracy through the politicization of the hegemonic norms that currently pervade social terrains towards alternative goals.

Technology, Literacy, Technoliteracy: Definitions

"Technological literacy is a term of little meaning and many meanings" (Todd, 1991). Upon first consideration, seeking a suitable definition of "technology" itself appears to be overly technical. Surely, in discussions concerning technology, it is rare indeed that people need to pause so as to ask for a clarification of the term. In a given context, if it is suggested that technology is either causing problems or alleviating them, people generally know what sort of thing is due for blame or praise.

Yet, the popular meaning of "technology" is problematically insufficient in at least two ways. First, it narrowly equivocates technological artifacts with "high-tech," such as those scientific machines used in medical and biotechnology, modern industrial apparatus, and digital components like computers, ICTs, and other electronic media. This reductive view fails to recognize, for instance, that indigenous artifacts are themselves technologies in their own right, as well as other cultural objects that may once have represented the leading-edge of technological inventiveness during previous historical eras, such as books, hand tools, or even clothing. Secondly, popular conceptions of technology today make the additional error of construing technology as being merely object-oriented, identifying it as only the sort of machined products that arise through industry. In fact, from the first, technology has always meant far more. Its complexity is reflected in recent definitions of technology as "a seamless web or network combining artifacts, people, organizations, cultural meanings and knowledge" (Wajcman, 2004: 106), or as that which "comprises the entire system of people and organizations, knowledge, processes, and devices that go into creating and operating technological artifacts, as well as the artifacts themselves" (Pearson and Young, 2002).

These broader definitions of technology are supported by the important insights of John Dewey. For Dewey, technology is central to humanity and girds human inquiry in its totality (Hickman, 2001). In his view, technology is evidenced in all manner of creative experience and problem-solving. Technology should extend beyond the sciences proper, according to Dewey, as it encompasses not only the arts and humanities, but the professions, and the practices of our everyday lives. In this account, technology is inherently political and historical, and in Dewey's philosophy it is strongly tethered to notions of democracy and education, which are considered technologies that intend social progress and greater freedom for the future.

Dewey's view is hardly naïve, but it is unabashedly optimistic and hopeful that it is within the nature of humanity that people may be sufficiently educated so as to be able to understand the problems that they face and that they can experimentally produce and deploy a wide range of technologies so as to solve those problems accordingly. While we agree with Dewey's constructivist and activist take on technologies, we also recognize that the present age is potentially beset by the unprecedented problem of globalized technological oppressions in many forms.

To this end, we seek to highlight the insights of radical social critic and technology theorist Ivan Illich (Kahn and Kellner, *forthcoming*). Specifically, Illich's notion of "tools" mirrors the broad humanistic understanding of technology outlined so far, while it additionally distinguishes "rationally designed devices, be they artifacts or rules, codes or operators . . . from other things such as food or implements, which in a given culture are not deemed to be subject to rationalization" (Illich 1973: 22). Consequently, Illich polemicizes for "tools for conviviality," which are technologies mindfully constructed and used to work within the balances of both cultural and natural limits. In our view, technology so defined will prove useful for the twenty-first-century technoliteracy challenged to meet the demands of a sustainable and ecumenical world.

One of the great insights of Marshall McLuhan is that new media produce new environments in which people live and navigate (1964). For instance, electricity produced entirely new urban and living spaces as well as new sciences that contributed to the development of contemporary physics as well as made new technologies, including the Internet. For McLuhan, a new technology of communication creates a new environment and he has theories of progression of stages of society and culture depending on dominant media, moving from oral culture through print culture and electronic media. New media for McLuhan require new literacies and we would argue that he provides an important rationale for reconstructing education and developing the multiple technoliteracies we are discussing in this study in order to properly perceive, navigate, and act in the new technological envionment.

"Literacy" is another concept, often used by educators and policy makers, but in a variety of ways and for a broad array of purposes. In its initial form, basic literacy equated to vocational proficiency with language and numbers such that individuals could function at work and in society. Thus, even at the start of the twentieth century, literacy largely meant the ability to write one's name and decode popular print-based texts, with the additional goal of written self-expression only emerging over the following decades. Street (1984) identifies these attributes as typical of an autonomous model of literacy that is politically conservative in that it is primarily economistic, individualistic, and is driven by a deficit theory of learning. On the other hand, Street characterizes ideological models of literacy as prefiguring positive notions of collective empowerment, social context, the encoding and decoding of non-print-based and print-based texts, as well as a progressive commitment to critical thinking-oriented skills.

In our conception, "literacy" is not a singular set of abilities but is multiple and comprises gaining competencies involved in effectively using socially constructed forms of communication and representation. Learning literacies requires attaining competencies in practices and in contexts that are governed by rules and conventions and we see literacies as being necessarily socially constructed in educational and cultural practices involving various institutional discourses and pedagogies. Against the autonomous view that posits literacy as static, we see literacies as continuously evolving and shifting in response to social and cultural changes, as well as the interests of the elites who control hegemonic institutions. Further, it is a crucial part of the literacy process that people come to understand dominant literacy codes as "hegemonic." Thus, our conception of literacy follows Freire and Macedo (1987) in conceiving literacy as tethered to issues of power. As they note, literacy is a cultural politics that "promotes democratic and emancipatory change" (viii) and it should be interpreted widely as the ability to engage in a variety of forms of problem-posing and dialectical analyses of self and society.

Based on our definitions of "technology" and "literacy" it should be obvious that, holistically conceived, literacies are themselves technologies involving meta-inquiry processes that serve to facilitate and regulate technological systems. In this respect, to speak of "technoliteracies" may seem inherently tautological. On the other hand, however, it also helps to highlight the constructed and potentially reconstructive nature of literacies, as well as the educative, social, and political nature of technologies. In today's educational context of ever multiplying information and entertainment technologies, technoliteracy is inevitably associated with proficiencies in new media and technology. More than ever, we need philosophical reflection on the ends and purposes of education and on what we are doing and trying to achieve in our educational practices and institutions. Such would be a technoliteracy in its deepest sense.

Hence, we see contemporary technoliteracies as involved with the need to comprehend and make use of proliferating high-technologies, and the political economy that drives them, towards furthering radical democratic understandings and transformations of our lives, as well as a democratic reconstruction of education. In a world inexorably undergoing processes of globalization and technological transformation, we cannot advocate a policy of clean hands and purity, in which people shield themselves from new technologies and their transnational proliferation. Instead, technoliteracies must be deployed and promoted that allow for popular interventions into the ongoing (often antidemocratic) economic and technological revolutions taking place, thereby potentially deflecting these forces for progressive ends like social justice and ecological well-being.

Consequently, technoliteracies encompass the computer, information, critical media, and multimedia literacies presently theorized under the concept "multiliteracies" (Cope and Kalantzis, 2000; Luke, 2000, 1997; Rassool, 1999; New London Group, 1996). But whereas multiliteracies theory often remains focused upon digital technologies, with an implicit thrust towards providing new media job skills for the Internet age, we seek to explicitly highlight the social and cultural appropriateness of technologies and provide a critique of the media and information economy as technocapitalist (Best and Kellner, 2001; Kellner, 1989), while acknowledging its progressive potentials. Thus, we draw upon the language of "multiple literacies" (Lonsdale and McCurry, 2004; Kellner, 2000) to augment a critical theory of technoliteracies that we develop in this study.

Functional and Market-Based Technoliteracy: The United States

> From being a Nation at Risk we might now be more accurately described as a Nation on the Move. As these encouraging trends develop and expand over the next decade, facilitated and supported by our ongoing investment in educational technology . . . we may be well on our way to a new golden age in American education. (U.S. Department of Education, 2004)

The fledging Internet, then known as the ARPANET due to its development as a research project of U.S. Defense Advanced Research Projects Agency (DARPA), was still a year away when the *Phi Delta Kappan* published the following utopian call for a computer-centric technoliteracy:

> Just as books freed serious students from the tyranny of overly simple methods of oral recitation, so computers can free students from the

drudgery of doing exactly similar tasks unadjusted and untailored to their individual needs. As in the case of other parts of our society, our new and wondrous technology is there for beneficial use. It is our problem to learn how to use it well. (Suppes: 423)

However, it was mainly not until *A Nation at Risk* (1983) that literacy in computers was popularly cited as particularly crucial for education. The report resurrected a critique of American schools made during the cold-war era that sufficient emphases (specifically in science and technology) were lacking in curriculum for U.S. students to compete in the global marketplace of the future, as it prognosticated the coming of a high-tech "information age." Occurring in the midst of the first great boom of personal computers (PCs), *A Nation at Risk* recommended primarily for the creation of a half-year class in computer science that would: "equip graduates to (a) understand the computer as an information, computation, and communication device; (b) use the computer in the study of the other Basics and for personal and work-related purposes; and (c) understand the world of computers, electronics, and related technologies" (National Commission on Excellence in Education, 1983).

While *A Nation at Risk* declared that experts were then unable to classify "technological literacy" in unambiguous terms, the document clearly argues for such literacy to be understood in more functional understandings of computer (Aronowitz, 1985; Apple, 1992) and information (Plotnick, 1999) literacy. Technology, such as the computer, was to be seen for the novel skill sets it afforded and professional discourse began to hype the "new vocationalism" in which the needs of industry were identified as educational priorities (Grubb, 1996). Surveying this development, Stephen Petrina (2000) concludes, "By the mid-1980s in the US, technology education and technological literacy had been defined through the capitalist interests of private corporations and the state" (183) and Besser (1993) underscores the degree to which this period was foundational in constructing education as a marketplace.

The 1990's saw the salience and, to some degree, the consequences of such reasoning as the World-Wide Web came into being and the burgeoning Internet created an electronic frontier "Dot-Com" economic boom via its commercialization in a range of personal computing hardware and software. In the age of Microsoft and America Online, computer and information skills were indeed increasingly highly necessary. Al Gore's "data highway" of the 1970s had grown an order of magnitude to become the "information superhighway" of the Clinton presidency and the plan for a "Global Information Infrastructure" was being promoted as "a metaphor for democracy itself" (Gore, 1994) as social and technological transformation ignited globally under the pressures of the "new economy" (Kelly, 1998).

By the decade's end, technological literacy was clearly a challenge that could be ignored only at one's peril. Yet, in keeping with the logic of the 1980s, such literacy was again narrowly conceived in largely functional terms as "meaning computer skills and the ability to use computers and other technology to improve learning, productivity, and performance" (U.S. Department of Education, 1996). Specifically, the department located the challenge as training for the future which should take place in schools, thereby taking the host of issues raised by the information revolution out of the public sphere proper and reducing them to standardized technical and vocational competencies for which children and youth should be trained. Further, technological literacy, conceived as "the new basic" (U.S. Department of Education, 1996) skill, became the buzz word that signified a policy program for saturating schools with computer technology as well as training for teachers and students both. Thereby, it not only guaranteed a marketplace for American ICT companies to sell their technology, but it created entirely novel spheres for the extension of professional development, as teachers and administrators began to be held accountable for properly infusing computer technology into curricula.

Come the time of the Bush administration's second term, the U.S. National Education Technology Plan quoted approvingly from a high schooler who remarked, "we have technology in our blood" (U.S. Department of Education, 2004: 4), and the effects of two decades of debate and policy on technoliteracy was thus hailed as both a resounding technocratic success and a continuing pressure upon educational institutions to innovate up to the standards of the times. Interestingly, however, the plan itself moved away from the language of technological literacy and returned to the more specific term "computer literacy" (13). Still, in its overarching gesture to the *No Child Left Behind Act of 2001*, which had called for technology to be infused across the curriculum—meaning the use of multimedia computers and the Internet across the arts and sciences—and for every student to be "technologically literate by the time the student finishes the eighth grade, regardless of the student's race, ethnicity, gender, family income, geographic location, or disability" (U.S. Congress, 2001), the United States demonstrated its ongoing commitment to delimit "technological literacy" in the functional and economistic terms of computer-based competencies.

Technoliteracy for Sustainable Development: The United Nations

Who benefits, who loses? Who pays? What are the social, environmental, personal, or other consequences of following, or not following, a particular course of action? What alternative courses of action are available? These questions are not always, and perhaps only rarely, going to yield agreed answers, but addressing them is arguably fundamental to any educational program that claims to advance technological literacy for all. (Jenkins,1997)

In order to chart trajectories in technoliteracy at the international level, we now turn to a brief examination of the United Nations' Project 2000+: Scientific and Technological Literacy for All. In 1993, UNESCO and eleven major global agencies launched Project 2000+ in order to prepare citizens worldwide to understand, deliberate on, and implement strategies in their everyday lives concerning "a variety of societal problems that deal with issues such as population, health, nutrition and environment, as well as sustainable development at local, national, and international levels" (Holbrook, et al., 2000: 1). The project's mission underscores the degree to which the United Nations conceives of technological literacy as a social and community-building practice, as opposed to an individual economic aptitude. Further, in contradistinction to the functional computer literacy movements found in the United States context, the U.N.'s goal of "scientific and technological literacy" (STL) for all should be seen as connected to affective-order precedents such as the "public understanding of science" (Royal Society, 1985) and "science-technology-society" (Power, 1987) movements.

Though directly inspired by the social development focus of 1990's World Declaration on Education, Project 2000+ also draws in large part from the Rio Declaration on Environment and Development agreed upon at the 1992 Earth Summit (UNESCO, 1999). While the Rio Declaration itself contains ample language focused upon the economic and other developmental rights enjoyed by states, such notions of development were articulated as inseparable from the equally important goals of "environmental protection" and the conservation, protection, and restoration of "the health and integrity of the Earth's ecosystem" (United Nations, 1992). "Sustainable development," defined as "development that meets the needs of the present without compromising the ability of future generations to meet their own needs" (Brundtland, 1987), cannot be properly separated from radical critiques of ecologically damaging political economy and other social behavior. Yet, neither can it be separated from the ability of people everywhere to gain access and understanding of the information that can help to promote sustainability. UNESCO does not make ICTs a centerpiece of STL projects, however. Of course, a major reason that UNESCO downplays an emphasis upon computer-related technology in its approach to technoliteracy is because the great majority of the illiterate populations it seeks to serve are to be found in the relatively poor and un-modernized regions of Latin America, Africa, and Asia, where an ICT focus would have less relevance at present. A more comprehensive reason, however, is that the United Nations has specifically adopted a nonfunctional commitment to literacy, conceiving of it as multiple literacies "which are diverse, have many dimensions, and are learned in different ways" (Lonsdale and McCurry, 2004: 5). STL, then, calls for understandings and deployments of appropriate technology the simplest and most sustainable technological means which can meet a given endas part of a commitment to literacy for social justice and human dignity. This is far different than in the United States, where technoliteracy has generally been reduced to a program of skills and fluency in ICTs.

Still, it would be incorrect to conclude that the United Nations is anticomputer. In fact, the institution is strongly committed to utilizing ICTs as part of its literacy and development campaigns worldwide (Wagner and Kozma, 2003; Jegede, 2002) whenever appropriate. But as it is also conscious of the ability of new technologies to exacerbate divides between rich and poor, male and female, and North and South, the United Nations promotes "understanding of the nature of, and need for, scientific and technological literacy in relation to local culture and values" (UNESCO, 1999). It also maintains that Scientific and Technological Literacy is best exhibited when it is embedded in prevailing traditions and cultures and meets people's real needs (Rassool, 1999). Consequently, while the United Nations finds that technoliteracy is a universal goal of mounting importance due to global technological transformation, STL programs require that various individuals, cultural groups, and states will formulate the questions through which they gain literacy differently and for diverse reasons (Holbrook, 2000).

Critical Multiple Technoliteracies

The critical understanding of technology, with which the education we need must be infused, is one that sees in it a growing capacity for intervention in the world, one that must necessarily be subjected to the political and ethical test . . . I mean here the ethic that is at the service of the peoples . . . not the narrow and mean ethic of profit and of the market. (Freire, 2004)

As we have seen, technoliteracy should be seen as a site of struggle, as a contested terrain used by the Left, Right, and Center of different nations and groups to promote their own interests, and so those interested in social and ecological justice should look to define and institute their own oppositional forms. Dominant corporate and state powers, as well as conservative and rightist groups, have been making serious use of high-technologies and education to advance their agendas. In the political battles of the future, then, educators (along with citizens everywhere) will need to devise ways to produce and use these technologies to advance a critical oppositional pedagogy that serves the interests of the oppressed. Therefore, in addition to more traditional literacies such as the print literacies of reading and writing, as well as other nondigital new literacies (Lankshear and Knobel, 2000) such as ecoliteracy (Kahn, 2004), cultural literacy, and social literacy, we argue that robustly critical forms of media, computer, and multimedia literacies need to be developed as subsets of a larger project of multiple technoliteracies that furthers the ethical reconstruction of technology, literacy, and society in an era of technological revolution.

Critical Media Literacies

With the emergence of a global media culture, multiple technoliteracies are arguably more important than ever, as media essentially are technologies. Recently cultural studies and critical pedagogy have begun to teach us to recognize the ubiquity of media culture in contemporary society, the growing trends toward multicultural education, and the need for a media literacy that addresses the issue of multicultural and social difference (Kellner, 1998). Additionally, there is an expanding recognition that media representations help construct our images and understanding of the world and that education must meet the dual challenges of teaching media literacy in a multicultural society and of sensitizing students and publics to the inequities and injustices of a society based on gender, race, and class inequalities and discrimination (Kellner, 1995). Also, critical studies have pointed out the role of mainstream media in exacerbating or diminishing these inequalities, as well as the ways that media education and the production of alternative media can help create a healthy multiculturalism of diversity and strengthened democracy. While significant gains have been made, continual technological change means that those involved in theorizing and practicing media literacy confront some of the most serious difficulties and problems that face us as educators and citizens today.

Developing critical media literacy and pedagogy also involves perceiving how media like film or video can also be used positively to teach a wide range of topics, like multicultural understanding and education. If, for example, multicultural education is to champion genuine diversity and expand the curriculum, it is important both for groups excluded from mainstream education to learn about their own heritage and for dominant groups to explore the experiences and voices of minority and excluded groups. Thus, media literacy can promote a more multicultural technoliteracy, conceived as understanding and engaging the heterogeneity of cultures and subcultures that constitute an increasingly global and multicultural world (Courts, 1998; Weil, 1998).

Critical media literacy not only teaches students to learn from media, to resist media manipulation, and to use media materials in constructive ways, but it is also concerned with developing skills that will help create good citizens and make them more motivated and competent participants in social life. As Dewey argued (1916), education is necessary to enable people to participate in democracy, for without an educated, informed, and literate citizenry, strong democracy is impossible. Moreover, there are crucial links between literacy, democracy, empowerment, and social participation in politics and everyday life. Hence, without developing adequate literacies, differences between "haves" and "have nots" cannot be overcome and individuals and groups will be left without the tools to navigate and challenge the emerging global economy, networked society, and culture of electronic media.

The technologies of communication are becoming more and more accessible to young people and ordinary citizens, and can be used to promote education, democratic self-expression, and social progress. Technologies that could help produce the end of participatory democracy, by transforming politics into media spectacles and the battle of images, and by turning spectators into cultural zombies, could also be used to help invigorate democratic debate and participation (Kellner, 2003b). In fact, they must be used in this latter fashion, for, as Carmen Luke has written, "unless educators take a lead in developing appropriate pedagogies for these new electronic media and forms of communication, corporate experts will be the ones to determine how people will learn, what they learn, and what constitutes literacy" (2000: 71).

Critical media literacy should therefore be conjoined with the project of radical democracy as it is concerned to develop and utilize technologies that will enhance democratization and participation. In this respect, critical media literacy takes a comprehensive approach that teaches critical attitudes and provides experimental use of media as technologies of social communication and change (Hammer, 1995; 2006). Some educators, such as Len Masterman (1985), have proposed that the goal of media literacy should be a sort of "critical autonomy" that will empower people to be independently critical of the media. On the other hand, "critical solidarity" (Ferguson, 2001) has been proposed as necessary to teach people to interpret and implement media within humanistic, social, historical, political, and economic contexts such that they can better understand the interrelationships and consequences of living and acting within a media culture. We feel that the dichotomy that opposes critical autonomy and solidarity is best mediated and so favors a critical media literacy that can work to foster both independent and interdependent critical media thinkers for a more democratic world.

Critical Computer Literacies

To fully participate in a high-tech and global society, people should cultivate innovative forms of computer literacy in ways that go beyond standard technical notions. Critical computer literacy involves learning how to use computer technologies to do research and gather information, to perceive computer culture as a contested terrain containing texts, spectacles, games, and interactive multimedia, as well as interrogation of the political economy, cultural bias, and environmental effects of computer-related technologies (Park and Pellow, 2004; Grossman, 2004; Plepys, 2002; Heinonen, Jokinen, and Kaivo-oja, 2001; Bowers, 2000).

The emergent cybercultures can be seen as a discursive and political location in which students, teachers, and citizens can all intervene, engaging in discussion groups and collaborative research projects, creating websites, producing innovative multimedia for cultural dissemination, and cultivating novel modes of social interaction and learning. Computers can thereby enable people to actively participate in the production of culture, ranging from dialogue and debate on public issues to the creation and expression of their own cultural forms. Thus, computers and the Internet can provide opportunities for multiple voices, alternative online communities, and enhanced political activism (Kahn and Kellner, 2005). However, to take part in this culture requires multiple forms of technoliteracy.

For, not only are accelerated skills of print literacy necessary, which are often restricted to the growing elite of students who are privileged to attend adequate and superior public and private schools, but in fact it demands a critical information literacy as well. Such literacy would require learning how to distinguish between good and bad information, identifying what Burbules and Callister (2000) identify as misinformation, malinformation, messed-up information, and mostly useless information. In this sense, information literacy is closely connected with education itself, with learning where information is found, how to produce knowledge and understanding, and how to critically evaluate and interpret information sources and material. It also raises profound questions of power and knowledge, concerning the definitions of high and low-status knowledge, who gets to produce and valorize various modes of information, whose ideas get circulated and discussed, and whose get marginalized.

Critical Multimedia Literacies

With an ever-developing multimedia cyberculture, beyond popular film and television culture, visual literacy takes on increased importance. On the whole, computer screens are more graphic, multisensory, and interactive than conventional print fields, something that disconcerted many of us when first confronted with the new environments. Icons, windows, mouses, and the various clicking, linking, and interaction involved in computer-mediated hypertext dictate new competencies and a dramatic expansion of literacy within the context of skills.

Visuality is obviously crucial, compelling users to perceptively scrutinize visual fields, perceive and interact with icons and graphics, and use technical devices like a mouse to access the desired material and field. But tactility is also important, as individuals must learn navigational skills of how to proceed from one field and screen to another, how to negotiate hypertexts and links, and how to move from one program to another if one operates, as most now do, in a window-based computer environment. Further, as voice and sound enter multimedia culture, refined hearing also becomes part of the aesthetics and pedagogies of an expanded technoliteracy, and that should allow for multiple methods of learning (Gardner, 1999).

Contemporary multimedia environments necessitate a diversity of types of multisemiotic and multimodal interactions, involving interfacing with word and print material and often images, graphics, as well as audio and video material (Hammer and Kellner, 2001). As technological convergence develops apace, individuals will need to combine the skills of critical media literacy with traditional print literacy and new forms of multiple technoliteracies to access, navigate, and participate in multimediated reality. Reading and interpreting print was the appropriate mode of literacy for an age in which the primary source of information was books and print media, while critical multimedia literacy entails reading and interpreting a plethora of discourse, images, spectacle, narratives, and the forms and genres of global media culture. Thus, technoliteracy in this conception involves the ability to engage effectively in modes of multimedia communication that include print, speech, visuality, tactility, and sound, within a hybrid field that combines these forms, all of which incorporate skills of interpretation and critique.

Reconstructing Technoliteracy

> We are, indeed, designers of our social futures. (New London Group, 1996)

Adequately meeting the challenge issued by the concept of technoliteracy raises questions about the design and reconstruction of technology itself. As Andrew Feenberg has long argued (1991, 1995, 1999), democratizing technology often requires its reconstruction and re-visioning by individuals. "Hackers" have redesigned technological systems, notably starting the largely anti-capitalist Open Source and Free Software movements, and indeed much of the Internet itself has been the result of individuals contributing collective knowledge and making improvements that aid various educational, political, and cultural projects. Of course, there are corporate and technical constraints in that dominant programs and machines impose their rules and abilities upon users, but part of re-visioning technoliteracy requires the very perception and transformation of those limits. Technoliteracy must help teach people to become more ethical producers, as well as consumers, and thus it can help to redesign and reconstruct modern technology towards making it more applicable to people's needs and not just their manufactured desires.

Crucially, alternative technoliteracies must become reflective and critical, aware of the educational, social, and political assumptions involved in the restructuring of education, technology, and society currently under way. In response to the excessive hype concerning new technologies and education, it is important to maintain the critical dimension and to reflect upon the nature and effects of emergent technologies and the pedagogies developed as a response to their challenge. Many advocates of new technologies, however, eschew critique for a more purely affirmative agenda.

For instance, after an excellent discussion of new modes of literacy and the need to rethink education, Gunther Kress argues that we must move from critique to design, beyond a negative deconstruction to more positive construction (1997). But rather than following such modern logic of either/or, critical pedagogues should pursue the logic of both/and, perceiving design and critique, deconstruction and reconstruction, as complementary and supplementary rather than as antithetical choices. Certainly, we need to design alternative pedagogies and curricula for the future, as well as developing improved social and cultural relations, but we need also to criticize misuse, inappropriate use, over-inflated claims, and exclusions and oppressions involved in the introduction of ICTs into education. Moreover, the critical dimension is more than ever necessary as we attempt to develop contemporary approaches to technoliteracy, and design more emancipatory and democratizing technologies. In this process, we must be critically vigilant, practicing critique and self-criticism, putting in question our assumptions, discourses, and practices, as we seek to develop technoliteracies and pedagogies of resistance (Kellner, 2004).

In sum, people should be helped to advance the multiple technoliteracies that will allow them to understand, critique, and transform the oppressive social and cultural conditions in which they live, as they become ecologically informed, ethical, and transformative subjects as opposed to objects of technological domination and manipulation. This requires producing multiple oppositional literacies for critical thinking, reflection, and the capacity to engage in the creation of discourse, cultural artifacts, and political action amidst widespread technological revolution. Further, as active and engaged subjects arise through social interactions with others, a notion of convivial technologies must come to be a part of the kinds of technoliteracy that a radical reconstruction of education now seeks to cultivate.

As we have argued, the project of reconstructing technoliteracy must take different forms in different contexts. In almost every cultural and social situation, however, a literacy of critique should be enhanced so that citizens can name the technological system, describe and grasp the technological changes occurring as defining features of the emerging global order, and learn to experimentally engage in critical and oppositional practices in the interests of democratization and progressive transformation. As part of a truly multicultural order, we need to encourage the growth and flourishing of numerous standpoints (Harding, 2004) on technoliteracy, looking out for and legitimizing counter-hegemonic needs, values, and understandings. Such would be to propound multiple technoliteracies "from below" as opposed to the largely functional, economistic, and technocratic technoliteracy "from above" that is favored by many industries and states. Thereby, projects for technoliteracies can allow reconstructive opportunities for a better world to be forged out of the present age of unfolding crisis.

References

Apple, M. (1992). "Is new technology part of the solution or part of the problem in education." J. Beynon and H. Mackay (ed.), *Technological Literacy and the Curriculum*. London: The Falmer Press, 105–124.

Aronowitz, S. (1985). "Why should Johnny read?" *The Village Voice Literary Supplement*, (May).

Besser, H. (1993). "Education as Marketplace." In R. Muffoletto and N. Knupfer (ed.). *Computers in Education: Social, Historical, and Political Perspectives.* Cresskill, NJ: Hampton Press.

Best, S. and Kellner, D. (2001). *The Postmodern Adventure: Science, Technology, and Cultural Studies at the Third Millennium.* New York and London: Guilford Press and Routledge.

Bowers, C. (2000). *Let Them Eat Data: How Computers Affect Education, Cultural Diversity, and the Prospects of Ecological Sustainability.* Athens, GA: University of Georgia Press.

Brundtland, G. et al. (1987). *Our Common Future*: Report of the World Commission on Environment and Development. Oxford: Oxford University Press.

Burbules, N. and Callister, T. (1996). "Knowledge at the crossroads." *Educational Theory*. Vol. 46(1): 23–34.

Burbules, N. and Callister, T. (2000). *Watch IT: The Risks and Promises of Information Technology*. Boulder: Westview Press.

Bromley, H. and Apple M. (ed.). (1998). *Education/Technology/Power: Educational Computing as Social Practice*. Albany, NY: State University of New York Press.

Castells, M. (1996). The Information Age: Economy, Society and Culture Vol. I: *The Rise of the Network Society*. Cambridge: MA. Blackwell Publishers.

Cope, B., and Kalantzis, M. (ed.). (2000). *Multiliteracies: Literacy Learning and the Design of Social Futures*. New York: Routledge.

Coppola, N. (1999). "Greening the Technological Curriculum: A model for Environmental Literacy." *Journal of Technology Studies*. Vol. 25(2): 39–46.

Courts, P. (1998). *Multicultural Literacies: Dialect, Discourses, and Diversity.* New York: Peter Lang.

Dewey, J. (1916). *Democracy and Education: An Introduction to the Philosophy of Education.* Carbondale and Edwardsville: Southern Illinois University Press.

Dyrenfurth, M. (1991). "Technological literacy synthesized." In M.Dyrenfurth and M. Kozak (eds), *Technological Literacy*. Peoria, IL: Glencoe, McGraw-Hill: 138–186.

Feenberg, A. (1991). *Critical Theory of Technology.* New York: Oxford University Press.

Feenberg, A. (1995). *Alternative Modernity.* Berkeley: University of California Press.

Feenberg, A. (1999). *Questioning Technology.* New York and London: Routledge.

Ferguson, R. (2001). "Media education and the development of critical solidarity." *Media Education Journal,* 30: 37–43.

Freire, P. (2004). *Pedagogy of Indignation.* Boulder, CO: Paradigm Publishers.

Freire, P. and Macedo, D. (1987). *Literacy: Reading the Word and the World.* Westport, CT: Bergin & Garvey.

Gardner, H. (1999). *Intelligence Reframed: Multiple Intelligences for the 21st Century.* New York: Basic Books Inc.

Gore, A. (1994). "Remarks prepared for delivery." Speech at the International Telecommunications Union (Buenos Aires:). Online at: http://263.aka.org.cn/Magazine/Aka4/gorestalk.html

Grossman, E. (2004). "High-tech Wasteland." *Orion.* July/August. Online at http://www. itu.int/itu-d/wtdc/wtdc1994/speech/gore_ww2.doc

Grubb, W. (1996). "The new vocationalism-What it is, what it could be." *Phi Delta Kappan, 77*(8): 535–546.

Hammer, R. (1995). "Strategies for Media Literacy." P. McLaren, R. Hammer, D. Sholle, and S. Reilly (eds.). *Rethinking Media Literacy: A Critical Pedagogy of Representation.* New York: Peter Lang: 225–235.

Hammer, R. (2006). Teaching Critical Media Literacies: Theory, Praxis and Empowerment.

Hammer, Rhonda and D. Kellner. (2001). "Multimedia pedagogy and multicultural education for the new millennium." *Current Issues in Education.* Vol. 4(2). Online at: http://cie.ed.asu.edu/volume4/number2/ *InterActions: UCLA Journal of Education and Information Studies.* Vol. 2(1), Article 6. Online at: http://repositories.cdlib.org/gseis/interactions/vol2/iss1/6

Harding, Sandra (ed.). (2004). *The Feminist Standpoint Theory Reader: Intellectual and Political Controversies.* New York and London: Routledge.

Hayden, M. (1989). "What is technological literacy?" *Bulletin of Science, Technology and Society,* 119: 220–233, STS Press.

Heinonen, S., Jokinen, P., and Kaivo-oja, J. (2001). "The ecological transparency of the information society." *Futures.* Vol. 33: 319–337.

Hickman, L. (2001). *Philosophical Tools for Technological Culture.* Bloomington: Indiana University Press.

Holbrook, J., Mukherjee, A., and Varma, S. (eds) (2000). *Scientific and Technological Literacy for All.* UNESCO and International Council of Associations for Science Education. Delhi, India: Center for Science Education and Communication.

Illich, I. (1973). *Tools for Conviviality.* New York: Harper and Row.

Jegede, O. (2002). *An Integrated ICT-Support for ODL in Nigeria: The Vision, the Mission and the Journey so Far.* Paper prepared for the LEARNTEC-UNESCO 2002 Global Forum on Learning Technology. Karlsruhe, Germany.

Jenkins, E. (1997). "Technological Literacy: Concepts and Constructs." *Journal of Technology Studies*. Vol. 23(1): 2–5.

Kahn, R. (2004). "Towards Ecopedaogy: Weaving a Broad-based Pedagogy of Liberation for Animal, Nature, and the Oppressed People of the Earth." K. Mundel and D. Schugerensky (eds). *Lifelong Citizenship Learning, Participatory Democracy and Social Change.* Toronto: University of Toronto.

Kahn, R. and Kellner, D. (2005). "Oppositional Politics and the Internet: A Critical/Reconstructive Approach." *Cultural Politics*, vol. 1, no. 1. Berg Publishers: 75–100.

Kahn, R. and Kellner, D. (*forthcoming*). "Paulo Freire and Ivan Illich: Technology, Politics, and the Reconstruction of Education." C. Torres (ed.) *Paulo Freire and the Possible Dream.* Urbana, IL: University of Illinois Press.

Kellner, D. (1989). *Critical Theory, Marxism and Modernity.* Baltimore, MD: Johns Hopkins University Press.

Kellner, D. (1995). *Media Culture: Identity and Politics Between the Modern and the Postmodern.* New York, NY: Routledge.

Kellner, D. (1998). "Multiple Literacies and Critical Pedagogy in a Multicultural Society." *Educational Theory*, 48: 103–122.

Kellner, D. (2000). "Globalization and New Social Movements: Lessons for Critical Theory and Pedagogy." N. Burbules and C. Torres (eds), *Globalization and Education: Critical Perspectives.* New York: Routledge.

Kellner, D. (2002). "Theorizing Globalization." *Sociological Theory* (November), 20: 3, 285–305.

Kellner, D. (2003a). *Media Spectacle.* London and New York: Routledge.

Kellner, D. (2003b). *From 9/11 to Terror War: The Dangers of the Bush Legacy.* Lanham, MD: Rowman & Littlefield.

Kellner, D.. (2003c). "Toward a Critical Theory of Education." *Democracy & Nature*, vol. 9, no. 1. Taylor and Francis: 51–64.

Kellner, D. (2004). "Technological Transformation, Multiple Literacies, and the Re-visioning of Education." *E-Learning.* vol. 1, no. 1.

Kellner, D. (2005). *Media Spectacle And The Crisis Of Democracy: Terrorism, War, And Election Battles.* Boulder, CO: Paradigm Publishers.

Kellner, D. and Share, J. (2005). "Toward Critical Media Literacy: Core concepts, debates, organizations and policy." *Discourse: Studies in the Cultural Politics of Education.* Vol. 26(3), September: 369–386.

Kelly, K. (1998). *New Rules for the New Economy.* Fourth Estate, London.

Kovel, J. (1983). "Theses on Technocracy." *Telos*, No. 54 (Winter).

Kress, G. (1997). "Visual and Verbal Modes of Representation in Electronically Mediated Communication: the potentials of new forms of text." In I. Snyder (ed.) *Page to Screen: taking literacy into the electronic era.* Sydney, Australia: Allen & Unwin: 53–79.

Lankshear, C. and Knobel, M. (2000). "Mapping postmodern literacies: A preliminary chart." *The Journal of Literacy and Technology.* vol.1, no.1, Fall. Online at http://www.literacyandtechnology.org/v1n1/lk.html

Lankshear, C. and Snyder, I. (2000). *Teachers and Technoliteracy: Managing Literacy, Technology and Learning in Schools*. Sydney, Australia: Allen and Unwin.

Lewis, T. and Gagel, C. (1992). "Technological literacy: A critical analysis." *Journal of Curriculum Studies*. Vol. 24(2): 117–138.

Lonsdale, M. and McCurry, D. (2004). *Literacy in the New Millennium*. Adelaide, Australia: NCVER.

Luke, C. (1997). *Technological Literacy*. Melbourne, Australia: National Languages and Literacy Institute. Adult Literacy Network.

Luke, C. (2000). "Cyber-schooling and technological change: Multiliteracies for new times." In B. Cope and M. Kalantzis (ed.), *Multiliteracies: Literacy, Learning, and the Design of Social Futures*. South Yarra, Australia: Macmillan: 69–105.

Luke, A. and Luke, C. (2002). "Adolescence Lost/Childhood Regained: On Early Intervention and the Emergence of the Techno-Subject." *Journal of Early Childhood Literacy*, Vol. 1(1): 91–120.

Masterman, L. (1985). *Teaching the media*. New York: Routledge.

McLaren, P, Hammer, R., Sholle, D and Reilly, S. (1995). *Rethinking Media Literacy: a critical pedagogy of representation*. New York: Peter Lang.

McLuhan, M. (1964). *Understanding Media: The Extensions of Man*. New York: Signet Books.

National Commission on Excellence in Education. (1983). *A Nation at Risk: The Imperative for Educational Reform*. Washington, DC: U.S. Government Printing Office.

National Telecommunications & Information Administration. (2002). *A Nation Online: How Americans are Expanding Their Use of the Internet*. Online at http://www.ntia.doc.gov/ntiahome/dn/nationonline_020502.htm

New London Group. (1996). "A Pedagogy of Multiliteracies: designing social futures." *Harvard Educational Review*. Vol. 66: 60–92.

O'Tuathail, G. and McCormack, D. (1999). "The Technoliteracy Challenge: Teaching Globalization Using the Internet." *Journal of Geography in Higher Education*, Vol. 22: 347-361.

Park, L and. Pellow, D. (2004). "Racial formation, environmental racism, and the emergence of Silicon Valley." *Ethnicities*. Vol. 4(3): 403–424.

Pearson, G and Young A.. (2002). *Technically Speaking: Why All Americans Need to Know More About Technology*. Washington, DC: National Academies Press.

Petrina, S. (2000). "The Politics of Technological Literacy." *International Journal of Technology and Design Education* 10, no. 2: 181–206.

Plepys, A.(2002). "The grey side of ICT." *Environmental Impact Assessment Review*. Vol. 22: 509–523.

Plotnick, E. (1999). Information literacy. ERIC Clearinghouse on Information and Technology, Syracuse University. ED-427777.

Postman, N. (1985). *Amusing Ourselves to Death*. New York: Viking-Penguin.

Postman, N. (1992). *Technopolis: the surrender of culture to technology*. New York: Random House.

Power, C. (1987). "Science and technology towards informed citizenship." *Castme Journal.* Vol. 7, 3: 5–18.

Rassool, N. (1999). *Literacy for sustainable development in the age of information.* London, UK: Multilingual Matters Ltd.

Royal Society. (1985). *The public understanding of science.* London: Royal Society.

Selfe, C. (1999). *Technology and Literacy in the Twenty-First Century: The Importance of Paying Attention.* Carbondale, IL: Southern Illinois University Press.

Street, B. (1984). *Literacy in theory and practice.* Cambridge, UK: Cambridge University Press.

Suppes, P. (1968). "Computer Technology and the Future of Education." *Phi Delta Kappan.* April: 420–423.

Todd, R. (1991). "The natures and challenges of technological literacy." In M. Dyrenfurth & M..Kozak (eds.) *Technological literacy.* Peoria, IL: Glencoe, McGraw-Hill: 10–27.

Trend, D. (2001). *Welcome to Cyberschool: Education at the Crossroads in the Information Age.* Lanham, Md: Rowman & Littlefield.

UNESCO. (1994). *The Project 2000 + declaration: The way forward.* Paris, France: UNESCO.

UNESCO. (1999). *Science and Technology Education: Philosophy of Project 2000+.* The Association for Science Education. Paris, France: UNESCO.

United Nations. (1992). *Report of the United Nations Conference on Environment and Development.* Rio de Janeiro, Brazil: UNCED.

U.S. Congress. (2001). *No Child Left Behind Act of 2001.* Public Law 107–110. Washington, DC.

U.S. Department of Education. (1996). *Getting America's Students Ready for the 21st Century—Meeting the Technology Literacy Challenge, A Report to the Nation on Technology and Education.* National Education Technology Plan. Washington, DC.

U.S. Department of Education. (2004). *Toward a New Golden Age in American Education: How the Internet, the Law, and Today's Students are Revolutionizing Expectations.* National Education Technology Plan. Washington, DC.

Waetjen, W. (1993). "Technological Literacy Reconsidered." *Journal of Technology Education.* Vol. 4(2): 5–11.

Wagner, D. and Kozma, R. (2003). "New Technologies for Literacy and Adult Education: A Global Perspective." Paper for NCAL/OECD International Roundtable. Philadelphia, PN. Online at http://www.literacy.org/ICTconf/PhilaRT_wagner_kozma_final.pdf

Wajcman, J. (2004). *Technofeminism.* Malden, MA: Polity Press.

Weil, D. (1998). *Toward a Critical Multicultural Literacy.* New York: Peter Lang.

Wells, H.G. (1938). *World Brain.* New York: Doubleday.

CHAPTER 17

Rethinking Technological Literacy for the Global Network Era

Leonard J. Waks

In this chapter I explain the relationship between globalization and technological literacy. After accounting for the notion of technological literacy that emerged in the 1970s and 1980s in the developed nations, I argue that this notion must be reshaped to fit the needs of the emerging global network society. That is, a renewed conception of technological literacy education must be developed to take account of changes in the global economy, including the widespread use of networked computer technologies.

In section 1 I review the conception of technological literacy developed in the 1970s and 1980s to respond to the technological problem-situation of that time. In section 2, I consider the impact of globalization on the emerging world-occupational structure and the fundamental role of networked technologies in today's rewarding and secure jobs. Finally, in section 3, I explain why this new technological problem-situation compels educators to reshape earlier notions of technological literacy education, and offer suggestions assigning larger roles to use of networked computers.

Section 1: The Technology Problem and the Rise of Technological Literacy

The notion of "technological literacy" education emerged in the late 1970s and early 1980s in the United States and other developed nations, particularly in the English-speaking world, as a response to specific social and economic factors of that time. Two somewhat conflicting motivations shaped initial technological literacy efforts, and I will consider these as they arose in the American context.

The first was the awareness of a "technology problem"—the erosion of the ideology of progress through science and technology, which had dominated Western ideology in the first half of the twentieth century. This ideology was severely challenged by various "techno-shocks" after 1950. A selective list specific to the United States would include: the atomic bomb in 1945; the creation of the hydrogen bomb in 1952 and its spread to the USSR in 1953; thalidomide babies in the late 1950s; the destruction of habitat due to agricultural pesticides, brought to public attention by Rachel Carson in 1962 in *Silent Spring*; the use of napalm, a jellied form of gasoline produced by the Dow Corporation from 1965–1969 as an incendiary weapon for U.S. forces in Vietnam; and the failure and cover-up at the Three Mile Island nuclear reactor in Pennsylvania in 1979, eerily forecast earlier that year in the thriller *The China Syndrome*.

The steady flow of these shocks prompted deeper, and more comprehensive, worries about technology and the environment, fostered by antiwar and environmental teach-ins on university campuses during the late 1960s, the publication of the first *Whole Earth Catalog* in 1968, and the first Earth Day in 1970. In response, nongovernmental organizations were created to fight the misuse of science and technology, and to promote an environmentally sustainable and peaceful world. These included the Union of Concerned Scientists, established at MIT in 1969; Friends of the Earth, founded by David Brower in 1969 (and successful, two years later, in preventing funding for the proposed American Supersonic Transport); and Greenpeace, organized in 1971 to promote a "green and peaceful planet." Worries about the long-range effects of industrial technologies were sharpened by the computer models of planetary collapse in *The Limits to Growth*, a 1972 report of the Club of Rome, a worldwide group of scientists, economists, businessmen, and political leaders. These developments challenged activists and educators to develop new educational means for controlling technological developments and protecting the environment. During the Carter administration years (1976–1980) American educators first sought federal funding for school and college courses in environmental and technological literacy, to enable participation by young citizens in the informed resolution of environmental and technological issues. Similar courses were also developed in Great Britain, Western Europe, and Australia.

The second motivation for technological literacy education in the United States came from the other end of the political spectrum. In the 1970s, American industry faced stiff competition in the global marketplace. International comparisons of U.S. and foreign students had also revealed that the former lagged behind their international competitors on measures of science-and-math achievement. *A Nation at Risk*, issued by President Ronald Reagan's Department of Education in 1983, blamed America's declining dominance over the world economy on its ineffective schools. The report called on American schools to require all students to take demanding courses in science, math, and computer science, and to learn how to use computers as tools in all academic subjects. The root idea of technological literacy in the report was mastery of computer skills for knowledge use in the workplace.

Initial Models of Technological Literacy Education

Each of these two conflicting motivations—controlling technological developments to promote peace and protect the environment versus mastering technology to dominate world markets—appealed to one of the two dominant American political parties. The two were tactically merged in the American technological literacy efforts of the 1980s. New courses in science paid greater attention to technological applications, and employed computer simulations as tools for modeling. Computer literacy programs were introduced. "Technology education," a field of general education featuring broad understanding of complex technological artifacts and systems in their social and environmental contexts, gradually replaced "industrial-arts education" as a school curriculum area.

Because of the overlapping concerns about technology and the environment, some influential efforts in technology education ran parallel to those in environmental education. Both were affected by the social movement activism of the time. The environmental movement was paralleled by a movement opposing harmful, incautious, or budget-busting technological developments: nuclear weapons and nuclear power, the star-wars space defense system, super-sonic transport, high-tech "big science" projects such as the super-conducting supercollider. This movement was tagged as being "anti-technology."

Social movement activism affected both environmental and technological literacy education. In addition to (a) mere cognitive *understanding* of scientific and technical matters, these "literacies" added (b) social issue awareness, (c) critical value assessment, and (d) ameliorative social action as prominent components. This four-component model became entrenched as an international "paradigm" as a result of the 1975 Belgrade Charter on environmental education and the 1977 Intergovernmental Conference Report on environmental education issued in Tblisi, Georgia,

USSR. Under the leadership of Harold R. Hungerford, the components of environmental education identified at Tbilisi were defined in concrete terms (Hungerford et al., 1980) and environmental literacy curricula embodying them were developed, implemented, and evaluated. Hungerford and his co-workers also extended the four-component paradigm to technological literacy efforts. At roughly the same time, "science, technology and society" (STS) education, a field initiated by a shaky coalition of school and college teachers responding in quite different ways to technological issues, also emerged as an influential shaper of technological literacy education, when the coalition's leaders organized a series of annual "Technological Literacy Conferences." Hungerford and his co-workers, especially Peter Rubba, Randall Weisenmeyer, Trudi Volk, and John Ramsey, rapidly saw STS as a useful platform for their technological literacy efforts, and developed, implemented, and evaluated STS curricula that paralleled those in environmental education. Their model consolidated efforts in technological literacy by extending the conceptual model and research base that Hungerford had established for environmental education to technological literacy. Environmental and technological literacy came to overlap to such a great extent that several scholars (e.g., Disinger, (1985/1986) declared them to be identical.

One great appeal of the "science, technology and society" notion was its open texture—its ability to incorporate and integrate components of technology-related education supported by both ends of the political spectrum—enriched scientific and technical content and capability on the one hand, plus critical value assessment and social action on the other. Another was its capacity to generate sequenced teaching-learning units in every existing curriculum site: science, social studies, math, language arts, and vocational education. STS thus offered useful and relevant opportunities for teachers in all fields. STS also provided a way of integrating the entire school curriculum by coordinating units from the pre-existing subject matter areas; unlike environmental education and technology education, STS promised to achieve its important goals without necessarily demanding a new curriculum or subject matter site of its own.

Subsequent developments of technological literacy education embodied the familiar four-component learning process that (a) engaged the interest of learners and in this way increased their awareness of problems, (b) conveyed scientific and technical knowledge related to those problems, (c) guided student investigations of the problems, and (d) assisted in analyzing results and coming to decisions leading to actions to address the problems.

The science and technology content already in the school curriculum was accepted as a given background for these STS units, as was the pre-selection and sequencing of subject matters typical of school curriculum designs. Technology-related problems were selected to amplify this content and demonstrate its real-world significance. The ozone hole, for example, was a good choice because it related familiar technological objects (refrigerators, aerosol sprays) and familiar health problems (UV radiation and skin cancer) to accessible, yet fascinating, atmospheric chemistry. The study of these problems could readily be sequenced according to Hungerford's four-phase model.

Student investigations of the selected problems were seen as akin to discipline-based research projects, and were used as adjuncts to, or replacements for, laboratory experiences in science, design efforts in technology education, or projects in social studies. Students linked textbook knowledge from the subjects they were studying to the selected problems, in order to formulate questions and state hypotheses. They then gathered data, subjected it to analysis, constructed physical or mathematical models, drew inferences, stated results, and applied these to the social or environmental problems motivating the question for investigation.

Guided student-actions were envisioned for the most part as ameliorative individual and collective action steps addressing long-range social problems of technology linked, for example, to environmental protection, occupational health and safety, and population growth. The public was made aware of such problems through efforts of nongovernmental organizations and by popular books detailing the "100 things you can do to save the earth." Young people learned to recycle, plant trees, turn down air conditioners and use bicycles instead of automobiles. Classes engaged in environmental clean-up projects, and tested water quality in nearby rivers.

Roadblocks to Implementation

While the STS idea of technological literacy was widely embraced, programs as implemented typically either neglected the third and fourth components (involving issue investigation, decision-making and social action), or reserved them for gifted and motivated learners. The activities in these components were unpredictable; they were difficult for teachers to manage, and overly challenging for many students. Unlike the first and second stages (awareness and content learning), which fit easily into the standard curriculum format of preselected and presequenced content, learning objectives, and standardized tests, the investigation and social action phases involved unique, creative, learning. They did not generate standardized learning outcomes for tests. On the contrary, they took teacher time and effort away from activities that did. They also involved controversial issues, and frequently generated negative feedback from conservative parents and groups insisting that schools "stick to the facts."

Significantly, these technological literacy efforts also predictably found little support in developing nations. A central concern of the environmental movement was the exponential growth of population, and this issue divided the developed and developing worlds. Population growth came to public awareness through the publication of Paul Erlich's *The Population Bomb* by the Sierra Club in 1968, and the establishment of Zero Population Growth, a highly visible nongovernmental organization, the same year. Although Erlich focused on effects of population growth in the developed world, with its high-consumption lifestyle, most of the population growth was actually taking place in developing regions including Asia and Latin America. The planetary collapse predictions in *The Limits to Growth* relied upon the spread of industrial technologies and high-consumption urban lifestyles to these regions.

As a result, the "antitechnology" and environmental movements became vulnerable to charges of "Gringoism"—rich Americans telling people in poor nations to stop having so many children and to slow their pace of industrial development. Naturally those in the developing nations rejected this message. They saw their growing populations as resources for industrial development, and refused to buy into "limits to growth." On the contrary, they demanded the transfer of industrial technology and technical knowledge from the developed world to stimulate their economic growth and to free themselves from dependency upon the rich nations. Instead of succumbing to the economic dominance of the richest nations, they sought to increase their own share of domestic and global markets.

Subsequent economic and technical developments did not work out as the elites in developing nations hoped, but the process of globalization after 1980 did integrate the economies and technological infrastructures of these nations into an emerging global network society, to which we now turn.

Section 2: Globalization and Networked Computers

Economic and Technological Globalization

The current stage of *economic* globalization began after World War II, when the economies of Europe and Asia were shattered by the war and the United States had surplus capital for investment. The world economy was in a state of chronic under-supply, and American firms faced little competition in international trade. They increased their direct foreign investments, creating foreign subsidiaries throughout the world making mass-produced products for global markets. Under these noncompetitive conditions American firms could set world prices for mass-produced goods, and could secure labor cooperation by passing along some part of their excess profits to unionized industrial workers as wages and benefits above world levels. But by the 1970s European and Asian economies had recovered sufficiently to compete with American firms on a global scale. American firms responded to this competition during the 1970s and 1980s by initiating aggressive anti-union practices, by shifting low-skilled production jobs to non-union plants in the South or poor nations in Asia and Latin America, and by greatly expanding low-wage service-sector industries. European and Japanese firms also began outsourcing routine jobs to low-wage nations in their regions and beyond. Notions of techno-logical literacy emerging at that time, however, did not pay close attention to those trends.

The globalization of *digital information technology networks* began in the early 1990s, after technological literacy efforts were set in place. The growth of digital networks was accelerated by the need to coordinate the far-flung production and marketing activities of large multinational firms. The first commercial Internet Service Provider opened for busi-ness in 1990, and the World-Wide Web was introduced at CERN in 1991. In 1992 the World Bank went online, followed by the White House and United Nations in 1993 (Howe, 2001). Commercial use of the World-Wide Web grew rapidly by the mid 1990s.

The driving forces of the growth of digital networks included the rapid technical advances and price declines in computer chips, satellites, and fiber-optic cables which facilitated growth in television, telephony, FAX, and the Internet, turning the global information grid into a seam-lessly integrated resource, "the biggest machine ever made" (Dizard, 1997: 1). By the end of 2001 the Internet was growing in the United States at the rate of two-million users a month. 143 million Americans were online (54 percent of the population), an increase of 26 million in 13 months. Schools and colleges also went online, and 75 percent of 14–17-year-olds and 65 percent of 10–13-year-olds were Internet users by 2002 (NTIA, 2002).

Economic and Technical Convergence: Network Enterprise

The convergence of these economic globalization and network technology developments enabled a reorganization of transnational enterprises: large, vertically organized firms with foreign subsidiaries were transformed into global "networks" of downsized flagship firms, small supplier firms, competitor firms, government agencies, and universities in strategic alliances.

These "meta-national" firms, unlike the traditional transnational firms rooted in a distinct "home" country, do not take knowledge from the corporate center in the United States, Western Europe, or Japan, incorporate it into a mass-produced product, produce it in their own subsidiaries, and ship it to markets in "less-developed areas." Rather, they are true "network enterprises" depending upon technical and managerial knowledge, experience, and market intelligence from employees and network associates all over the world, connected by in-person and electronic links, to produce small-batch, customized, intermediate, and consumer products for rapid shipment to highly differentiated global markets.

The Global Movement of Jobs and Workers

Economic elites in developing nations have as a result become more tightly linked to their counterparts in the developed nations and more essential to their far-flung enterprises. Meta-national firms draw talent from developing nations to the "global city" planning centers to work on projects that employ their nations' labor or offer products to their markets. Meanwhile the poorest residents of poor nations, in which traditional rural economic roles have deteriorated, are forced to seek livelihoods in their own nations' growing urban economies or to migrate (Sassen, 1994; Richmond, 2002).

Robert Reich's distinction between routine production workers and in-person service workers (Reich, 1992) explains one important division in workers from developing nations. Sophisticated manufacturing can now be performed throughout the world, and jobs will tend to move to nations with reliable, low-cost workers. The largest proportion of employees and sub-contractors of some companies based in developed nations are now located in developing nations. This increases the low-wage routine production sectors of developing nations. But many jobs, both complex and routine, require in-person contact. If you want a brain tumor operated on, or, at the other end of the spectrum, a Walmart facility cleaned, you must find an in-person surgeon or facility cleaner. For this reason in-person workers across the economic spectrum migrate to wealthier nations with favorable markets for their services.

Globalization and Workforce Reorganization

The formation of global networks and network enterprises competing in global markets has brought about changes in workforce organization in all affected societies. To enhance competitiveness, many firms in developed nations have re-engineered their work systems, employing cross-functional teams of "knowledge workers" (Brown et al., 2001) using knowledge and information in novel ways for rapid response to global opportunities (Applebaum et al., 2000). They have also cut costs by automating many complex work tasks and relying on low-cost, low-skill routine workers, at home and abroad. These workers serve increasingly on a part-time or contingent basis, without job security or health insurance (Cappeli, 1999). In poor nations, the formal economy increasingly has a similar structure of knowledge and routine workers, but also relies heavily on informal workers, for example in food preparation and recycling used parts for machinery.

The Four Occupational Categories in the Global Economy

High-Tier Knowledge Professionals
One important group of knowledge workers includes the elite knowledge-professionals, labeled "symbolic analysts" by Robert Reich (Reich, 1991). These workers acquire, permute, and recombine knowledge and information to generate new products and services, while in the process generating new knowledge and information that can be distributed through their networks for "knowledge reuse" (Castells, 1996). Charles Grantham projects a continuing evolution toward a "team-of-teams" approach in the creative sectors of the economy, where elite professional-knowledge workers come together from throughout the world, "blending interdisciplinary skills focusing on a particular project, completing the project, then disbanding the team as each of its workers move on to other projects" (Grantham, 2000). The most important asset in the productive process is no longer production capital but the knowledge that moves with such workers from one project to another. Elite knowledge-professionals thus relate in a new way to the means of production, becoming a distinct "*knowledge class.*"

High-Skill Production Workers
The jobs of many front-line production workers in today's networked workplaces have been radically restructured (Applebaum et al, 2000: 3–4). The late 1980s saw modest introduction of self-directing work teams that make and implement decisions without top–down control. The terms "process re-engineering" and "high-performance work systems" refer to such innovations. Employee participation in self-directing work teams in the United States was low in 1990, when among

6.5 million workers in companies responding to a survey, only 300, 000 (5 percent) were in self-directing teams (Levine, 1995: 3–7). But since then, many firms have increased the use of self-managing teams. The spread of digital information technologies converged in the 1990s with these workplace organization practices. Information technologies are fundamentally different from earlier innovations because information-based tools are highly malleable. They are reprogrammable, and the same equipment can perform a wide variety of customized functions. They reduce retooling time, and create opportunities for economies of scope. They have a built-in capacity for data collection and analysis to support decision-making (Ducatel, 1994; Applebaum, 2000).

"Smart" networked environments call for an increase in skills among front-line production workers as a result of both information technologies and worker participation practices. In these environments, the required skill-sets shift from manual and craft skills to higher-level cognitive skills including abstract reasoning, because the workers are removed from the physical processes of moving and making. They are system controllers, able to program and maintain their machines, as well as to interpret the data read-outs that the machines produce.

Information technologies fit best in settings in which workers and managers cooperate directly in production processes (Ducatel, 1994). Workers in these environments require additional "soft" skills in communication and group decision-making. Eileen Applebaum uses the term "high performance work systems" to refer to work situations in which new organizational processes and information technologies have converged. In these systems front-line workers require information processing and communications skills (Applebaum, 2000), must be able to carry out a wide range of tasks. This flexibility presupposes training in the use of networked computers. They also must develop "interpersonal and behavioral skills, to take on supervisory and coordination functions, and to interact effectively with other workers and managers" (Applebaum, 2000: 208). Prior cross-cultural and cross-class experiences are very valuable in acquiring these soft skills.

Cappelli and his co-authors (1999) have noted that American firms have moved more slowly toward high-skill systems than competitors in Japan and Western Europe, because the larger scale of American production accommodates mass production, long-established traditions of top-down management have been difficult to change, and low-wage minority and immigrant workers are plentiful. Thus the advantages of low-skill mass production using low-cost routine labor remain strong in many segments of American industry. These advantages are also strong in developing nations with large populations of displaced rural workers.

Routine Production and In-Person Service Workers

The direct result of globalization in neo-liberal developed nations such as the United States and the United Kingdom has been a widening income division between high-skill and low-skill segments of the economy, and a relative reduction of the former and expansion of the latter. The routine worker category is growing rapidly while the middle-tier is declining, causing an "hour-glass" shaped distribution with less room in the middle and more at the bottom. The "routine worker" category contains a high proportion of women including single heads of households, disadvantaged minorities, and recent immigrants from developing nations (including illegal aliens), in, for example, material moving, fast-food and low-end retail and healthcare occupations, and as handlers, helpers, and laborers (Amiratimadi and Wah, 2002: 94). Unlike industrial workers of the 1950s, a large proportion of today's routine workers work in temporary or part-time "contingent" work. From 1970 to 1992 the total payroll of American temporary employees in real terms rose an astounding 3,000 percent (Weinbaum, 1999). While many American routine workers are drawn from poor native-born black and Hispanic groups, a substantial fraction of both blacks and Hispanics in the American labor force are foreign born. In New York City three quarters of recent immigrants have come from such poor third-world countries as Haiti, Nigeria, Jamaica, the Dominican Republic, Ecuador, and Columbia. Since 1980 there has been a very substantial increase in the proportion of the new immigrants in lower-tier occupations, and a substantial decline in their real and relative earnings (Amiratimadi and Wah, 2002: 96). These workers form a growing *working poor* class.

Informal Underclass Workers

Estimates indicate that from 20 percent to 70 percent of the mega-urban workforce in the developing world works in the informal economy (the average of various estimates is 50 percent), altogether outside the government-regulated and taxed system of employment (Simon, 1998). These workers sell hot food or used clothing from make-shift booths, or repair bikes and cars on the streets, or shine shoes, sort and recycle rubbish or used machines, or sell sex services. These informal workers are essential to the economies of these cities, as they feed and clothe a large part of the population, and supply used parts that keep capital equipment operating. They provide a low-cost infrastructure to maintain low production costs in the formal sector of the economy. They comprise a *working underclass* outside the official social system. Network technology skills can upgrade the job prospects of routine workers, and facilitate opportunities for college-level occupational training. In surprising ways, these skills can also enhance the work tasks and incomes of informal workers, by reorganizing informal work into individual and collective business enterprises. Network technologies can, moreover, also be useful in delivering knowledge work and entrepreneurial skills even to young people who have left formal schooling for informal work. I discuss these points in the next section.

Section 3: Reconstructing Technological Literacy

The New Problem of Technological Literacy Education

The global technology problem-situation today, as outlined in the previous section, is very different from the problem-situation motivating the initial conceptions of technological literacy. A new and more relevant conception is therefore needed.

Two changes are especially important. First, the world population in 1970 was approximately 3.7 billion. Today it stands at 6.4 billion, an increase of 73 percent in just less than a quarter century. World population growth, however, has dropped from over 2 percent in 1970 to just over 1 percent today, and is not, in itself, the pressing issue it was in 1970, though the annual *numerical* increase in population remains more or less constant. Second, globalization has integrated most nations in Asia, Latin America, and Eastern and Central Europe into the world economy, and digital production and communications technologies have also integrated their populations into the global techno-structure. Seoul, Korea is not only the largest city in the world, but also the city with the highest level of digital delivery of government services and participation in democratic action (E Governance Institute, 2003). Brazil, with its notorious mega-city "favelas" (urban shanty-towns), is also the first nation in the world to establish a completely electronic voting system, with 406,000 electronic ballet boxes (Belos, 2002). As networked enterprises spread, networked computers are found throughout the workplaces of the developing world, and are spreading to schools and youth centers. With concerted effort, networked computers can now be made widely available for education.

The conceptions of technological literacy introduced in the 1970s and 1980s have, as a result, three primary shortcomings from a contemporary standpoint.

First, even a quarter-century ago the populations of the largest metropolitan regions were much smaller and less ethnically diverse than today. In global society, migrants from developing nations surge into the metropolitan regions of developed nations. They perform in-person services at every income level from medical specialist to hospital orderly. The cities of the developing nations, in turn, draw migrants from ethnically diverse groups in the surrounding rural areas. The megacity seaports, with their long histories as trading centers, are particularly diverse. Initial conceptions of technological literacy made passing reference to ethnically diverse students in central city schools of developed nations. Today, ethnic and linguistic diversity is the dominant feature of urban education, and because of the greater diversity of the urban workforce, soft skills in cross-group communication are understood to be essential in work settings. A relevant contemporary conception of technological literacy would place concerns of ethnic diversity, social stratification, and school exclusion and isolation, front and center.

Second, while the initial conceptions certainly encouraged project-based learning, their model projects did not essentially involve networked computers or the manipulation of real-time data. These initial conceptions were forged shortly after the introduction of microcomputers into schools, and long before the introduction of the World-Wide Web. Computers in most workplaces and schools at that time were weak, stand-alone machines. The economic and technical convergence of globalization leading to "knowledge work" and "networked enterprise" had not yet taken place. Today, however, "the machine *is* the network." An ever-increasing proportion of educational facilities have some networked computers, and school projects, organized both on and off site, can gradually approximate the problems faced by skilled knowledge workers. An up-to-date conception of technological literacy must take account of this basic fact.

Third, the initial notions of technology literacy education tied technology-related learning to established curriculum sites such as science, math, social studies, language arts, and vocational/technical education. Technological literacy education was essentially a component of the secondary-school curriculum. Today metropolitan education can be conceived not merely as an official "school system," but as a "network" with nodes that include government-funded official and alternative private and charter schools, learning centers, detention facilities, extracurricular programs operated by nongovernmental agencies, and home-schools. As a result, the assumption can no longer be made that that curriculum designs requiring the preselection and presequencing of subject matters are most appropriate. Technological literacy educators must be open to experimentation with less-structured "post-curricular" designs (Green, 1995). A contemporary conception of technological literacy education should, moreover, be relevant to educational efforts throughout the network, both within and beyond the formal school curriculum.

Reconstructing Technological Literacy

Leaders in technological literacy education still remain committed to the paradigms established a quarter century ago. They are, nonetheless, recognizing some limitations that constrain the implementation of their preferred models. Hungerford and Volk, for example, recently complained that despite more than twenty years of hard work, environmental and technological literacy education remain inadequate, inconsistent, and scattered, with practitioners consistently ignoring research findings (Hungerford and Volk, 2003). Technology educators protest that despite new standards that explain the "what," "how," and "why" of technological literacy, the "where" and "when" remain elusive (Meade and Dugger, 2005), and grumble that school leaders, "deluded" that teaching students how to use networked computers will convey technological literacy, waste huge sums on purchasing, installing and connecting them (Weber, 2005).

In light of these frustrations, the time may be ripe for a more fundamental reconsideration of technological literacy education for the global network era. We can build on the initial process model of technological literacy education, which, as stated earlier, involved (1) raising awareness and engaging the interest of learners in technology-related problems, (2) conveying scientific and technical knowledge related to those problems, (3) guiding student investigations of the problems, and (4) assisting in the analysis of results to promote practical decision-making and student action. Each of these components, however, can be reconsidered in light of economic globalization and the spread of computer networks. I will take the components one at a time.

Engagement

For today's learners the primary challenge stemming from the global network environment is to avoid getting trapped in the routine or informal occupational sectors. A secondary school diploma no longer is a ticket to advantageous occupational opportunities. As a result, participants in today's technological literacy efforts can no longer assumed to be committed school students. They may instead be disadvantaged youths at risk for dropping out, or part- time students working in the informal economies of developing nations (e.g., as trash recyclers or commercial sex workers), or young adult immigrants from poor countries. Recruiting and engaging members of each of these groups in educational projects pose distinct problems. The problems engaging them are rarely the abstract problems that typified earlier technological literacy efforts: environmental pollution, depletion of industrial materials, or protection of endangered species. Often they are problems of immediate personal survival.

Young people from all social groups are, however, for better or worse, more attracted than ever to new technologies such as cell phones, game players, and the Internet, and even children from poor families have surprising savvy in playing computer games and surfing the web. Technological literacy educators, using a kind of pedagogical jiu-jitsu, can turn this pre-existing attraction into a peg for significant learning experiences. Learners will acquire the skills of knowledge workers only if they engage with environments that support contemporary knowledge acquisition and use. Instead of complaining about the costs of computer networking, technological literacy educators should seize the opportunities for engagement (and subsequent awareness, investigation, decision-making and action) that this strong emotion-based attraction to technology provides

Conveying Scientific and Technological Knowledge and Skill

Initial models of technological literacy education were designed to fit into school curriculum sites and they accepted the standard curriculum as a given background. The problems appropriate for technological literacy education, however, change as we consider *all* learners including the poor, minority, and immigrant learners increasingly populating urban areas and educational networks, and taking their specific needs into account. Those on the verge of dropping out of school, or in alternative schools or informal educational settings, are not captive audiences. They only become engaged when lessons address their own pressing problems and interests, as they perceive them, in concrete ways. Technological literacy educators in such settings, as a result, cannot preselect curriculum content based on standard topics in the secondary curriculum. Instead, content selection requires continuous inputs and feedback from learners.

An example illustrates this point. Homeless trash recyclers in San Paulo formed a cooperative with the assistance of a nongovernmental organization, and established a profitable and efficient business by using networked computers to locate trash, organize inventory, and link with markets. The program was able to recruit them and provide technological knowledge and skill because the young workers, from the beginning, helped shape the program to meet their needs.

Guiding Student Investigations
The concept of "issue investigations" in early formulations of technological literacy education was shaped by a notion of "investigation" that was too academic. Despite the official goal of "science and technology for all," the issue investigations in technological literacy education served primarily to bolster research skills useful for college preparation. Poor students from inferior primary schools lacked the complex academic skills and background knowledge to perform such investigations. In implementing technological literacy, the phases involving investigations or discovery learning were often neglected, or used selectively for academically gifted or motivated students.

Even capable students from disadvantaged groups saw no obvious pathways leading from their present life situation to college and the professional workforce, moreover, so many of them were not motivated to engage personally in these intellectually demanding investigations. The root idea of guiding student's use of knowledge and information in inquiries that generate new knowledge and information relevant for practical decisions and actions, however, remains valid today. It needs, however, to be conceived in a broader, less-exclusively academic, way.

In today's "knowledge society," knowledge professionals and high-skilled production workers use complex background knowledge from their educations and their out-of school experiences, in unpredictable ways. They combine it with flows of real-time data and information, and knowledge modules such as online software tutorials, to respond to ill-structured problems and make decisions under conditions of uncertainty. To connect technological literacy with mature use of technology, the model of knowledge discovery and use in technological literacy education should be that of the "generalized knowledge worker." Scientific research and engineering design should be understood merely as special, limit cases of "investigation" in knowledge work.

This simple idea has three immediate implications.

First, problems selected for investigation must be broadened to include those affecting the immediate economic and social challenges of all learners, across the socioeconomic spectrum. While these include problems of broad social significance and intellectual interest, they also include problems of personal economic survival, health, safety and shelter, basic labor rights, and protection from exploitation and child trafficking. The educational efforts of some non-governmental organizations are exemplary, and can often serve as models for school-based programs.

Second, full weight should be given to the vernacular knowledge of young people. Educators often downplay community-based, real-world knowledge, using official school knowledge to "trump" the knowledge young people bring to school. In the process, they unwittingly render learners "ignorant" in the school setting. But vernacular knowledge ("street smarts") is highly relevant to problems that can be treated in technology education. Young trash recyclers in third world cities, for example, know more about the sources of, and markets for, machine parts than schoolteachers and even manufacturers. Their day to day work experiences *are* investigations of these matters. Today, these street smarts include skills in playing computer games, in web surfing, and even in reconfiguring computer hardware.

Third, in the problems under investigation, even those of the trash recyclers, networked computers can be used as practical tools for gathering, storing, and manipulating information, and for acquiring knowledge on an as-needed or just-in-time basis.

Guiding Student Decision and Action

While participation in the ameliorative projects of nongovernmental organizations was given rhetorical support in initial conceptions of technological literacy, it was rarely central to technology literacy education as implemented in schools. Many young people, both rich and poor, moreover, were too engaged in their own problems to take much interest in abstractions like "the environment" or "future generations." Today, however, nongovernmental organizations often recruit and train young people to "take action" on their *own* behalf, and the schools should link their students to these organizations. In Indonesia, for example, KOMPAK seeks to increase the awareness of Jakarta's child workers about their labor rights, and to protect them from exploitation and trafficking, through computer games and simulations. In Nicaragua, the Ben Linder cyber café in Managua offers free computer education and Internet access to poor young people, and serves as a hub for community centers throughout the nation.

Networked Learning and Technological Literacy

A greater synergy in metropolitan education can be attained through systematic cooperation between the school and nongovernment sectors in the broader educational network. As noted above, local "nodes" in such networks now include mainstream schools, but also alternative schools, home schools, learning centers, and facilities organized by nongovernmental organizations.

Significant learning could be promoted by adopting learning designs incorporating problem-solving tasks gradually approximating adult roles as networked knowledge workers. Today, interactive computer networks have spread to educational and cultural institutions, learning centers, libraries, and homes, making new forms of learning, approximating the conditions of knowledge work, practicable. The networks can be used to connect "front-line" educators (whether teachers, librarians, parents or social activists) to a vast world of networked "back-line" sources of knowledge, information, and expertise. These "back-line" sources might include knowledge workers in government, industry, the university, and nongovernmental organizations. Networked educational "knowledge workers," linking students and schools to back-line resources, could reconstruct schools as "network enterprises."

An explicitly recognized "networked school" organization for a metropolitan region could coordinate the local "front-line" educational facilities and educators and regional "back-line" facilities, educators, and resource people. The "back-line" structure could be used to organize virtual activities connecting diverse groups of young people throughout the region and providing them with many opportunities for hands-on use of computers for problem solving. It could also bring these diverse learners together from time to time, as appropriate given the society's goals for interethnic and interclass solidarity, for significant in-person project-based learning. These in-person cross-cultural and cross-class experiences in networked-computer environments would be valuable for spreading "soft skills" throughout the region. They could be coordinated with preliminary and follow up learning at local sites, using network technologies (e-mail, distance learning, list-servers, websites) to maintain "virtual" inter-group contact. I refer to this kind of network organization as a "networked common school" (Waks, 2004).

Summary

Globalization refers to the broad integration of economic activity and broad spread of computer networks on an essentially worldwide basis. The convergence of economic and technological developments has enabled a radical restructuring of enterprise, including a reorganization of the global division of labor. A four-fold division of the labor force has resulted, with a growing gap between knowledge professionals and high skill production workers on the one hand, and routine production and service workers in the contingent economy and informal workers on the other.

Some segments of industry in the developed world rely increasingly on knowledge workers, but many segments, especially in the United States, still compete on the basis of economies of scale in mass market production and use of low-skill, low-cost routine labor. Routine workers are drawn primarily from native-born disadvantaged minorities and recent immigrants from poor nations. They compete for low-wage work without job security or health benefits. Developing nations in the global economy also employ knowledge professionals and highly skilled production workers, but a large part of the workforce exists in the informal economy, outside the government-administered system of employment and taxation.

Knowledge work requires a high level of academic preparation, flexible thinking and problem solving capabilities, and human relations skills—especially abilities to cooperate in highly diverse work teams. Schools in the developed world with a conventional curriculum offer many students few opportunities for high-level academic achievement, flexible thinking and problem solving skills, or positive inter-group experiences. As a result, the students are poorly prepared for college or knowledge work. Their bleak future prospects inhibit attachment to school and academic learning. A large proportion of young people in the developing world lack basic access to secondary education, and are subject to great risks of exploitation and abuse.

The reconstruction of technological literacy education would seek to engage all learners, from all sectors of society, in learning tasks approximating those of knowledge workers in the global network economy. Technological literacy education should now be reconceived to emphasize the use of networked computers in addressing complex, poorly structured problems, including the urgent economic, social, and personal problems today's students face.

Some educational out-reach activities of nongovernmental organizations offer exemplary models for this kind of education. In many cases they offer the only educational lifeline for child workers lacking access to secondary education, and hence to the academic knowledge and skills required for knowledge work. Some have successfully used networked computers to assist informal workers in converting their work situations into individual or collective business enterprises. Others have provided Internet access to poor young people as a means of bringing them together and providing them with health and education benefits, and to rally them in support of their own basic human rights.

The metropolitan educational organization within which technological literacy education functions can now be reconceived as a network, rather than merely as a system of official schools. Through the extensive use of networked computers this network can arrange activities bringing learners together across ethnic and class lines, can facilitate technological literacy through project-based learning in both face to face and virtual environments, and can help to forge a synergy among the metropolitan region's educational providers, including schoolteachers, youth workers, social activists in nongovernmental organizations, business people, and parents involved with home schooling.

References

Amirahmadi, H. and Wah, T. (2002). "New York City: A social profile and alternative economic futures." *Journal of Urban Technology*. 91, 85–107.

Applebaum, E., Bailey, P. and Kalleberg, A. (2000). *Manufacturing Advantage: Why High Performance Work Systems Pay Off*. Ithaca, NY: Cornell University Press.

Belos, A. (2002). "From jungle to capital the voting is electronic." *The Guardian* October 5, 2002. At http://www.guardian.co.uk/international/story/ 0%2C3604%2C805092%2C00.html

Brown, P., Green, A., and Lauder, H. (2001). *High Skills: Globalization, Competitiveness, and Skill Formation*. Oxford: Oxford University Press.

Cappelli, P. (1999). *Employment practices and business strategies*. Oxford: Oxford University Press

Castells, M. (1996). *The Rise of Network Society*. Cambridge: Blackwell.

Dizard, W. (1997). *Meganet:How the Global Communications Network will Connect Everyone on Earth* . Boulder, CO: Westview.

Ducatel, K (ed.). (1994) . *Employment and Technical change in Europe: Work organization, Skills and Training*. Hants, Aldershot: Edward Elgar.

E-Governance Institute. (2003). *Digital governance in municipalities worldwide: An assessment of municipal websites throughout the world*. Rutgers University. Newark, New Jersey, Grantham, C.(2000). *The Future of Work. The Promise of the New Digital Age*. New York: McGraw-Hill.

Green, B. (1995). "Post curriculum possibilities: English teaching, cultural politics, and the postmodern turn." *Journal of Curriculum Studies*, 27: 4, 391–409.

Howe, W. (2001). *A Brief History of The Internet*. Available online at http:// www.wathowe.Com/navnet/history.html

Hungerford, H., Peyton, R. B., and Wilke, R. (1980). "Goals for curriculum development in environmental education." *Journal of Environmental Education*, 11, 42–47.

Hungerford, H. and T. Volk. (2003). "Notes from Harold Hungerford and Trudi Volk." *Journal of Environmental Education* 43: 2, 4–6.

Levine, D. (1995). *Reinventing the Workplace: How Business and Employees can both win*. Washington D.C., Brookings.

Meade, S. and W. Dugger. (2005). "Presenting the program addenda to ITEA's technological literacy standards." *Technology Teacher*. 64: 6, 26–29.

NTIA (National Telecommunications and Information Administration) (2002). *A Nation Online: How Americans are Expanding their use of the Internet*. Available online at ntia.doc.gov/ntiahome/dn/index.html

Richmond, A. (2002). "Globalization: implications for immigrants and refugees." *Ethnic and racial studies*, 25: 5, 707–728.

Reich, R. (1992). *The Work of Nations: Preparing Ourselves for 21st Century Capitalism*. New York: Vintage.

Sassen, S. (1994). *Cities in a World Economy*. Thousand Oaks: Pine Forge.

Simon, P. (1998). "Informal responses to crises of urban employment: an investigation into the structure and relevance of small-scale informal retailing in Kaduna, Nigeria." *Regional Studies* 32, 6.

Waks, L. (2004). "The concept of a 'Networked Common School." *E-Learning* 1: 2, (317–328).

Weber, K. (2005). "Proactive approach to technological literacy". *Technology Teacher*. 64: 7, 28–31.

Weinbaum, E. (1999). "Organizing labor in an era of contingent work and globalization." Chapter 2 in B. Nissen, (Ed.) *Which Direction for Organized Labor?* Detroit: Wayne State University Press, 37–58.

CHAPTER 18

From Knowledge to Information: Virtual Classrooms or Automated Diploma Mills?

Michael A. Peters

Martin Heidegger's Philosophy of Technology

Everywhere we remain unfree and chained to technology, whether we passionately affirm or deny it. But we are delivered over to it in the worst possible way when we regard it as something neutral for this conception of it, to which today we particularly like to do homage, makes us utterly blind to the essence of technology. (Heidegger, 1997: 4)

I begin with a quotation from Martin Heidegger because even though the essay "The Question Concerning Technology" was delivered in 1953—some forty-five years ago—it remains one of the most profound statements concerning technology that has been made. Heidegger's essay has not only become a philosophical classic but also has remained an important source of inspiration for a generation of philosophers writing of the nature of technology, including Herbert Marcuse and Jürgen Habermas of the Frankfurt School, and those like Michel Foucault and Jacques Derrida whom we might call "poststructuralists."

I begin with Heidegger also because I want to avoid an approach that seeks to develop explanations of technology in relation to education from within the field of education, so to speak. If anything, the nature of technology and its relation to education needs to be explained in terms of a very broad picture. Heidegger provides a perspective for considering technology in this way, and in doing so he confounds our taken-for-granted assumptions about modern technology. In terms of the received view technology is something that stands in a subsidiary, instrumental, and temporal relation with modern science. Modern physical science begins in the seventeenth century; historically it is seen as achieving a kind of take-off in Europe by 1750, and its institutionalization through royal societies, learned societies, and universities also dates from a considerably earlier period, with the establishment of the Royal Society in 1660. Machinic technology, by contrast, is pictured as beginning in the eighteenth century and is seen essentially as the "handmaiden" to science, regarded as an application of "pure" or applied science.

With his perspective Heidegger, however, reverses the chronological order of the received view and ontologically prioritizes technology over science. He distinguishes technology in its various manifestations from its essence that is *not* technological and describes this essence by returning to the Greek concept of *techné*, which relates to the activities and skills of the artisan. The essence of technology, Heidegger maintains, is a *poiesis* or "bringing forth" which is grounded in revealing (*aletheia*). As he says: "The essence of modern technology shows itself in what we call Enframing . . . It is the way in which the real reveals itself as standing-reserve" (Heidegger, 1977: 23). This essence then encapsulates a "productionist metaphysics" because the concept of "standing reserve" refers to resources that are stored in anticipation of consumption. Ingrid Scheibler (1993: 116) explains that modern technology, for Heidegger, "is linked to a particular mode of conceiving our relation to the world—of bringing forth—through a process that objectifies the world." Scheibler goes on to explain that for Heidegger the essence of technology is part of the broader project of understanding the relation of this mode of objectifying experience to the tradition of Western metaphysics, which means that the question concerning technology cannot be thought apart from the critique of Western metaphysics (see also Peters, 2002).

Heidegger (1977: 4) poses the question quite forthrightly:

> According to ancient doctrine, the essence of a thing is considered to be what the thing is. We ask the question concerning technology when we ask what it is. Everyone knows the two statements that answer our question. One says: Technology is a means to an end. The other says: Technology is a human activity.

Two definitions are furnished: the instrumental and the anthropological. Heidegger goes on to question the instrumental and the will to mastery that such a conception entails. This is the source, in part, for the notion of instrumental rationality, a purely technical reason that Habermas, along with other members of the Frankfurt School, contrast strongly to practical reason. Heidegger's account strongly influenced Foucault's notions of technologies of domination and of self, and is central to the way in which new information-and-communications technologies have the power to restructure or reformat our subjectivities and identities. Heidegger's analysis of the "will to will" foreshadows the critical concern with cybernetics and self-regulating system that take on a cultural significance of their own.

The Question Concerning Technology was one of Heidegger's later works. Based on four lectures delivered in 1949 the book captured Heidegger's ontological approach to a war-torn Europe and elaborated his concern for a technical nihilism. The question of European nihilism he inherited directly from Nietzsche, and the catastrophe of Europe after the war, he described in terms of the confrontation with global technology. Yet as we have already seen for Heidegger, 'technology's essence is nothing technological' (1977: 4). It is a system—*Gestell*—an all-encompassing view of technology, described as a mode of human existence. Heidegger is careful not to pose as an optimist or pessimist; his account is one that relates technology back to a critique of the Western metaphysical tradition and focuses upon the way machinic technology can alter our mode of being, distorting our actions and aspirations. It is based also on a history of philosophy that illuminates the *longue dureé* of Western cultural development.

Heidegger's account of technology has been criticized on a number of grounds. Andrew Feenberg (1996), for instance, writes:

> Translated out of Heidegger's own ontological language, he seems to be saying that technology constitutes a new type of cultural system that restructures the entire social world as an object of control. This system is characterized by an expansive dynamic, which invades every pretechnological enclave and shapes the whole of social life. The instrumentalization of man and society is thus a destiny from which there is no escape other than retreat. The only hope is a vaguely evoked spiritual renewal that is too abstract to inform a new technical practice. As Heidegger explained in his last interview, "Only a god can save us" from the juggernaut of progress.

Feenberg's criticism is that Heidegger's argument is so abstract that it does not permit him to "discriminate between electricity and atom bombs, agricultural techniques and the Holocaust." All different forms and instances of technology are merely different expressions of an identical enframing, which we can only transcend through the recovery of a deeper relation to being: "And since he rejects technical regression while leaving no room for a modern alternative, it is difficult to see in what that relation would consist beyond a mere change of attitude." In a footnote (n. 3) Feenberg argues, "Heidegger envisages change in "technological thinking," but how is this change supposed to effect the design of actual devices? The lack of an answer to this question leaves me in some doubt as to the supposed relevance of Heideggers' work to ecology."

Feenberg's criticisms are well taken, but granted that Heidegger's account of technology is dressed up in the ontological language of "being" and related to the question of European nihilism and a critique of the Western metaphysical tradition, his account is necessarily very general. His account is also a philosophical account and does not allow theoretical discriminations between different forms of technology in the way that a socially and culturally embedded theory of technology might (see Feenberg, 1999 and see the "Theory of Technology" website at http://carbon.cudenver.edu/~mryder/itc_data/tech_theory.html which includes a number of full text-articles by Feenberg). (It must be remembered that Heidegger was writing before the PC revolution and well before the development of the widespread use of the new communications and information technologies.) Perhaps, one should judge the fecundity of philosophical argument by its richness and complexity, on the one hand, and by the different levels of interpretation it permits, on the other. On these criteria we can appreciate the way in which Heidegger's text (and writings more generally) have helped to stimulate a critical philosophy of technology, carried on in different ways by Marcuse, Habermas, Foucault, and Dreyfus.

The Shift from Knowledge to Information

The inspiration for this chapter also springs directly from the work of Jean-François Lyotard (1984) and his analysis of "knowledge in computerized societies." As he argues in *The Postmodern Condition*: "Our working hypothesis is that the status of knowledge is altered as societies enter what is known as the postindustrial age and cultures enter what is known as the postmodern age" (Lyotard, 1984: 3). His now-famous analysis in terms of the logic of *performativity* is prophetic for anyone who has lived through the last couple of decades in so-called advanced-liberal or neoliberal states. As he writes:

"Knowledge is and will be produced in order to be sold, it is and will be consumed in order to be valorized in a new production; in both cases, the goal is exchange." (4)

Lyotard's analysis of the "postmodern condition" is a review of the status of knowledge in advanced societies under the impact of technological transformation. As such Lyotard's prophetic and strategic analysis accomplishes the same end as Heidegger's philosophy in that it clearly involves a critique of the Western metaphysical tradition, a tradition in which Lyotard sees technology playing a fundamental role. And yet Lyotard is more specific than Heidegger, providing an account of the way in which technological developments underwrite the expansion of global capitalism.

He uses the term "postmodern condition" to describe the state of knowledge and the problem of its legitimation in the most highly developed societies. In this he follows sociologists and critics who have used the term to designate the state of Western culture "following the transformations which, since the end of the nineteenth century, have altered the game rules for science, literature and the arts" (Lyotard, 1984: 3). Lyotard places these transformations within the context of the crisis of narratives, especially those Enlightenment metanarratives concerning meaning, truth, and emancipation that have been used to legitimate both the rules of knowledge of the sciences and the foundations of modern institutions.

By "transformations" Lyotard is referring to the effects of the new technologies since the 1950s and their combined impact on the two principal functions of knowledge—research and the transmission of learning. Significantly, he maintains, the leading sciences and technologies have all been based on language-related developments—theories of linguistics, cybernetics, informatics, computer languages, telematics, theories of algebra—and their miniaturization and commercialization. In this context, Lyotard argues that the status of knowledge is permanently altered: its availability as an international commodity becomes the basis for national and commercial advantage within the global economy; its computerized uses in the military are the basis for enhanced state security and international monitoring. Knowledge, as he acknowledges, has already become the principal force of production, changing the composition of the workforce in developed countries. The commercialization of knowledge and its new forms of media circulation, he suggests, will raise new ethico–legal problems between the nation-state and the information-rich multinationals, as well as widening the gap between the so-called developed societies and the third world.

This is a *critical* account theorizing the status of knowledge and education in the postmodern condition which focuses upon the most highly developed societies. It constitutes a seminal contribution and important point of departure to what became known in the 1980s—in part due to Lyotard's work—as the modernity/post modernity debate, a debate which has involved many of the most prominent contemporary philosophers and social theorists (see Peters, 1995, 1996a). Lyotard's *The Postmodern Condition* is a book that directly addresses the concerns of education, examining the education and knowledge futures under conditions of global knowledge capitalism. Many of the features of Lyotard's analysis of the "postmodern condition"—an analysis nearly three decades old—now appears to be an accepted part of our experience in Western advanced-liberal societies.

Lyotard's critique leads us directly to the central question of legitimation of knowledge and education. If the Enlightenment idealist and humanist metanarratives have become bankrupt and the state and corporation must abandon or renounce them, where can legitimacy reside? Lyotard, in his critique of knowledge capitalism, suggests that the State has found its only credible goal in power. Science and education are to be legitimated, in de facto terms, through the principle of *performativity*, that is, through the logic of maximization of the system's performance, which becomes self-legitimating in Niklas Luhmann's (1982) sense.

It is this account that has proved so potent in analyzing the changes to economic and social policy that have taken place in the Western world with the ascendancy of neoliberalism. Education, not so long ago regarded as a universal welfare right under a social democratic model of the postwar settlement, has been recast as a leading sector of the economy and the basis of an entrepreneurial culture and knowledge economy. Lyotard's *The Postmodern Condition* (1984) provides an understanding and critique of the neoliberal marketization of education in terms of the systemic, self-regulatory nature of global capitalism. His work in general provides a clear account of the way in which the "new technologies" concern language. The substitution of automata for natural sequences carried out by the cortex renders language "informational" and, at the same time, it recenters science, technology, and economy in the following ways:

- The exteriorization of knowledge in relation to the knower;
- The introduction of fragmented activities and strongly hierarchized organization in research [in which the laboratory becomes a post-industrial workshop];

- An increased technologicization of knowledge where the new machines (such as particle accelerators, supercomputers, electronic telescopes, lasers), and their institutional routines help shape new kinds of research;
- The spread of automata to the so-called tertiary sectors of production, including the "elevation" of qualifications (new *métiers*), specialization in the tasks of the "employees," of the "inferior and average ranks of management," of the "ideas people" and "decision makers"; and
- The multiplication of commodities with integrated automata and, more generally, with an integrated language (the logical language of microprocessors) used in both production and consumption (developed from Lyotard, 1993: 16).

"Informatization" increases the concentration of the means of production of knowledge while allowing for its decentralization; it causes "technological unemployment" and devalues the productive labor; and it disperses the horizons of everyday life by transforming the relationship to wealth, encouraging the individual initiative of the user. Perhaps, most importantly, and rekindling the inspiration of Heidegger, Lyotard asserts that by informatizing language, the new technologies informatize the social bond, transforming our institutions and (inter)subjectivities.

I have developed these points and conceptual relationships in bullet points below. They emphasize the importance of information in a so-called global "information economy"; it hypothesizes a new kind of information capitalism predicated on the shift from knowledge to information.

Capitalism/Knowledge/Information

- Transformation of society from industrial to service to information economy.
- Transformation from analog to digital processing technologies.
- Transformation from knowledge to knowledge management, and from knowledge management to the articulation of fragmentary flows of information.
- Exponential growth of knowledge and emergence of the knowledge industry.
- Transformation from late capitalism to ad hoc transnational managerial capitalism and bricolage entrepreneurialism in postindustrial nations.

- Increased gaps between richer and poorer, in terms of both economic and cultural/informational capital.
- Increased problematic nature of property in general (including the technology of reproduction; intellectual property).

The following bullet points map the importance of these shifts specifically for education and begins to provide a basis for theorizing what I have called the "technologising of education."

Information/Education: "The Technologizing of Education"

- Commodification of education and knowledge.
- Increased splitting of academic fields, discourses, languages; homogenization under "theory."
- Commercialization of the university, alliance of business and education—that is, "the business of education," "education of business," "private–public partnerships."
- The growth of private training and education establishments and erosion of traditional "providers."
- Globalization of education, including the franchising and satellite broadcasting of educational programs and degrees and the development of private virtual universities.
- The recasting of "student" as "consumer" and teacher/lecturer as "provider."
- Increased interpenetration of "school," "university," and "home," "workplace" and "homeplace"—collapse of modernist enclosures or institutional spaces.
- The growing significance of the paradigm of "the copy" generating new legal, ethical issues concerning copyright, patent, plagiarism.
- The radical concordance of sound, text, and image involving a transition from book culture to image culture.
- The power of new information technologies to restructure consciousness and identity.

In this context, Mark Poster's path-breaking *The Mode of Information* (1990) provides an important set of arguments for consideration by anyone interested in the relation between education and technology. Poster is interested in developing a poststructuralist strategy for writing the contemporary history of the new communications. He wants to reconfigure "in theory certain phenomenon so that their disruptive potential can be recognized and perhaps in time be acted upon" (20). This leads him to invoke Marx's concept of the mode of production in relation to the history of communications to suggest that "history may be periodised by variations in the structure . . . of symbolic exchange, but also that the current situation gives a certain fetishistic importance to 'information'" (6). His main thesis, which he then investigates in relation to the work of Daniel Bell, Michel Foucault, Jacques Derrida, and Lyotard, is summarized in the following passage:

> Every age employs forms of symbolic exchange which contain internal and external structures, means and relations of signification. Stages in the mode of information may be tentatively designated as follows: face-to-face, orally mediated exchange; written exchanges mediated by print; and electronically mediated exchange. If the first stage is characterized by symbolic correspondences, and the second stage is characterized by the representation of signs, the third is characterized by informational simulations. In the first, oral stage, the self is constituted as a position of enunciation through its embeddedness in a totality of face-to-face relations. In the second, print stage the self is constructed as an agent centered in rational/imaginary autonomy. In the third, electronic stage the self is decentered, dispersed, and multiplied in continuous stability. (6)

If Poster is doing history here it is a kind of Foucauldian "philosophical" history for he defines himself primarily in relation to the history of the philosophy of the subject. In interviews with Poster (Peters and Marshall, 1995; Peters, 1996b) I questioned "the mode of information" and asked whether he thought the history of education was also governed and to some extent determined by these same stages. He replied that he thought the stages were applicable to history of education (while acknowledging that such history was not reducible to them) and stated that he believed that electronic technologies will profoundly affect the "modern student," agreeing with Richard Lanham (1993) that "the multimedia computer, hypertext programs and internet connectivity will likely undermine existing forms of authority, encourage visual over textual literacy and open new forms of communications."

I was interested to test to what extent Poster's thesis still shared some features with a Marxist philosophy of history and to what extent he was committed to technologically-derived stages of history. I was interested in the extent to which historical "stages" implied a linear progression of development and the way in which the notion of "stages" runs against the explicit rejection of periodizing that characterizes Lyotard's work. Poster admitted that stage theories of history are associated with grand narratives of progress and indicated that he had used "stage theory" in *The Mode of Information* for analytic purposes only. He argued that a stage theory can avoid the suggestion of progress and the function of legitimation, while still serving as a heuristic for empirical study and pointed to Foucault's theory of genealogy as one strong solution for configuring succeeding epochs as differential or discontinuous. He wanted to expand Foucault's notion to include *simultaneity* as well as discontinuity. By doing so, he suggested, we "might somehow envision periods not canceling each other but introducing possibilities of reconfiguration in which combinations of repetition and difference result in, to allude to Benjamin's term, new constellations."

In the interview, I focused on Poster's interpretation of Lyotard, ("Lyotard and Computer Science") in *The Mode of Information*. At one point in Poster's discussion he indicates that Lyotard distinguishes two narratives which furnish science with legitimation: the idea of progress in Britain, France, and the United States on the one hand, and the idea of education "as promoting the health of the nation . . . in Germany" (1990: 143), on the other. While there have existed metanarratives for the legitimation of science and education in the past it seemed clear that in the "postmodern condition" computerization and new communications-technologies provide a new ground or a relegitimizing narrative for science and development through education. In pursuing this thought I was referring to the way in which education is now regarded less as a universal welfare right of all citizens of a community and more as the means for the development of human capital in the "productive" areas of science and technology, which is seen as necessary for national competition within an increasingly global economy. This kind of discursive recasting of education policy according to the economic imperatives of science and technology, in part, lay behind the past popular iconography surrounding an ideology that motivated American educational reformers in the 1960s during the sputnik era, the "Space-Wars" scenario of the 1980s, and the more recent perceived threat to the world competitiveness of American enterprise in the 1990s. Within the discourse of "the second media age," focusing upon the economic benefits of the "information superhighway," education has been recast in terms of policy discourse as a new legitimizing metanarrative for "technoscience," to use Lyotard's term. In other words, far from encouraging a suspicion of metanarratives (Lyotard's famous definition of the postmodern condition), neo-liberal governments have developed new master narratives of national development that seem to wield great discursive power.

Poster, in response to this observation, referred to Lyotard's concern of the instrumentalisation of education and he acknowledged that the exact status of what Lyotard calls "performativity" is left somewhat ambiguous. Poster agrees that "performativity is part of the modern metanarrative, but one that de-emphasizes the values of freedom and equality. It is sort of an alegitimate legitimacy, an effort to be self-justifying without any adequate attention to justice as a category." He also agreed that there is a strong current of technoscientific utopianism in the United States which constituted a new metanarrative.

Neo-liberal economic theory is just catching up with the approach to "knowledge institutions" developed by Lyotard nearly two decades ago, albeit in a different register. Much of what has been written on the new communications-technologies by educationalists, including philosophers of education, tends towards accepting an instrumentalising view of the educational use of the new communications-technologies—a view which Heidegger, Lyotard and Poster, in their different ways, warn us against. There is a disturbing apolitical tendency in much of this work. It is the case that there is an *educational* focus to the relations between neoliberalism, globalization, and the new communications-technologies.

The Search for the Virtual Class

The notion of the "information society" passed into the sociological literature soon after Daniel Bell (1973) and Alain Touraine (1974) had written on "post-industrialism" in the late sixties. Bell had focused upon the centrality of theoretical knowledge and the social and institutional changes required for the "knowledge society." Touraine predicted the rise of new social movements associated with the shift to post-industrialism. His analysis led him to emphasize the way in which social life, including education, was being increasingly integrated into the realm of production. During the seventies and eighties the notion of the information society became part of a theory-laden and contested discourse about the future of advanced liberal societies. The debate had begun much earlier. The "cybernetics group," including Norbet Weiner, Claude Shanon, Von Neuman, and, perhaps surprisingly, the anthropologists Margaret Mead and Gregory Bateson, had met regularly during the 1940s to talk about systems theory and its applications. Together they had helped shape the culture of the cold war. During the 1960s, Fritz Machlup and Marc Porat charted the employment effects of an emerging U.S. information-economy and argued for productivity gains from investment in the information sector. Several generations of sociologists, economists, philosophers of technology, geographers, engineers, and politicians have debated the meaning and significance of the technical transformations wrought by communications and information technologies in the post-war period.

One particular contemporary variant of this discourse on the 'information society' is closely tied to neoliberalism; it is wildly utopian; it uses a hyperbolic language of "revolution" and attempts to conjure up a vision of the future; it emphasizes universal and abstract techno-fix solutions to social and economic problems; it focuses upon the technical transformation of society, highlighting the commercial benefits; and it approaches technology in general as something that, in itself, is neutral, denying the necessity of social or political analysis.

Manuel Castells (1989) has argued that there is a historical coincidence of the restructuring of capitalism and the rise of the informational mode of development resulting in the formation of a specific techno–economic paradigm. The restructuring of capital, involving the appropriation of a significantly higher share of surplus from the production process and a changed pattern of state intervention away from political legitimation and social redistribution to establishing conditions that are favorable for capital accumulation, could never have been accomplished without the development of the technological and organizational potential of internationalism. He argues, "There is an interactive effect between the new form of capitalism and the technological revolution and new forms of organization have been adopted" (29).

Some years ago John Tiffin and Lalita Rajasingham wrote a book that "presents a vision of what education and training could become as information technology develops." Their *In Search of the Virtual Class: Education in an Information Society* (1995) is an example of what I describe above. The book promises a great deal but is disappointing in what it delivers. Tiffin held the David Beattie chair of communications studies at Victoria University in New Zealand and Dr Rajasingham is senior lecturer in the same department. They have all the right credentials and experience. The acknowledgments make clear that the Network College of Communication in the Pacific acted as a sounding board and the Telecom Corporation of New Zealand and Ameritech supported their research. (As the authors make clear, "The 1990s is the decade of telecommunications" (102) and "the learner-centered, market-driven model of education" (85) based on telelearning in cyberspace is their panacea). The book is dedicated to their adopted country—New Zealand—("First country to give women the vote . . . to make university education universally available . . . to develop a national telelearning network"), and yet there is no further reference to New Zealand, nothing that applies distinctively to New Zealand, its society or culture. The vision could be equally applied anywhere in the world; in fact, it is touted as *the* global solution to the problem of modern education.

The vision that Tiffin and Rajasingham put forward is encapsulated in a little story they tell about Shirley who goes off to school by donning her school helmet to enter the virtual world of her virtual school. Her father is already "teleworking"; the family are to go "teleshopping" later; Shirley is "telelearning." With nanotechnology, the helmet is more likely to be a "datasuit as a second skin which eliminates the stimuli from the real world and replaces it by stimuli from a computer" (137). Curiously, the authors believe this futuristic long-term vision will sustain us. While they refer to the science fiction of William Gibson (*Neuromancer*) and others, they do not seem to want to acknowledge the implicit critique that bubbles beneath the surface of this genre.

The justification for such a vision lies in systems theory, "education is communication"—("the classroom is a communication machine" [20])—and communication is defined in terms of three functions: transmission of information, its storage, and its processing. This constitutes the "new paradigm of education," which is based upon the choice of telecommunications rather than transport. It is a paradigm that is seen to overcome the traditional problems of space, storage and time of conventional education. In addition, it is seen to be learner-centered, problem-focused, flexible, accessible, and much cheaper. Anyone can access information at any time and both the home and the workplace will become communication systems for education. Education becomes the global educational utility based upon forms of teleconferencing and the virtual class is the place where, following Bucksminster Fuller, "we can learn to think globally and act locally" (187). Such a global educational utility in New Zealand would presumably be provided and controlled more by Telecom than the state (or perhaps, a consumer-driven education could be contracted-out?).

Frankly, the underlying concept of education here is very technocratic. This is not to suggest that Shanon's work on communication systems is not important or useful or, even, that systems theory does not have interesting applications in education (for example, Gregory Bateson's notion of "double-loop learning' and Chris Argyris" work). It is to say that technically driven understandings of education, or technologically deterministic concepts, require careful scrutiny. There is a huge literature that deals with these questions in a theoretically sophisticated way. I would like to briefly mention in this context the work of

Mark Poster (1990), Anthony Smith (1996), and Tim Luke (1989, 1998) (see also Peters, 1996a, 1996c; Peters and Lankshear, 1996).

Tiffin and Rajasingham have provided a *forbidding* vision; one that is frightening in its technical simplicity and one seemingly unaware of the political context or social consequences of the rationalistic cybernetic epistemology underlying it. This is a great pity given the opportunity for critique, especially when it is most required. Various ministers of education have characteristically defined information technology as one of the three forces that will shape higher education in the twenty-first century (along with increased demand and internationalization). While mention is often made of information technology in terms that implicitly underlie the reform of higher education, it is not examined or analyzed as a condition of higher education in either national or international contexts, except as a cost-cutting measure or more flexible delivery mode. Tiffin and Rajasingham's technical vision acts only as a grim reminder of what education might become in the "brave new world."

Automated Diploma Mills?

Some years ago David Noble (1998) drew our attention to events at two large North American universities that signal we have moved into the era of automation of higher education. (His book of the same title was published in 2002.) He mentions that through its "Instructional Enhancement Initiative" UCLA has become the first major university to make mandatory the use of computer telecommunications technology in the delivery of higher education. Meanwhile at York University in Toronto, faculty ended a two-month strike taken partly in response to unilateral administrative initiatives in the implementation of instructional technology. At both universities, the administrations had spawned its own subsidiaries, in partnership with the private-sector companies, committed to the commercial development of online education.

Noble suggests, "at the very outset of this new age of higher education, the lines have already been drawn in the struggle which will ultimately determine its shape. On the one side university administrators and their myriad commercial partners, on the other those who constitute the core relation of education: students and teachers."

He goes on to suggest the campus has been identified as a major site of capital accumulation—a transformation involving two phases focusing upon the conversion of ideas into intellectual property: the first began twenty years ago with the commodification of the research function of the university and transformed scientific and engineering knowledge into commercially viable proprietary products that could be owned and bought and sold in the market. The second, which has only begun recently, entails the commodification of the educational function of the university, and involves the transformation of courses into courseware, the activity of instruction itself into commercially viable proprietary products that can be owned and bought and sold in the market. As he argues, "In the first phase the universities became the site of production and sale of patents and exclusive licenses. In the second, they are becoming the site of production of—as well as the chief market for—copyrighted videos, courseware, CD-ROMs, and Web sites."

The second transformation of higher education is driven by corporate trainers, technozealots, university administrators, and the vendors of the network hardware, software, and "content," such as Apple, IBM, Bell, the cable companies, Microsoft, and the edutainment and publishing companies Disney, Simon and Schuster, Prentice-Hall, etc. who see higher education as a multi-billion-dollar industry.

Universities throughout North America, Noble (1998) warns, are rapidly being overtaken by this second phase of commercialization. There are the stand-alone virtual institutions like University of Phoenix, the wired private institutions like the New School for Social Research, the campuses of state universities like the University of Maryland and the new Gulf-Coast campus of the University of Florida (which boasts no tenure). On the state level, the states of Arizona and California have initiated their own state-wide virtual university projects, while a consortia of western "Smart States" have launched their own ambitious effort to wire all of their campuses into an online educational network. In Canada, a national effort has been undertaken, spearheaded by the Telelearning Research Network centered at Simon Fraser University in Vancouver, to bring most of the nation's higher education institutions into a "Virtual U" network.

The commodification of university instruction raises issues about the introduction of new technologies of production for the faculty traditional labor. As teachers are drawn into a production process designed for the efficient creation of instructional commodities their activity is restructured and, accordingly, their autonomy, independence, and control over their work is reduced. Workplace knowledge and control is concentrated more and more into the hands of the administration. Noble (1998) explains:

> Once faculty and courses go online, administrators gain much greater direct control over faculty performance and course content than ever

before and the potential for administrative scrutiny, supervision, regimentation, discipline and even censorship increase dramatically. At the same time, the use of the technology entails an inevitable extension of working time and an intensification of work as faculty struggle at all hours of the day and night to stay on top of the technology and respond, via chat rooms, virtual office hours, and e-mail, to both students and administrators to whom they have now become instantly and continuously accessible. The technology also allows for much more careful administrative monitoring of faculty availability, activities, and responsiveness.

David Noble provides the antidote to the utopian techno-dreams of Tiffin and Rajasingham. He provides a grounded analysis of a kind of contemporary history of the university which focuses upon a deskilling of faculty and the administrative monitoring and control of their knowledge. Noble's view is based upon his own recent experiences at York University: he thinks we are moving inexorably towards automated diploma mills. I find Noble's analysis consistent with the critical view of technology I outlined above by reference to Heidgger, Lyotard, and Poster. But it is not to say that this is the way things must be or that technology will be exploited by capital against labor.

Acknowledgments

Parts of this chapter are based upon a paper entitled "The Question Concerning Virtual Technology in Higher Education—The Shift from Knowledge to Information" in Peters and Roberts, 1998.

References

Bell, D. (1973). *The Coming of Post-Industrial Society*. New York: Basic Books.

Castells, M. (1989). *The Informational City: Information Technology, Economic Restructuring, and the Urban-Regional Process*. Oxford, UK; New York, NY: Blackwell.

Feenberg, A. (1996). *From Essentialism to Constructivism: Philosophy of Technology at the Crossroads* at http://www-rohan.sdsu.edu/faculty/feenberg/talk4.html (accessed June 22, 2005).

Heidegger, M. (1977). *The Question Concerning Technology*. W. Lovitt, trans. New York: Harper and Row.

Lanham, R. (1993). *The Electronic Word: Democracy, Technology and the Arts*. Chicago and London: University of Chicago Press.

Luhmann, N. (1982). *The Differentiation of Society*. New York: Columbia University Press.

Luke, T. (1989). *Screens of Power: Ideology, Domination and Resistance in Informational Society.* Urbana: University of Illinois Press.

Luke, T. (1998). "Discipline and discourse in the digital domain: The political economy of the virtual university." In M. Peters and P. Roberts (eds), *Virtual Technologies in Tertiary Education.* Palmerston North: Dunmore Press.

Lyotard, J.-F. (1984). *The Postmodern Condition: A Report on Knowledge*, trans. G. Bennington and B. Massumi. Minneapolis: University of Minnesota Press.

Lyotard, J.-F. (1993). "New technologies." In: J.-F. Lyotard, *Political Writings*, trans. B. Readings and K. Geiman. Minneapolis: University of Minnesota.

Noble, D. (1998). "Digital diploma mills: The automation of higher education." *First Monday.* http://www.firstmonday.org/issues/issue3_1/noble/ (accessed June 22, 2005).

Noble, D. (2002). *Digital Diploma Mills: The Automation of Higher Education.* Monthly Review Press.

Peters, M. and Lankshear, C. (1996). "Critical Literacy and the Digital Text." *Educational Theory*, 46: 1, Winter (51–70).

Peters, M. and Marshall, J. (1995). "An interview with Mark Poster." *Media Studies* 2: 1 (45–53).

Peters, M. (ed.) (1995). *Education and the Postmodern Condition.* Foreword by J.-F. Lyotard, Westport, CT and London: Bergin & Garvey.

Peters, M.(1996a). "Cybernetics, cyberspace and the politics of university reform." *Australian Journal of Education*, 40: 2 (163–177).

Peters, M.(1996b). "Education and the mode of information: an interview with Mark Poster." *New Zealand Journal of Educational Studies*, 31:1 (3–12).

Peters, M. (1996c). "Information, ideology, power: an interview with Timothy W. Luke." *Sites: A Journal for South Pacific Cultural Studies*, 33 (144–159).

Peters, M. (1996d). *Poststructuralism, Politics and Education.* Westport, CT and London: Bergin & Garvey.

Peters, M. (ed.) (2002). *Heidegger, Education and Modernity.* Lanham, Boulder, NY, Oxford: Rowman & Littlefield.

Peters, M. and Roberts, P. (1998). "Virtual technologies in tertiary education." In: J. Weiss, J. Nolan, J. Hunsinger, and P. Trifonas (eds), *The International Handbook of Virtual Learning Environments.* Springer International Handbook of Education. The Netherlands.

Poster, M. (1990). *The Mode of Information: Poststructuralism and the Social Context.* Cambridge: Polity Press.

Scheibler, I. (1993). "Heidegger and the rhetoric of submission: technology and passivity." In V. Conley (ed.), *Rethinking Technologies*, 115–142. Minneapolis and London: University of Minnesota Press.

Smith, A. (1996). *Software for the Self: Technology and Culture.* London: Faber and Faber.

Tiffin, J. and Rajasingham, L. (1995). *In Search of the Virtual Class: Education in an Information Society.* London and New York: Routledge.

Touraine, A. (1974). *The Post-Industrial Society.* London: Wildwood House.

Notes on Contributors

Frank Banks (BA, MA, C.Phys., M.Inst.P.) is director of the innovative flexible PGCE course at the Open University (OU). Until recently he served as a sub-dean with particular responsibility for teacher professional development courses in Education, and was a visiting professor in the School of Engineering and Advanced Technology, Staffordshire University. After working for eleven years as a school teacher of technology, engineering science, and science, at both secondary and primary levels, he is currently a senior lecturer in the Centre for Research and Development in Teacher Education (CReTE), where he has contributed to a number of initial and in-service teacher education courses at all levels. His subject expertise is in science and technology and his research interests are the links between those school subjects, and in teacher professional development, particularly when using new communications technologies. He has authored or edited twelve books and handbooks for teachers, including editing *Teaching Technology* published by Routledge, and over fifty academic papers in the fields of science and technology education, teacher professional knowledge, and teacher education.

Dr. David Barlex is a senior lecturer in education at Brunel University and an acknowledged leader in design-and-technology education, curriculum design, and curriculum-materials development. He is director of the Nuffield Design and Technology project, which has produced an extensive range of curriculum materials widely used in primary and secondary schools in the United Kingdom. He is educational manager of Young Foresight, an initiative that has developed approaches to teaching and learning that enhance students' ability to respond creatively to design & technology activities. He is curriculum adviser to the Electronics in Schools project, which aims to increase the number of pupils studying electronics-based design-and-technology courses. In 2002 he won the DATA Outstanding Contribution to Design and Technology Education award. David's research activity stems from his conviction that there should be a dynamic and synergic relationship between curriculum development and academic research. He currently pursues this activity through partnerships with researchers in the United Kingdom and Canada. He has presented work regularly at international conferences and published in the Journal of Design and Technology and the International Journal of Technology and Design Education Research.

John R. Dakers lectures at the University of Glasgow in the Department of Educational Studies. His research interests include technology education, the philosophy of technology, technological literacy and creating communities of learners in technology education settings. He has written extensively on these subjects in international journals and books, acted as guest editor in several journals, and delivered international presentations at various conferences around the world, including keynote presentations. He presents guest lectures at several universities around Europe including Finland and Sweden. He has acted as consultant to the European Commission for the past years on matters relating to increasing recruitment to science, mathematics and technology subjects.

He acted as conference director for a major international conference on "pupils Attitudes Towards Technology" (PATT) held in Glasgow in 2003 and co-edited the peer-reviewed conference book with Marc J. de Vries from the Netherlands. Serving on the editorial board of two international Journals, he is about to take up assistant editor of the Scottish Educational Review early next year. He is currently acting as section editor in the forthcoming international handbook on technology education.

Wendy Dow is a lecturer in Educational Studies at the University of Glasgow. She has worked collaboratively on a range of projects in Design and Technology Education and has carried out research into a number of areas pertaining to the area. She presents papers on technology on a regular basis at technology conferences such as DATA, CRIPT, and PATT. Moreover, she has papers published in the DATA Journal and the International Journal of Technology and Design Education.

Her main research interests are the effect of implicit theories on pedagogy and learning and factors affecting motivation. Her interest in technology education combined with her wider cross-curricular background and research interests has added an important dynamic to projects, helping both to identify important cross curricular issues as well as the factors which make technology education a unique and important part of the Scottish five to fourteen curriculum.

Wendy co-directed an evaluation of the *Nuffield Design and Technology* materials adapted for Scottish primary and secondary schools, and is currently acting as an associate consultant to the

European Commission on a project designed to increase interest in Mathematics, Science and Technology in a European context.

Andrew Feenberg holds the Canadian Research Chair in Philosophy of Technology in the School of Communication of Simon Fraser University. He is the author of *Lukacs, Marx and the Sources of Critical Theory* (Oxford University Press, 1986), *Alternative Modernity* (University of California Press, 1995), *Questioning Technology* (Routledge, 1999), and *Transforming Technology* (Oxford University Press, 2002). He is also co-editor of *Modernity and Technology* (MIT Press, 2003). In addition to his work on critical theory and philosophy of technology, Dr. Feenberg is recognized as an early innovator in the field of online communication. He is currently directing a project for improving software for online discussion forums under a grant from the U.S. Department of Education.

J. Britt Holbrook received his Ph.D. in philosophy from Emory University in August 2004. He taught at Emory and at Georgia State University before relocating to Dallas, Texas in the Fall of 2004. In January 2005, he became research assistant professor within the Department of Philosophy and Religion Studies at the University of North Texas. Holbrook's research focuses on the role philosophers might play in addressing the relations between science, technology, society, and humanity (not to mention individual human beings). He has authored several articles on the U.S. National Science Foundation's Second Merit Review Criterion, which requires proposers and reviewers to address and assess the "broader societal impacts" of grant proposals.

Don Ihde is distinguished professor of philosophy and director of the Technoscience Research Group in the Department of Philosophy, Stony Brook University, NY. He is the author of thirteen books, many of which are about the philosophy of technology. Recent publications include: *Chasing Technoscience: Matrix of Materiality* (Indiana, 2003) with Evan Selinger; *Bodies in Technology* (Minnesota, 2002); *Expanding Hermeneutics: Visualism in Science* (Northwestern University Press, 1998); and *Postphenomenology: Essays in the Postmodern Context* (Northwestern University Press, 1993).

Tim Ingold is professor of social anthropology at the University of Aberdeen. He has carried out ethnographic fieldwork among Saami and Finnish people in Lapland, and has written extensively on comparative questions of environment, technology and social organisation in the circumpolar North, as well as on evolutionary theory in anthropology, biology and history, on the role of animals in human society, and on issues in human ecology. His current research interests are in the anthropology of technology and in aspects of environmental perception. He has edited the *Companion Encyclopedia of Anthropology* (1994) and was editor of *Man* (the Journal of the Royal Anthropological Institute) from 1990 to 1992. He is a Fellow of the British Academy and of the Royal Society of Edinburgh. He served on the Anthropology panel for the 2001 Research Assessment Exercise, and is currently a member of the Research Grants Board and the International Advisory Committee of the Economic and Social Research Council. His major publications include *Evolution and Social Life* (1986), *The Appropriation of Nature* (1986), *Tools, Language and Cognition in Human Evolution* (co-edited with Kathleen Gibson, 1993), and *Key Debates in Anthropology* (1996). His latest book, *The Perception of the Environment*, was published by Routledge in 2000.

Richard Kahn is a doctoral candidate in the Graduate School of Education at UCLA. He is a co-editor of *Theory, Facts, and Interpretation in Educational and Social Research* (Rodn "WOM," 2004) and has written extensively with Douglas Kellner on the critical theory of technology and education, including "New Media, Post-Subcultures and Technopolitics" in *Media and Cultural Studies: Keyworks* (Blackwell, 2005) and "Oppositional Politics and the Internet: A Critical/ Reconstructive Approach" in *Cultural Politics* 1(1). Additionally, he works to theorize and promote ecopedagogy and in this respect he serves as the research associate in ecopedagogy for the UCLA Paulo Freire Institute.

Steve Keirl lectures at the University of South Australia in design and technology (D&T) education, ethics, and critical enquiry. He has taught D&T in primary and secondary schools in Australia and England and has been involved in D&T teacher education, in-service programs and post-graduate programs at universities for over ten years. He was chair of the Technology Expert Working Group and subsequently principal writer for the D&T Learning Area of the South Australian Curriculum Standards and Accountability Framework. He was also a TaskForce member for the national Investigation into the Status of Technology Education in Australian Schools and a researcher for the OECD investigation into Technology Education in Australia.

Steve's research interests include the relationships amongst ethics, curriculum, pedagogy, democracy, and D&T. These might be summarised as "explorations of Technological Literacy." Steve has published extensively including thirty-four peer-reviewed papers and chapters. He has led numerous forums and workshops, and has given invited papers and keynote addresses, both nationally and internationally. He is referee for several D&T conferences and journals.

Douglas Kellner is George Kneller Chair in the Philosophy of Education at UCLA and is author of many books on social theory, politics, history, and culture, including *Camera Politica: The Politics and Ideology of Contemporary Hollywood Film*, co-authored with Michael Ryan; *Critical Theory, Marxism, and Modernity; Jean Baudrillard: From Marxism to Postmodernism and Beyond; Postmodern Theory: Critical Interrogations* (with Steven Best); *Television and the Crisis of Democracy; The Persian Gulf TV War; Media Culture*; and *The Postmodern Turn* (with Steven Best). Recent books include a study of the 2000 U.S. presidential election, *Grand Theft 2000: Media Spectacle and the Theft of an Election*, and *The Postmodern Adventure. Science, Technology, and Cultural Studies at the Third Millennium* (co-authored with Steve Best). His most recent books are *Media Spectacle* and another from 2003 September 11, *Terror War, and the Dangers of the Bush Legacy*.

Richard Kimbell was the first professor of Technology Education in London University. He has taught technology in schools and been course director for undergraduate and postgraduate courses of teacher education. Between 1985–1991 he directed the Assessment of Performance Unit (APU) project for the Department of Education and Science—assessing the technological capability of 10,000 pupils in 700 schools throughout England Wales and or them Ireland. In 1990, he founded the Technology Education Research Unit (TERU) at Goldsmiths College London as the base from which to manage his expanding research portfolio. In the subsequent period, research sponsors include research councils (eg., ESRC, NSF [USA]), industry (eg., LEGO, BP), government departments (eg., DfES, DfID), as well as professional and charitable organisations (eg., Engineering Council, Royal Society of Arts, Design Museum).

He has published widely in the field and his latest book *Assessing Technology* (a study of international trends in curriculum and assessment in technology, spanning Europe, the United States, and Pacific Rim nations) won the "Outstanding Publication of the Year" Award (1999) at the International Technology Education Association Conference in Minneapolis, the United States. He has been commissioned to prepare reports for the Congress of the United States, UNESCO, NATO, and the British Council. He has written and presented television programmes and he regularly lectures internationally.

Prof. Robert McCormick (B.Sc., MA, Ph.D.) is internationally known in technology education, having made major keynote speeches to conferences and publishing widely with over 100 books, articles, and papers. He has worked for the last thirty years in curriculum and teaching studies, including (technology education) at postgraduate level. He was consultant to distance learning institutions in Pakistan and China, on TE to the (American Association for the Advancement of Science), and on a European Commission feasibility study on education in China. He directed a large United Kingdom Economic and Social Research Council funded research study on problem solving in TE, and a government-funded inservice programme for design and technology teachers, providing 1000 schools with training through 16 institutions, and through the Open University. He was director of the Learning Schools Programme, to train 150,000 United Kingdom teachers in the use of information communication technology in the classroom and is currently carrying out research on it. He is co-director of the ESRC Teaching and Learning Resarch Programme project on learning how to learn, and a Department for Trade and Industry project on promoting electronics in schools, and a lead partner in EC projects on learning objects (ICT), ICT research and policy links, and on peer review of ICT innovation.

Mike Michael is professor of sociology of science and technology at the Sociology Department, Goldsmiths College, University of London. His interests include public understanding of science, mundane technology, technoscience and everyday life, biotechnological innovation, and culture. His most recent books are *Reconnecting Culture, Technology and Nature: From Society to Heterogeneity* (Routledge, 2000) and (with Alan Irwin) *Science, Social Theory and Public Knowledge* (Open University Press, 2003).

Carl Mitcham received his Ph.D. in philosophy from Frodham University and has taught at Brooklyn Polytechnic University and the Pennsylvania State University before joining the faculty at the Colorado School of Mines in 1999. His publications include *Philosophy and Technology: Readings in the Philosophical Problems of Technology* (1972, 1983) and *Thinking through Technology: The Path between Engineering and Philosophy* (1994). He currently serves as editor-in-chief of a multi-volume, international *Encyclopedia of Science, Technology, and Ethics* forthcoming from Macmillan Reference.

Patricia Murphy is a reader in education and has a history of leading research in science and technology in primary and secondary phases of education, starting with her work with the APU national monitoring programme of science performance in schools (deputy director 1985–1987). It was in this period that she began her research into gender and achievement in science and technology specifically and gender and teaching and learning more specifically. She is well-known international figure in this field having published many books, articles, and chapters and contributed regularly at international conferences. She has developed and contributed to a range of postgraduate professional development courses and initiatives for teachers in curriculum and teaching studies. She co-directed a large UK ESRC funded research project *Problem Solving in Technology Education*. Since 1996 she has been continually involved in directing projects evaluating and refining curriculum materials to enhance creativity in teaching and learning. These projects include the evaluation of the Nuffield *Primary Design & Technology* materials and the evaluation of the Design Council's *Millennium Products* for KS3(key stage 3) students. In 2000–2001 Patricia directed the evaluation of the national Young Foresight programme which aims to foster creative thinking and problem solving within the KS3 D&T curriculum. She currently co-directs the DTI funded project, *Electronics in Schools*.

Michael A. Peters is research professor of education at the University of Glasgow (UK). He also holds adjunct professorships in the School of Education at the University of Auckland (NZ) and in the Department of Communication Studies at the Auckland University of Technology. He has research interests in educational theory and policy, and in contemporary philosophy. He has published over 150 articles and some twenty books in these fields, including most recently: *Poststructuralism and Educational Research* (2004) with Nick Burbules; *Derrida, Deconstruction and Education* (eds.) (2004); *Critical Theory and the Human Condition* (eds.) (2003); *Futures of Critical Theory* (eds.) (2003); *Heidegger, Education and Modernity* (2002) (ed.); *Poststructuralism, Marxism and Neoliberalism: Between politics and theory* (2001); *Nietzsche's Legacy for Education: Past and present values*, (2001) (eds.); *Wittgenstein: Philosophy, postmodernism, pedagogy* (1999) with James Marshall; *Poststructuralism, politics and education* (1996).

Joseph C. Pitt received his Ph.D. from The University of Western Ontario. He has been on the faculty of Virginia Tech since 1971 where he is professor of philosophy and serves as head of the department of philosophy. He is the author of three books, the most recent being *Thinking About Technology*, and the editor of ten more including *New Directions in the Philosophy of Technology* (with E. Byrne). An associate editor of *Techné, The Journal of the Society for Philosophy and Technology*-he is the founding editor of *Perspectives on Science, historical, philosophical, social*. His current work focuses on the impact of technological developments on scientific change.

Marc J. de Vries (M.Sc., Ph.D.) is an affiliate professor at the Delft University of Technology and an assistant professor at the Eindhoven University of Technology, both in the Netherlands. His research into pupils' attitudes towards technology initiated the PATT conferences that now serve as an international platform for discussions on various issues related to technology education. In the Netherlands he co-authored textbooks for technology education at the lower secondary level, co-edited television programs about technology for the same age level, co-founded the Dutch Technology Teachers' Association, and was a technology teacher educator. He is currently the editor-in-chief of the *International Journal for Technology and Design Education*, published by Springer. A special issue of that journal, co-edited by him, was on transforming philosophical perspectives into mental images through technology education. He wrote a book on the history of the main research laboratory of the Philips Electronics Company. His current research is in the philosophy of technology, and based on that he recently published a book that introduces the philosophy of technology for nonphilosphers.

Leonard J. Waks is professor emeritus of educational leadership and policy studies at Temple University. He received a Ph.D. in philosophy from the University of Wisconsin (1968), and has taught Philosophy at Purdue, Stanford, and Penn State, where he was also a professor in the science, technology and society program. He was a co-founder of the U.S. National Technological Literacy Conferences, which celebrate their twentieth anniversary in 2004. He is the author of *Technology's School* (1995) and more than sixty scholarly articles and book chapters. His current research explores educational arrangements emerging in global network society.

Author Index

Subject Index